Britain's Achilles Heel

Britain's Achilles Heel

Our Uncompetitive Pound

John Mills

CIVITAS

First published May 2017

© Civitas 2017
55 Tufton Street
London SW1P 3QL

email: books@civitas.org.uk

Paperback edition ISBN 978-1-906837-86-0 and
hardback edition ISBN 978-1-906837-87-7

Independence: Civitas: Institute for the Study of Civil Society is
a registered educational charity (No. 1085494) and a company
limited by guarantee (No. 04023541). Civitas is financed from a
variety of private sources to avoid over-reliance on any single
or small group of donors. All publications are independently
refereed.

All the Institute's publications seek to further its objective of
promoting the advancement of learning. The views expressed are
those of the authors, not of the Institute, as is responsibility for
data and content.

Designed and typeset by Typetechnique

Printed in Great Britain by
Berforts Ltd

Contents

Preface

This book is about questions of evident importance to which there appear to be no obvious answers. Why is economic growth and prosperity in the world so patchy and unstable? Why are countries in the East doing so much better in growth terms than those in the West? Why have incomes for so many people in both Europe and the USA stagnated for long periods? Why is there so much inequality – and debt? Are all these conditions inevitable or are there more effective ways of ordering our economic affairs which could achieve better results?

There is not much disagreement about the conditions which most people would like to see attained. They would like to see a combination of reasonably rapid economic growth and living standards, as near full employment as is achievable, relatively stable prices, not too much inequality and a sustainable future. But for much of the world, including most of the West, this is not what is being delivered. Is this because such a combination of goals is simply unattainable? Or is it because there are policies which we are not applying but which we ought to be using which could produce much better results? If so, how do we determine what they are?

The message in this book is that there are better policies available and that a study of our economic history, and the ideas which have shaped it, is capable of showing what they might be. The approach adopted is to review in parallel both how our economies have developed and how thinking about economic policy has evolved, to enable us to learn lessons from successive phases of our economic history on what went well and what went badly and what guidance might be gleaned from them for the future.

The Industrial Revolution was all about increasing productivity, the growth rate and thus living standards, a phenomenon which the world had never seen before at least on anything like the same scale. Why did this happen when and where it did? The steady but uneven spread of industry in the nineteenth century and up to World War I, initially mainly in the western world, but subsequently more widely, contains important lessons about how to maintain economic momentum. The two world wars and the period between them provided a kaleidoscope of good and bad economic outcomes, from which there is much to be learnt. The post-war period, especially in the West, was far more successful than anything before or after it but proved to be unsustainable. Was it really necessary that this happened?

In fact, the 1970s saw stagflation – a combination of higher inflation and slower growth – in a new policy environment as Keynesianism was replaced by monetarism. Why did this reduction in economic performance occur and was it inevitable? Following the fall of the Berlin Wall in 1989, the 1990s and the early years of the twenty-first century seemed to exhibit a sustainable 'Great Moderation', until the crash came in 2008 followed by almost no growth at all, at least measured by GDP per head in the West, while the East romped ahead. The problem now in much of Europe, the USA and Japan is to achieve any increase in living standards, especially for the bulk of the population, excluding the already well-off and the super-rich. What has gone wrong? Are these conditions really inevitable or are there policies which could produce much better outcomes? These are some of questions to which this book attempts to offer answers.

Even if different policies did succeed in producing more economic growth, would they be sustainable or would more output run up against environmental and resource constraints which would make more of further growth impossible to attain – or not worth achieving even if it could be? What about other economic objectives, such as full employment, reasonably stable prices, sustainability and avoiding unnecessarily extreme inequality? Full-time employment for nearly all the population is a relatively new concept, born out of the regular jobs which flowed from industrialisation and the decline in agriculture. At a time most people scratched a living in subsistence agriculture, there were relatively few full-time jobs. Inflation on anything like the scale seen in the 1970s is also a new phenomenon in most countries, except for during wars or their immediate aftermath. An ounce of gold retained the same sterling value – £3. 17s 9d – with occasional usually short breaks – from 1711 to 1931.[1] Sustainability was first highlighted in a major way by the Club of Rome in their report published in 1972[2] and global warming or climate change only began to hit the headlines during the last quarter of the twentieth century.[3] Inequality has always been with us but it became much less extreme between 1914 and 1945, then widened only very slowly up to 1970 and has since become far greater. There are, therefore, plenty of issues which need to be addressed, other than just getting the economy to grow more rapidly, if more successful economic policies are to be pursued than those we have seen recently, especially in the West.

Of course there are no very easy and obvious solutions to all our economic problems. If there were, no doubt they would have been implemented long ago. The question, nevertheless, is whether, even if we cannot reach nirvana, we ought to be able to do substantially better than we are now. The conclusion reached in this book is not that the problems we face are insoluble but that in a number of key respects the policy framework within which our political and administrative leaders work is flawed, so we could do better. There are important lessons from the past which we have failed to learn and gaps in our economic understanding which have led to policies being implemented which are much less effective and successful than they might be.

The thesis in this book is that there is too little clear understanding about what actually produces economic growth and what will and will not encourage it to happen; too little appreciation of what potentially can be done to provide everyone who wants to work with a productive and well-paid job; too much fear of price increases and too little concern about very low or negative inflation; too much insouciance about the destabilising impact of footloose capital moving round the world; far too little worry about the enormous increase in credit and debt which has taken place especially during the early part of the twenty-first century; and much too little concern about the imbalances there are in the world economy between countries, particularly in the West, with chronic balance of payments deficits and others which pile up surpluses every year. Capitalism and globalisation have been remarkably successful in lifting many millions of people out of poverty over recent decades but at the cost of generating imbalances in the world economy which are in danger of choking off future progress.

There is also a very large political dimension to the problems currently faced, particularly by the western world. While many people are generally content with their lot in life there is a very significant minority who are not. Broadly speaking, these are the people who have not seen their fortunes improved by globalisation as their jobs and lifestyles have become more insecure and their incomes have stagnated or declined. They are the working and middle class sectors of society who have watched with increasing anger, especially as conditions for them have stubbornly not improved post the 2008 crisis, the rich getting richer, those directly responsible for the crash remaining largely unscathed, and inequality of opportunity, incomes and life chances generally becoming more and more marked. These are the people who voted for Donald Trump (b. 1946) in the USA, for UKIP in the UK and who may elect other protest parties right across Europe in forthcoming elections.

The danger is that, as a result of waning belief in the capacity of our ruling elites to find reasonably effective solutions to our economic problems, the social cohesion which allows civilised democratic politics to work successfully is being eroded away. Moderate left- or right-of-centre political parties have seen their share of the vote tumbling, to be replaced by support for a variety of different protest parties from left and right, with largely populist agendas. Some of them, at least, have racist, xenophobic or millenarian goals which are barely compatible with liberal democracy, or which may positively prefer to replace the tolerance which makes moderate politics work with more authoritarian regimes. The danger in places like Europe is not that nation states will go to war with each other. It is that civil society will break down with, at worst, riots and force, drifting into authoritarianism, replacing the proper use of the ballot box.

The search for more effective economic policies is not, therefore, just a matter of raising living standards among people who are already, by any historical measure, much better off than their forebears. Increasing real incomes to pay for higher living standards may be almost universally desired but this is not the whole of the endgame. We also need to generate economic conditions which are broadly acceptable to the vast majority of the population and not just to those who are doing well. In particular, we need to heal the divisions, as far as we can, between those who have done well out of globalisation and trade liberalisation and those who have not. The purpose of this book is to erect some signposts as to how this might be done.

Author

John Mills is an entrepreneur and economist who has long been involved with political affairs. He is the founder and chairman of John Mills Limited (JML), which specialises in selling high volume consumer products, using audio-visual methods for promoting their sale both in the UK and in many other countries – about 85 at the last count. His main interests as an economist are the UK's relationship with the EU and the relatively poor performance of western economies compared with those in the East.

He was for many years a senior Labour elected member of Camden Council, the London Boroughs Association and the Association of Metropolitan Authorities, and in the late 1980s he was Deputy Chairman of the London Dockland Development Corporation. He was chairman and then deputy chairman of Vote Leave, joint chairman of Business for Britain and the founder of Labour Leave, all campaigning for Brexit during the run-up to the June 2016 EU referendum. He is on the board of OpenDemocracy, vice-chairman of the Economic Research Council and chair of both The Pound Campaign and Labour Future, all concerned in different ways with the UK's economic and political prospects. He is a frequent commentator on TV and radio and he has a large number of published books, articles, pamphlets and tracts to his credit.

He is the author or joint-author of 10 books: *Growth and Welfare: A New Policy for Britain* (1972); *Monetarism or Prosperity* (with Bryan Gould and Shaun Stewart, 1982); *Tackling Britain's False Economy* (1997); *Europe's Economic Dilemma* (1998); *America's Soluble Problems* (1999); *Managing the World Economy* (2000); *A Critical History of Economics* (2002); *Exchange Rate Alignments* (2012); *Call to Action* (with Bryan Gould, 2015) and *The Real Sterling Crisis* (with Roger Bootle, 2016).

Acknowledgements

This is the eleventh book I have written either on my own or with others about economic policy and specifically about the British economy. It has always seemed to me that a booming export sector was the key to economic growth and that, to be successful at exporting, the price at which we try to sell our goods and services to foreign buyers has to be competitive. In turn, this had a lot to do with the exchange rate. Not many people, however, seem to agree with these insights and our steadily dropping share of world trade strongly indicates that UK policymakers have never paid much attention to this point of view. It seems so clear to me, nevertheless, that ignoring the strength of the pound, because it is such a key link with the rest of the world, is so obviously such a major strategic mistake that I have never understood why everyone else should have such difficulty in seeing that this was the case. The reality, however, is that most people don't think along the same lines as me. The result is that for all of the last 50 years during which I have been writing about economics, I have been in a small minority, with few people sharing my views. This book is therefore yet another attempt to try to persuade all those who are sceptical about my perceptions that there is some merit in what I have to say.

There are some people, however, who have shared my approach and I am deeply grateful to them for all the support which they have provided to me – and those who have worked with me – over the years. Sir Roy Harrod provided the endorsement needed to get my first book published in the early 1970s. Shaun Stewart, who sadly died in 1997, and Bryan Gould who left British politics in the 1990s to return to his native New Zealand, were very important allies in the 1980s and 1990s. We wrote a book together and umpteen pamphlets for the Fabian Society. When Bryan went back to New Zealand, Austin Mitchell MP took up the cudgels in his place. More pamphlets, campaigns and books followed, all to little avail, although the books evidently sold well enough for Palgrave Macmillan to keep publishing them. Tim Farmiloe, their academic department's publishing editor deserves a special mention as a truly loyal supporter, to whom I remain extremely grateful. One of the books I wrote for Palgrave Macmillan, *A Critical History of Economics*, was picked up by the main publishing house in China in 2006, translated into Mandarin and used as a textbook in Chinese universities. Draw what conclusion you like about this occurrence.

Moving beyond the crash in 2008 into the lacklustre performance of the UK economy in the early 2010s provided a further stimulus to action, not least because the sudden death of my wife, Barbara, left a big gap which provided more space for writing two more books, one on my own and another with Bryan Gould. At the same time the advent of the internet and social media made it possible to make contact with a much wider audience than was achievable previously. This got me started on blogging – to supplement more pamphlets, including four published by Civitas, thanks especially to its director, David Green – as well as monthly bulletins. These were partly organised through two campaigns which I chair, one called The Pound Campaign and the other Labour Future, both of which now have a very substantial social media presence and to whose staff I am very grateful, not least because they have a much more detailed knowledge of how to handle this new means of building up a big following than I have.

A particularly significant academic helper at this time was my old Oxford economics tutor, Professor John Black, and another important stimulus came from a long pamphlet/short book which I co-authored with Roger Bootle. Rather less successful was a series of publications on rebalancing the UK economy which I – jointly with the Politics and Economics Research Trust – sponsored from a variety of think tanks during 2016 and 2017. Most of their publications, with the notable exception of the one produced by the Centre for Progressive Capitalism – and with grounds for hope from the Institute for Public Policy Research – sadly stayed on safe supply-side ground, without trying to tackle the demand side which seemed to me to be so crucial to explore. There is therefore, in my view, still a big battle to be won.

All this activity has now culminated in the present book in which I have tried to pull together all the major interesting strands of thought which have emerged from the work I have done on economic policy over the years. Bringing this project to fruition requires also some very specific thanks. Steve Laughton, who has also been exceptionally supportive over a long period, has been very helpful with his comments and for preparing the glossary which can be accessed online. Daniel Bentley at Civitas has been a huge help in getting the book produced quickly, not least to avoid all the statistics it contains getting out of date. I have also been hugely lucky with my colleagues at JML, my family, and especially my partner Marjorie Wallace who has had weekends curtailed while the book was being written, for which I must apologise. I am very grateful to them all. It remains for me to hope that at least some of you, this time round, will at last be persuaded by the message this book contains.

John Mills
March 2017

Civitas is very grateful to the Nigel Vinson Charitable Trust for its generous support of this project.

Glossary

This book has been written in as plain English as possible, to make its arguments easily accessible to anyone interested in current affairs. It is impossible, however, to avoid references being made to concepts which are bound to be more familiar to economists than to other people. A major debt of gratitude is therefore owed to Steve Laughton who has prepared a glossary of economic terms which are used in the book, to help those who might be unfamiliar with them. This can be accessed directly, using the following URL: glossary.org.uk.

Introduction

Between 1950, shortly after World War II ended, and 2015, the world economy grew to 10.9 times its 1950 size, or by an average of 3.7% per year.[1] Of course, the population has also become much larger too, increasing over the same period from 2.6bn to 7.3bn, an average of 1.6% per annum.[2] Dividing the increase in GDP by the increase in population shows that GDP per head – a qualified proxy for living standards – rose over this 65-year period by a factor of 3.85, or by an average of 2.1% per annum.

Judged by anything achieved on any comparable scale previously in human history, these are astonishing figures. In 1945, only a small proportion of the world's population lived much above subsistence level, most of them in the industrialised West. Nowadays, the number of very poor people – those with incomes equivalent to $2 a day or less – has shrunk to about 12% of the world's population, down from 37% in 1990 and 44% in 1981.[3] Prosperity on a scale unimaginable to our ancestors has spread to most of the planet.

This has happened because the value of the work which the world's population has done has risen exponentially, although not because – on average – the number of hours worked per person has gone up. Some people, such as those employed in industrial occupations are now working shorter hours than their equivalents were 70 years ago while others, such as those who have moved out of subsistence farming into more productive occupations, are working more hours per week. The reason why so much more is achieved by the world's working population now than then is that there has been a huge increase in the value created per hour of work done. It is this increase in productivity which lifted output per head of the world's population to such a huge extent cumulatively over the whole 1950-2015 period.

The key to understanding what has made the world economy – and output per head – grow like this is to appreciate what has made this miraculous increase in productivity possible. It is not that people are working harder. Nor is it, beyond a limited extent, because they are working more intelligently, although some undoubtedly are. It is because they are working more effectively, which is a rather different concept. This happens mainly for three inter-related reasons. One is the application of machinery to work which previously had to be done without it. The second is the use of much more power than the human frame is capable of producing. The third is the application of technology to make things happen in a productive way which would not otherwise have occurred. It is these three processes which are very largely responsible for all the growth in output which the world has witnessed.

Of course investment in other areas, such as schools, hospitals, roads and rail, is also very important from a social point of view, but it has a very limited contribution to make as a source of increased output per hour and thus economic growth. The return on this type of investment is typically very low – indeed little more than the interest charges on the capital needed to finance it – so it does not produce enough extra gross value added to lift the whole economy very much, and sometimes not at all. Education and training are obviously also very important too but – critically – not sufficient on their own. They are a vital complement to physical investment for increasing output per hour but, as has been found almost everywhere, on their own they are much less effective than most people would like to believe they are.

The key to economic growth, therefore, is to arrange economic incentives so that the maximum feasible amount of investment goes into machinery, technology – especially in the digital and virtual world – and the power they need, which then, of course, needs to be complemented by appropriate education and training and other supply-side policies. Some economies have managed to do this on an extraordinarily extensive basis. The proportion of Chinese GDP which is reinvested in total has recently been hovering at close to 50%[4] of which about a third goes into the kind of industrial investment which produces the huge returns which have driven Chinese growth rates.[5] The world average ratio for gross capital formation as a percentage of GDP is about 26%.[6] Some economies, however, have done very much worse than this. In 2016, the proportion of UK GDP devoted to investment, net of expenditure on intellectual property, was just under 13%,[7] one of the lowest in the world, but much of western Europe and the USA have done little better. This has a lot to do with why productivity and real wage increases are stagnant and why, in consequence, the rates of economic growth of many western economies are so low.

Why have the Chinese devoted such a high proportion of their GDP to investment while in the UK the ratio has been so low? As always, there are complex reasons why such different outcomes have materialised, but at bottom it boils down to economic incentives. People will tend to react to the circumstances in which they find themselves in ways which they believe will maximise their economic advantage. If, for whatever reasons, it does not pay all those in a position to influence investment decisions to promote investment, it will not take place on any major scale – and vice versa. The keys to achieving a reasonably high rate of growth are therefore not, in principle, difficult to determine. They involve no more than identifying clearly those sectors of the economy in which investment most readily promotes increased output, and then providing an environment which provides the right incentives for getting it to take place.

Why has this not happened in much of the world, particularly across much of the West in recent years, especially since the 2008 crash? This book is about searching for an answer to this question. Why have our governments apparently been so bad at identifying what needs to be done and then providing the right incentives to make sure that what is really needed actually happens?

The way in which this book sets out to provide answers to these questions is by a combination of searching for what economic history can tell us, taking account of what people at the time thought were the major problems and what the solutions to them might be, and then looking back at what happened with the benefit of hindsight. Chapter 1 searches for what the world's economic history up to the outbreak of World War I might be able to tell us about why the Industrial Revolution did not really start to materialise until the eighteenth century and why it then only slowly spread, mainly initially through the western world, but leaving some countries growing much more rapidly than others. Chapter 2 turns to the turbulent period between the start of World War I and the end of World War II, when the main economic problems facing policymakers during the period between the wars were centred around the disruption caused by World War I and the huge levels of unemployment and unused capacity triggered by the catastrophic fall in demand which caused the slump.

Chapter 3 then looks at the golden period of economic growth and full employment, especially in the West, from the end of World War II to the early 1970s. Why did the policies which had initially been so successful end up in a quagmire of stagflation – a dire mixture of high inflation and very slow growth? Chapter 4 turns to the monetarist response to this policy conundrum. Inflation came down but at the cost of much slower rates of growth than had prevailed previously. What caused this slowdown to happen and could this have been avoided?

Chapter 5 then reviews what the implications of the neo-liberal policies – underpinned by much of the thinking which monetarist doctrines generated – turned out to be not only for the domestic economies of the West but to international trading relations, particularly globalisation and the rise of the East compared to the West. Why did the West suffer from far lower growth rates than the Pacific Rim, and how did this manage to help to generate the conditions which led to the 2008 crash? Chapter 6 then turns to what has happened since 2008 – disappointingly low rates of economic growth in the West, largely stagnant incomes for most people, rising inequality and consequent political instability. What alternative policies might be available to avoid the prospect for years ahead of little or no increase in real incomes for the bulk of the population? How can we avoid mounting resentment at the rich apparently getting richer while everyone else is squeezed, and the erosion of trust in the capacity of our political leadership to govern reasonably competently and fairly?

Chapter 7 then pulls together the lessons which it seems ought to be learnt from the history and analysis in the previous chapters. What policy changes need to be made to get the world economy on to a more stable footing, while avoiding the western world, with its liberal democratic values, being eclipsed by the more authoritarian rising powers in the East as a result of its inability to achieve a reasonable rate of economic growth? Economic expansion is not everything, however, and Chapter 8 looks at some of the other major hazards which humanity is facing if we are to have a sustainable future – world population pressures, possible limitations on resources, climate change and the tensions caused by mass migration. Chapter 9 then draws together conclusions about what needs to be done – and what may well happen if there is no improvement in the outcomes which we manage to achieve.

These are key questions to which it is extremely important that we find convincing answers. Hopefully, this book will help to influence and redirect economic policies in a positive and more successful direction than those we have espoused in recent decades.

1

Economic Evolution

Between the dawn of civilisation and the start of the Industrial Revolution, living standards for most people hardly rose at all. GDP per head, measured in 1990 US dollars, averaged an estimated $444 across the whole of the world at the time of Christ. By 1000 it had fallen slightly to $435 but by 1820, as the Industrial Revolution begun to get under way, over about 800 years it had risen to a world average of $667,[1] largely as a result of what was happening in the West where, by 1820, the figure was $1,130 compared with $573 in the East – much the same as it had been 300 years earlier. Over the next 200 years the world was transformed. By 1998, the figure for the West was $21,470 and for the East $3,120.[2]

Because there was a very significant increase in the world's population between the time of Christ and 1820 – from about 27m to just over 1bn[3] – there was a corresponding increase in world GDP, but growth in output as a result of rising population is a very different matter from growth which raises average living standards. Why was there so little increase in output per head among the world's population until the Industrial Revolution got under way? If essentially all that is required to secure significant productivity increases is machinery, power and technology, why did none of these components come together to any significant extent before about the middle of the eighteenth century? The reasons are complex and interlocking, but appreciating why for thousands of years living standards remained almost static, despite development of institutional improvements and intellectual discoveries upon which the Industrial Revolution eventually depended, sheds important light on what had to happen to enable it to get started.

The ancient world

The first recognisable states made their appearance in the Fertile Crescent, about 3700 BC. To enable them to function a fair degree of economic organisation must have been essential, and evidence shows that this had indeed materialised.[4] The form of government was very much from the top down, but could not operate without significant division of labour. An elaborate system for recording debts and obligations was required, which took the form of baked clay tablets, organised largely by the priesthood who formed the backbone of the state administration. This system provided an important step towards the creation of money, since the obligations recorded by the clay tablets could be transferred or assigned. Systems for keeping track of debts, owing from some and due to others, were thus created which were not quite money, because both the debtors and creditors were specific individuals or groups of people. It nevertheless provided a relatively flexible system for recording and discharging obligations, which was needed in an economy too big for everyone to know everyone else, and where there were too many debts and payment obligations for any one person to be able to keep track of them all.

The next stage was the invention of money proper. Barter tokens were minted by the Chinese in the second millennium BC, but true coinage was invented in the western world in Asia Minor about 700 BC, in the Kingdom of Lydia.[5] Originally made of electrum, a local natural amalgam of gold and silver, the first coins were produced by the fabled Croesus of Lydia (d. 546 BC) in the sixth century BC.[6] Their value, which then became separated from their intrinsic worth, had the major advantage of not requiring the involvement of any personal debtor or creditor. Their credibility depended solely in the trust of those who used them, backed by the state which issued them that others would recognise and accept them. The invention of coinage greatly increased the scope for trade, and it is no coincidence that the explosion in exchange of goods, and the establishment of colonies within the Mediterranean basin which followed, occurred over the next century or two after coins first appeared on the scene.

The ancient world, therefore, succeeded in developing the credit systems necessary to enable an extensive trade and commercial network to exist, to make it possible to establish large-scale states, to operate complex tax systems, and to form, maintain and fund large-scale armies. At first sight, it might appear that the Roman Empire, in particular, had all the necessary requirements to enable a beginning to be made on applying technology to the perennial problems of economic shortage. For nearly 400 years after the consolidation which took place under Caesar Augustus (63 BC–AD 14), it encompassed a large and varied area, where peace and order generally prevailed. There was a relatively efficient and impartial legal system. The Roman Empire was plagued intermittently by inflationary problems, but this did not stop there being substantial accumulations of capital. Interestingly, the Roman period is the only one when, until very recently, most of Europe was covered by a single currency. Some industrial processes, such as smelting, were well known. A considerable quantity of theory about scientific matters, mostly developed by the Greeks, was available. Indeed, a steam engine of sorts, used as a toy, had been developed by the Greek polymath Hero (c.10–c.70 AD), in Alexandria one of the centres of Greek learning.[7]

There was, therefore, a substantial artisan class, capable of contributing practical knowledge and experience to new ideas about production methods. The standards of education, especially among the more prosperous classes, were reasonably high. Both the Greeks and the Romans produced superb examples of civil engineering, varying from the Parthenon to the Roman road system, with about 40,000 miles of paved roads in use.[8] And yet, despite all of these apparently potentially favourable circumstances, there was almost no technological development at all for all of the hundreds of years during which the Roman Empire lasted. Why did nothing resembling the Industrial Revolution occur? There appear to be several reasons, of which the more significant form an interlocking pattern. They all throw light on why the Industrial Revolution, when it gathered pace in Europe in the eighteenth century, although arguably the most important event in human history, was also one whose trajectory was remarkably difficult to have foreseen.

First, there was nothing equivalent to the body of scientific knowledge that had accumulated in Europe by the time the Industrial Revolution got under way there, which was a very different matter from the speculations of ancient Greek philosophers. It is true that many of the early inventions which got industrialisation started in Britain were developed by highly skilled journeyman engineers rather than intellectuals. Examples are the flying shuttle invented by John Kay (1704-1779), which first appeared in 1733, the water frame (1769) from Richard Arkwright (1732-1792), the spinning jenny (1770) from James Hargreaves (1720-1758)[9] and the steam engines developed by Thomas Newcomen (1664-1729) as early as 1712 but greatly improved from 1769 onwards by James Watt (1736-1819).[10] Nevertheless, the climate of opinion in which all these people worked had undoubtedly been heavily influenced by the writings of proponents, such as Francis Bacon (1561-1626), of what came to be called the scientific method. This was the system of experimentation and verification on which technical advance was to be built. This was a far cry from the methods employed by the most influential intellectual leaders in the ancient world, particularly the most important Greek teachers such as Plato (427–347 BC) and Aristotle (384–322 BC), who relied much more on derivation of conclusions from first principles than on empirical experiments.

Second, the Industrial Revolution was not a complete break with the past, in the sense that new practical inventions suddenly started materialising in a way which had never happened before. On the contrary, it was an acceleration of a process which had been slowly gathering pace for hundreds of years, providing a much more formidable basis for advance than existed at any stage during the ancient world. As well as high-profile inventions such as the printing press, clocks, eyeglasses, and lateen sails, all of which were of crucial significance, there had been many other improvements in technology which had slowly accumulated over the centuries, or been imported from other parts of the world. These included the manufacture and use of gunpowder and paper, techniques for smelting many metals, and processes for handling a wide variety of other materials from glass and porcelain to marble and sugar.

Third, as well as technical knowledge, the Romans and Greeks lacked what may have been an equally crucial intellectual component, which was an adequate mathematical system. The whole of the ancient world operated on methods of counting such as Roman numerals. There was no true concept of zero. No calculations were possible which were more complicated than could be handled on an abacus. The universal modern numbering system was invented in India in the fourth century AD, and took 800 years to reach Europe via the Islamic Arab states. It was first publicised in the West by Leonardo Fibonacci (c.1170–c.1250), also known as Leonardo of Pisa, in his Book of the Calculator, which appeared in 1202, and which rapidly led to the adoption of the so-called Arabic – though originally Indian – notation first in Italy and then throughout Europe.[11] Not only did the new numbering system make it much easier to carry out relatively complicated calculations, it also made it possible for mathematics to develop much more complex ways of solving problems than had been possible previously. It is no coincidence that the advance of mathematics in Europe began to accelerate rapidly once the new notation had been introduced.

Fourth, another major requirement for the development of as complex a division of labour – and hence as complicated an economy – as the Industrial Revolution required, was a much more sophisticated credit system than the ancient world ever had. Until well into the Middle Ages, no true banks existed. Of course, before then, there were merchants who kept their stores of wealth in the form of gold coins, and who were willing to lend against their security, and there were plenty of money lenders and changers in the ancient world, many of them ex-slaves.[12] The inefficiency of the old mathematical systems, however, and the difficulties involved in maintaining records before printing and paper manufacture had been perfected, both militated against sophisticated banking operations. These problems were solved by the advent of the new mathematical notation, major improvements in paper production, the invention of double-entry bookkeeping, and the subsequent rapid development of accountancy as a profession. All added to the ease with which complicated records could now be kept. The result was the development of true banks, first in Italy and then throughout Europe, as great banking dynasties established themselves – the Medici in Italy, the Fuggers in Germany – with many smaller-scale banking enterprises following in their wakes.[13]

Fifth, even the development of banking proper left the economies of the time heavily dependent on adequate supplies of gold and silver to provide sufficient coinage to make the financial system operate. Some leverage could be provided by the use of financial instruments such as bills of exchange, used mainly to finance trade, but the scope was limited until the invention of the next major step forward, which was the introduction of paper currency. Although, again, there had been precedents in China, culminating in the first true bank note materialising there in the seventh century AD, the issuing of notes began in the West at the end of the seventeenth century,[14] led by the Bank of England, established in 1694 as a private corporation, the status it retained until it was nationalised in 1946.[15] Bank notes were not originally designed for general use, but were issued in large denominations, mostly for the financing of trade. Essentially, they were bearer cheques, drawn in the UK on the Bank of England. Their impact, however, was to make it possible to separate still further the limited availability of gold and silver and the increasing amount of credit which could be extended by the banking system as a whole, by creating facilities such as overdrafts, leveraged on the underlying precious metals.

Sixth, even apart from the shortage of technical opportunities, the unconducive intellectual climate, the lack of appropriate methods of calculation, and the undeveloped credit system, there may be another perhaps even more fundamental reason why the ancient world failed to industrialise. Its society was too regimented, too top-down, too stable and therefore, despite the wrenching changes which periodically took place at the top, too stagnant and lacking in vigour to embark on the kind of free-thinking progress that the Industrial Revolution required. Technical progress may also have been held back by the widespread existence of slavery, which both lowered the cost and social prestige attaching to productive labour.[16] It is no coincidence that much of the early impetus in Britain and elsewhere came from dissident, independent people, who were excluded because of their religion or for other reasons from the established mainstream, but who were not precluded by convention or fear of retribution from trying new ways of doing things. It was the combination of their attitude of mind with the availability of all the other components which the ancient world lacked which triggered the start of industrialisation on a scale which was completely irreversible once it got started, and which was to spread and transform the whole of the rest of the world.

Even if the ancient Mediterranean culture of the Greeks and Romans failed to give birth to industrialisation, it does not necessarily follow that it could not have begun somewhere else before it did in eighteenth-century Britain. Some of the factors required were available elsewhere, and perhaps most of them in some cases. There were major unified states in China, India and in the Islamic countries, and, for a considerable period, in central Asia too, as well as many smaller, reasonably stable polities, most of them with access to more technology than the ancient world possessed. In varying degrees, they were in touch with at least some of the cultural and intellectual developments taking place in Europe. The state which came closest to breaking through into industrialisation was China during the fifteenth century, but the progress made was snuffed out by the country's leaders, who turned back to traditional ways.[17] India, on the other hand, never showed any more signs of sustained industrial development than the Romans, despite the ability of the Mughal culture to build the Taj Mahal, its high point of excellence both in design and execution. Nor were smaller nations elsewhere any better at producing sustained economic growth. On the contrary, it was in Europe, divided into a large number of relatively small states, all in competition with each other, that there began to be a slow cumulative increase in living standards, starting early in the second millennium, which eventually produced the Industrial Revolution, and the transformation in prospects for humanity which it brought in train.

Machinery, technology and power

Understanding the way in which world economic history has unfolded depends largely on appreciating what economic growth actually entails and what makes it occur. What changed when the

Industrial Revolution got under way? What had not been happening before which then started to manifest itself on the scale and to the degree which made the radical difference to living standards which Table 1.1 portrays? This table shows estimates of GDP per head in different parts of the world before and after industrialisation got under way.

Table 1.1: Estimates of GDP per head in selected regions of the world during the last two millennia. (All figures are per year and in 1990 international dollars.)

Year	0	1000	1820	1998
Western Europe	450	400	1,232	17,921
Western Offshoots	400	400	1,201	26,146
Japan	400	425	1,130	21,470
Latin America	400	400	665	5,795
Eastern Europe (inc USSR)	400	400	667	4,354
Asia (exc Japan)	450	450	575	2,936
Africa	444	440	573	3,102

Source: Table 1-2 on page 28 in *The World Economy: A Millennial Perspective*, Angus Maddison, Paris: OECD, 2001.

Humanity has always been interested in higher living standards, which the strongest and most gifted members of society have always made sure that they enjoyed, with the most powerful frequently flaunting their income and wealth. Poorer people have always envied those who were richer and down the ages have strived to emulate their perceived good fortune. In democracies, as in more authoritarian societies, the popularity of governments turns heavily on their ability to deliver the increases in living standards which only economic growth can produce. The reason why, despite the attractions of doing so, it has often proved so difficult in practice for governments to produce sustained increases in productivity is that it is not so obvious what makes this possible and thus what to do to create the conditions when it will occur.

Increases in output per head can only be achieved when the value of whatever is produced by the average worker goes up – and in real terms. The Industrial Revolution demonstrated that this could happen essentially in three ways. The first was the development of machinery which could carry out far more quickly and accurately processes which would otherwise have had to be carried out by slower and often more fallible human labour. The second was to apply technology to production which would enable inputs to be combined together to produce much more valuable outputs than could be achieved without the know-how now being applied. The third was to use fuels – originally wood, charcoal and coal, but subsequently oil – greatly to increase the power which could be exercised and used in the production of goods and services.

All these ways of increasing output involved real increases in value added. If a new machine which makes two of something replaces one which makes one of the same thing, without any increase in inputs, output doubles. Similarly, if the use of technology combines together inputs which have only half the value of what is then produced, output is multiplied by two. And if the use of fuel doubles up the rate at which value can be created while all other inputs remain the same, again output goes up by 100%. This is what produces economic growth, and why a bulldozer is so much more productive than a shovel and a computer than a slide-rule. The key point to grasp is that no other economic activities will achieve these increases in real output on anything like the same scale. Many other kinds of investment are extremely important in social terms (in roads, schools, hospitals, rail and housing, for example) or for commercial reasons (building office blocks or opening new restaurants) but generally they all lack the capacity to add value to the economy as a whole at a rate much faster than the rate of interest on the investment needed to finance them. The Roman empire was good at producing almost all forms of social infrastructure but failed to achieve sustained increases in output per head. This was because it lacked the capacity to harness the key ingredients for doing so: mechanisation, technology and power.

The increases in productivity achieved by all forms of investment – those that produce high or low rates of return – are then disseminated throughout the economy. The extent to which this is done by any particular activity is measured by the social rate of return. This is the total return to society which comes from increased output. Some of it is reflected in higher wages, some in increased returns to whoever financed whatever investment was required, some in increased profitability for the organisation responsible, some in the form of better and/or cheaper products and some comes back to society in the form of increased tax receipts.

The key factor is that the social rate of return – especially in the right conditions – which can be achieved by machinery, technology and increased power, backed up by appropriate education and training and other supply-side inputs, is typically far higher than the private returns to those who may have invested in resources to make the increased output possible. Perhaps the most extraordinary case is that of the USA when, spurred on initially by Lend-Lease and then by wartime munition requirements, between 1939 and 1944 its economy grew in real terms by 84%, while the social rate of return per annum on investment soared to 164%.[18] Our own economic history also has at least one short period – during the middle of the 1930s – when exceptionally high returns were achieved with a 28% per annum total return on investment, on average, for the years between 1934 and 1937.[19] Japan, on the other hand achieved a social rate of return on investment of 35% for the whole of the period from 1950 to 1970.[20] Small wonder that at the end of this period, the Japanese economy was 5.0 times the size it had been at the beginning.[21] Compare this with the UK economy where the overall rate of return between 1950 and 1970 – taking into account all forms of investment – averaged 16% and between the beginning and the end of the period the economy grew by no more than 74%.[22]

While these returns are calculated for ratios covering the whole of the economies concerned, not all the recorded output increases in gross domestic product, (GDP), even if calculated in real terms, i.e. net of inflation, represent genuine increases in value added, at least in the same sense as those achieved by machinery, technology and increased power. This is because the very high increases in productivity achievable from these activities are not replicable across most of the rest of the economy, including large sections of the service sector. GDP simply measures the cash value added of all activity in the economy, some of which may go up without there being any real increase in utility.

The classic example is hairdressing where productivity increases since the Industrial Revolution started have effectively been zero.

It still takes about the same time and level of skill to carry out a haircut now as it did 250 years ago, but if hairdressers were paid in real terms now what they were then, there would be no-one available nowadays to cut anyone's hair. Instead what has happened is that the income earned by hairdressers has gone up in real terms more or less in line with those earned by those whose increases in output per hour have risen as a result of their increased productivity. At the same time the real in-use value of the goods produced – largely as a result of improvements in machinery, technology and again power – has risen dramatically while their price has fallen. The net result is that whatever level of economic growth is actually achieved, measured in the conventional way by enhanced GDP, is even more dependent on achieving rising living standards in real terms on the sectors which produce large increases in output per hour than might appear at first sight to be the case.

It is in this light that the figures in Tables 1.2a and 1.2b which need to be interpreted. These cover sufficiently long periods, to enable it to be seen clearly over a time-span which irons out short-term fluctuations where real growth was generated. In both the USA and the UK, manufacturing produced much the largest contribution to economic growth of any sector of the economy – 54% in the USA and 28% in the UK, despite the fact that as a percentage of GDP manufacturing contributed only 19% of GDP in the USA and 11% in the UK, averaged out over the periods concerned.

Where significant contributions to growth were achieved, other cases in the US were Wholesale Trade (20%), Agriculture (12%), and Transport & Utilities (11%). In the UK, where the classifications were done on a different basis, the sectors with particularly significant growth contributions were Information and Communications (23%), Science & Technology and Professional (17%) and Finance & Insurance (14%). In all of these sectors it is easy to see how relevant investment in mechanisation, technology and power must have been to the growth achieved.

The US has a large sector described as Services which has an appallingly bad productivity record, with employment nearly doubling but output per head falling by nearly 1% every year across the whole of the 20-year period covered by the figures. In

Table 1.2a: Changes in output per head of the US working population between 1977 and 1997

1977	Output value in constant 1992 $bn	Labour force (millions)	Output per head ($000s)		% GVA in 1977	% GVA in 1997	1977-1997 change in GDP % output
Manufacturing	796.5	19.7	40.5		18.6%	18.8%	0.2%
Construction	213.8	3.9	55.5		5.0%	3.8%	−1.2%
Mining	82.4	0.8	101.4		1.9%	1.5%	−0.4%
Sub total	1,092.7	24.3	44.9		25.6%	24.1%	−1.4%
Agriculture, Forestry & Fishing	61.1	4.1	14.7		1.4%	1.8%	0.3%
Transport & Utilities	346.8	4.7	73.6		8.1%	8.9%	0.7%
Wholesale Trade	201.0	4.7	42.6		4.7%	7.3%	2.6%
Retail Trade	364.5	13.8	26.4		8.5%	9.8%	1.3%
Finance, Insurance & Real Estate	742.7	4.5	166.3		17.4%	17.7%	0.3%
Services	712.5	15.3	46.6		16.7%	19.2%	2.6%
Statistical Discrepancy	37.3				0.9%	−0.6%	−1.5%
Not Allocated	−2.4				−0.1%	−0.3%	−0.3%
Government	717.4	15.1	47.4		16.8%	12.2%	−4.6%
1977 GDP	4,273.6	86.6	49.3		100.0%	100.0%	0.0%

1997	Output value in constant 1992 $bn	Labour force (millions)	Output per head ($000s)	Output per Head Percentage Changes from 1977 to 1997 Total % Change	Output per Head Percentage Changes from 1977 to 1997 Annual % Average	Weighted Average % of the Economy	1977-1997 Growth Contribution	1977-1997 Growth Contribution %
Manufacturing	1,369.9	18.7	73.4	81.4%	3.0%	18.8%	9.4%	54.2%
Construction	274.4	5.7	48.3	−13.1%	0.7%	4.2%	−0.3%	−2.0%
Mining	109.9	0.6	185.6	83.2%	3.1%	1.7%	0.9%	4.9%
	1,754.2	24.9	70.4	56.7%	2.3%	24.7%	8.6%	49.7%
Agriculture, Forestry & Fishing	127.6	2.9	44.5	201.8%	5.7%	1.6%	2.0%	11.7%
Transport & Utilites	644.3	6.4	100.8	36.9%	1.6%	8.6%	2.0%	11.2%
Wholesale Trade	532.0	6.6	80.0	88.0%	3.2%	6.3%	3.4%	19.8%
Retail Trade	713.5	22.0	32.4	22.7%	1.0%	9.3%	1.3%	7.5%
"Finance, Insurance & Real Estate"	1,286.0	7.1	181.4	9.1%	0.4%	17.6%	1.0%	5.7%
Services	1,398.6	36.0	38.8	−16.7%	−0.9%	18.3%	−1.9%	−10.8%
Statistical Discrepancy	−45.4					−0.1%	0.0%	0.0%
Not Allocated	−25.0					−0.2%	0.0%	0.0%
Government	884.0	19.6	45.2	−4.8%	−0.2%	13.9%	−0.4%	−2.3%
1997 GDP	7,269.8	125.6	57.9	17.3%	0.8%	100.0%	17.3%	100.0%

Source: Tables B.13, B.46 and B.100, *Economic Report to the President 1999*. Washington DC: US Government Printing Office 1999

the UK, there is no comparable statistical sector, but of the growth which was achieved a total of 68% came from Manufacturing (28%), Information and Communications (23%) and Professional, Science & Technology (16%), which between them contributed only 23% of GDP. All the remaining 77% of GDP only produced 32% of increased gross added value, even allowing for the bias involved in conventional GDP accounting in favour of services and against manufacturing as the cost of goods tends to fall while those of services are inclined to increase.

These figures also indicate a number of crucial features about investment and how to achieve economic growth. There is little indication that the social rate of return from investment in most social infrastructure – schools, hospitals, housing, etc – however desirable it may be on other grounds, does anything significant to produce economic growth, although transport infrastructure – road and rail – may have a more significant part to play. Nor does it suggest that education and training have as much of a role as is often supposed, unless combined with physical investment, again however much they may be valued for other reasons. Machinery and technology require skilled management when initial decisions about their use are made but, once installed, many of their operating requirements are comparatively simple and do not need particularly high levels of skill or training. On the contrary, the key requirements among the workforce are attributes such as thoroughness, dedication and timeliness.

The reality is that the natural environment for most large-scale investments in machinery and technology is in the profit driven private sector, primarily in light manufacturing and the heavily technology oriented parts of the service sector. There is a very important role for the government, however, and that is to ensure that the environment in which those sectors of the economy capable of achieving high rates of increase in output per hour are encouraged to undertake the investment in them which, in turn, will produce the returns needed to secure rapid increases in productivity. The key requirement here is that investment of this kind has a high chance of being profitable, and this is very largely a function of how competitive labour costs – adjusted for both

Table 1.2b: Changes in output per head of the UK working population between 1990 and 2015

	1990	Gross Value Added in constant £bn	Labour Force in '000s	Gross Value Added per Head	% GVA in 1990	% GVA in 2015	1990-15 Change in GDP % Output
A	Agriculture	£9.9	486	£20,465	1.0%	0.7%	−0.3
B	Mining and Quarrying	£47.4	137	£346,182	4.7%	1.9%	−2.8%
C	Manufacturing	£152.5	4,814	£31,676	15.3%	9.7%	−5.6%
D	Electricity, Gas, etc	£14.3	211	£67,896	1.4%	1.2%	−0.2
E	Water	£11.7	113	£103,796	1.2%	1.2%	0.0%
F	Construction	£92.5	2,128	£43,462	9.3%	6.1%	−3.1%
G	Wholesale Retail & Motor Trade	£107.3	4,363	£24,600	10.7%	11.6%	0.9%
H	Transportation and Storage	£42.4	1,327	£31,972	4.2%	4.4%	0.2%
I	Accommodation and Food	£29.9	1,592	£18,791	3.0%	2.7%	−0.3%
J	Information and Comms	£31.1	950	£32,705	3.1%	6.3%	3.2%
K	Financial & Insurance	£62.6	1,181	£53,027	6.3%	6.9%	0.6%
L	Real Estate	£86.9	242	£359,256	8.7%	11.7%	3.0%
M	Professional Science Tech	£42.0	1,490	£28,214	4.2%	8.0%	3.8%
N	Administration & Support	£28.3	1,291	£21,947	2.8%	5.2%	2.4%
O-Q	Government, Health and Edu	£199.7	6,447	£30,977	20.0%	18.1%	−1.8%
R-U	Other Services	£40.9	1,306	£31,309	4.1%	4.2%	0.2%
		£999.7	28,078	£35,604	100.0%	100.0%	0.0%

	2015	Gross Value Added in constant £bn	Labour Force in '000s	Gross Value Added per Head	Output per Head Percentage Changes from 1990 to 2015 Total % Change	Annual Average	Weighted Average % of the Economy	Growth Contribution	Growth Contribution %
A	Agriculture	£11.7	384	£30,568	49.4%	1.6%	0.83%	0.36%	0.9%
B	Mining and Quarrying	£30.6	76	£403,211	16.5%	0.7%	3.00%	0.43%	1.1%
C	Manufacturing	£155.0	2,614	£59,300	87.2%	2.5%	11.80%	9.03%	23.0%
D	Electricity, Gas, etc	£19.9	139	£143,295	111.1%	3.0%	1.31%	1.28%	3.3%
E	Water	£19.5	180	£108,261	4.3%	0.2%	1.20%	0.05%	0.1%
F	Construction	£98.3	2,118	£46,416	6.8%	0.3%	7.32%	0.44%	1.1%
G	Wholesale Retail & Motor Trade	£186.2	4,965	£37,510	52.5%	1.7%	11.27%	5.19%	13.2%
H	Transportation and Storage	£70.7	1,387	£50,978	59.4%	1.9%	4.34%	2.26%	5.8%
I	Accommodation and Food	£43.2	2,174	£19,888	5.8%	0.2%	2.81%	0.14%	0.4%
J	Information and Comms	£101.4	1,344	£75,449	130.7%	3.4%	5.08%	5.83%	14.9%
K	Financial & Insurance	£110.7	1,131	£97,868	84.6%	2.5%	6.65%	4.93%	12.6%
L	Real Estate	£187.3	501	£373,780	4.0%	0.1%	10.52%	0.37%	1.0%
M	Professional Science Tech	£127.9	2,569	£49,771	76.4%	2.3%	6.52%	4.37%	11.2%
N	Administration & Support	£83.7	2,692	£31,108	41.7%	1.4%	4.30%	1.57%	4.0%
O-Q	Government, Health and Edu	£291.2	8,342	£34,909	12.7%	0.5%	18.84%	2.10%	5.4%
R-U	Other Services	£68.2	1,782	£38,250	22.2%	0.8%	4.19%	0.81%	2.1%
		£1,605.6	32,398	£49,559	39.2%	1.3%	100%	39.2%	100.0%

Sources: Tables on Employees by Standard Industrial Classification (SIC) ONS reference LPROD02. Table on Value Added by SIC from ONS Table reference GDP (O) Low Level. All values are in constant prices Employment figures are from Q3. ONS include a qualification that some of the data provided is volatile. Users are therefore requested to take this into account when interpreting it.

their productivity and the exchange rate – are for any particular economy in the globalised market in which nowadays they almost all have to operate.

The productivity of any country's labour force depends partly on its level of training, particularly vocational training, but even more on the volume of accumulated capital assets (in this case mostly machinery) with which it is provided. One of the main reasons why German exports are so competitive, despite the relatively high wages which German workers are paid, is that the Germans both have a very well-trained labour force and very substantial accumulated machinery capital assets to support it. The UK suffers, correspondingly, because our educational system is poorly orientated towards vocational training and because our workforce is relatively so inadequately endowed with accumulated capital equipment.

Another perception which needs to be treated with a large measure of caution is that our future depends on high- rather than low- or medium-tech manufacturing activity. It is true that in the UK, and indeed across much of the western world, low- and medium-tech industrial, internationally-tradable activity has diminished in significance as unmanageable competition from the Far East has undermined its profitability and hence its viability, leaving to a large extent only high-tech activity still standing. This does not mean, however, that high-tech is inviolable – only that it is more difficult to attack from low-cost bases and that its complex supply chains, intellectual property, heavy branding, accumulated expertise and know-how give it protection in the short and medium term. In the longer run, however, as emerging economies gain expertise, they will be able to attack this sector too. The result may well be that it will also be eroded away by lower-cost competition.

The reality is that most manufacturing activity is not at the cutting edge of technology. Most of it relies on know-how and machinery which is widely and generally available. Where it gets sited in the world will then depend very largely on where total operating costs are competitive, which in the end boils down very largely to the rate at which unit labour costs are charged out to the rest of the world.

Given the situation which countries like the UK are in, however, where much of our industry has clearly been struggling to compete, there is a way of compensating for what would otherwise be our relatively high unit labour costs in those sectors of our economy which have to compete on world markets – a key underlying theme throughout this book. This is to use a lower exchange rate to enable us to charge out our labour costs at a rate which the rest of the world is prepared to pay. Since most of our exports are goods rather than services, this means adopting an exchange rate which will make our manufactures competitive on world markets.

Now we are getting close to seeing why some economies grow so much more rapidly than others. Given whatever the accumulated skills and industrial capital behind their workforce may be, any economy which has a competitive exchange rate will generate an environment where investment in machinery and technology will be profitable for investors. The profitability thus generated will attract able managers, who will then use their skills and abilities to run their businesses with better than average sales and investment strategies for the future. Investment as a percentage of GDP will go up. Exports will grow exponentially while imports will remain comparatively restrained. This is not what we see in the UK at the moment – or indeed in nearly all of the western world. It is, however, a familiar picture in many countries particularly along the Pacific Rim.

Economic history – and our prospects for the future – are therefore very largely determined by the effect which the policies pursued by governments have on the competitiveness of the economies for which they are responsible. This is the core variable which is traced through all of the following chapters. It is the comprehensive failure of policymakers in the West to realise the significance of their countries' competiveness, and what needs to be done in terms of fiscal monetary and exchange rate policies to achieve it, which is fundamentally the reason why the western world is in the unstable state it is in at present, both economically and politically.

The Industrial Revolution

The Industrial Revolution, which began in Europe in the eighteenth century, evidently rested on a foundation built over hundreds of years. Since the Middle Ages, and at least since the fourteenth century, there had been a slow increase in output per head in Europe, set back from time to time by pestilence, bad government and devastation caused by wars. This growth had come about partly as a result of improved agriculture, partly as a result of increased trade, based on the availability of an adequate credit system, but mainly because of the application of new ideas, some based on novel technology, to a wide variety of production processes.

To reiterate, the Industrial Revolution was built on the foundation of the slow accumulation of a large number of technical advances over hundreds of years. The advent of the printing press vastly reduced the cost of producing books, and thus of disseminating knowledge. The developments in ship design and navigation greatly decreased the costs of trading, while opening up large sections of the world which had previously been unknown to Europeans. The resulting exchange of products enabled gains from specialisation in the production of goods and agricultural products to be realised which had never been available before. There was a steady improvement in the working of metals, providing the basis for the production of machinery. The Renaissance and the Enlightenment provided a ferment of ideas, some of which fed through to industry to provide a much clearer explanation of how industrial processes worked. Not least of these were advances in mathematics, mentioned previously, which made it easier for calculations relating to production processes to be done quickly and accurately. At the same time, there was a steady accumulation of practical knowledge acquired by increasingly skilled labour forces, capable of putting new ideas into operation.

The Industrial Revolution quickened and began to gather pace faster in Britain during the eighteenth century than elsewhere, allowing the British to take over economic leadership from the Netherlands. During the previous two centuries, the Dutch had built up a formidable economy based on a combination of trade and commerce, which had provided a higher standard of living than had previously been achieved anywhere else. As was to happen so frequently in the future, however, the accumulation of wealth and financial power, which appeared to make the state so strong, gradually became its undoing. As financial interests, with their usual predilection for hard money, became increasingly dominant, the exchange rate rose, and the rising costs of doing business in the Netherlands, compared to elsewhere, caused economic activity to drift away, not least to Britain.[23] The Dutch economy stagnated, and its lead was lost, though the reasons why this occurred – essentially the same overvalued exchange rate problem which was to be Britain's undoing in the nineteenth century and subsequently – were not appreciated at the time, or for a long period to come.

In the meantime, Britain had moved further away from the feudal system of the Middle Ages than most other countries in Europe. There was a more highly developed system of contract law, and generally a less arbitrary system of government than on the continent. As a result of successfully developed trading patterns, there was a reasonably sophisticated banking system and accumulations of capital which could be mobilised for risk ventures. There was stable government. Above all, there was an entrepreneurial class, much of it, characteristically, excluded from mainstream political life in the form of the non-conformists, which was attracted to commerce and manufacturing. There were also major agricultural interests with much of the land owned by forward-looking landowners involved in exploiting new ideas in agricultural husbandry.

The Industrial Revolution thus got under way in Britain in textiles, pottery, mining and metal working, aided by improvements in transport such as the development of canals. A combination of outworking and factories led to big increases in output when production processes were broken down into individual specialised functions, as Adam Smith (1723–1790) accurately noted in *The Wealth of Nations*. This extremely influential book, published in 1776 at a remarkably early stage of the Industrial Revolution, contained an exceptionally powerful set of ideas about the changes taking place in the industrial and commercial worlds, and how government policy should be organised to take advantage of them. If the early pace in the development of economics set by Adam Smith had been maintained, the subsequent economic history of the world might have been very different.

Not only did the early Industrial Revolution involve rising

living standards on average for the British people compared to those elsewhere, it also greatly enhanced Britain's power in the world. This made it possible for the British to build and maintain a dominant navy and to deploy and finance the coalition of land forces which eventually won them victory in the Napoleonic Wars. Thereafter, it enabled the British to extend their control over ever-increasing areas of the world until, by three-quarters of the way through the nineteenth century, Britain ruled directly or indirectly about a quarter of the land surface of globe.[24] The accumulation of an empire on this scale undoubtedly provided Britain with ready access to raw materials and sources of supply of cheap food, as well as a partially protected export market. Earlier, profits from the slave trade had assisted the accumulation of capital, some of which helped to finance the Industrial Revolution in the UK.[25] The relative decline in the British economy as the territories the British controlled grew in number, however, calls into question whether this major endeavour as a whole entailed a net benefit. Faster economic growth elsewhere strongly suggests that the effort and bias in policy involved in building up and running the British Empire, and the cost of maintaining it, were more trouble than they were worth.

While France had a rather lower average standard of living than Britain in the early eighteenth century,[26] many of the other circumstances needed to get industry moving there were also in place. The French, however, were much slower to take advantage of the new opportunities available in manufacturing. Partly this was the result of the arbitrary characteristics of the *Ancien Régime*, which lacked the contract legal system introduced shortly after the 1789 French Revolution.[27] Partly it was a matter of social pressures, also related to the sense of values of the pre-revolutionary period, which held industry and commerce in relatively low esteem. The result was that French industry tended to concentrate on the manufacture of individually produced items, some of them widely recognised as being of exceptionally high quality, rather than moving to mass production methods. French furniture, tapestries, china and jewellery were internationally renowned, but the cottage industry techniques used for producing them were not the stuff of which industrial revolutions are made. Germany also suffered from disadvantages, many of them similar to those in France, compounded by the patchwork of small states which made up the country, each with its own tariff and economic policies. The southern areas of Europe, Spain, Portugal, Italy and Greece were all much poorer, and in a weaker position to start industrialising, as indeed remained the case for a century or more. The Netherlands, which had grown richer during the eighteenth century than anywhere else, faltered as its trading and financial success undermined its domestic industry – a story to be repeated many times in the years to come. It was therefore Britain which made the running for a long time into the nineteenth century.

Europe up to 1914

A recurrent theme in this book – indeed the most dominant one of all – is how crucially important exchange rates have been to the way economic history has evolved. This has been especially so at times when trade and capital flows have been liberalised. Nevertheless, it is remarkable how little their impact, particularly on foreign trade but with ramifications across the whole economy, has been taken into account by policymakers. Nowhere is this truer than in the case of the UK, which has a long history of ignoring the impact of competitiveness on our foreign trade position, with dire consequences for the rest of the economy.

An all too typical – and important – early case took place before the Industrial Revolution had really begun. During the reign of William III (1650-1702), which lasted from 1689 to 1702, the silver coinage which was circulating in the country had been debased by clipping.[28] The effect was to devalue the clipped silver currency in relation to gold. As a result, by 1695, the rate of exchange between gold guineas and silver coins, which had previously been 20 to one, had risen to 30 silver coins per gold guinea. Much of the international trade of the time was conducted in silver shillings. What should be done? Should the value of the silver coinage be allowed to remain at 30 shillings to the guinea, or should its value be driven up to 20?

Leading contestants in the dispute which followed were Sir Isaac Newton (1642–1727), who advocated the former view, and the philosopher John Locke (1632–1704), who favoured the latter. The King accepted Locke's deflationary advice – a dismal and ominous portent for the future. The consequences, as Newton predicted, were falling prices and depressed business conditions. Newton nevertheless became Master of the Mint, and in 1711 he fixed the value of the pound at £3 17s 9d per ounce of gold. Apart from suspensions during and following the Napoleonic Wars and World War I, and two short breaks during the nineteenth century caused by temporary financial panics, this parity remained intact until 1931.

The next major controversy over macro-economic policy in the UK took place towards the end of the Napoleonic Wars. The strain imposed on the British economy during the long wartime period, stretching almost without a break from 1793 to 1815, had stimulated output. The economy was much larger and more productive at the end of the wars than it had been at the beginning. The high level of demand had, however, led to substantial inflation, which had nearly doubled the price level during the war years. Britain had gone off the gold standard in 1797 because the country's banks of the time could not meet the demand for cash caused by the threat of invasion. Too many holders of their bank notes wished to change them into gold. The banks were therefore freed to increase the note issue without gold backing, both in response to the increase in government borrowing to finance the wars, as well as the additional demand for money resulting from expanding national output. By 1810, prices had risen an estimated 76%[29] compared with 1790, and this was of course reflected in the price of gold, which had risen proportionately.

Had prices risen because the money supply had been increased? Or was extra money required to accommodate the growing need for cash as both prices rose and the size of the economy became larger, with the fundamental causes of inflation lying elsewhere? This controversy – still central to economic policy formulation – was the key issue addressed by the *Report from the Select Committee on the High Price of Gold Bullion*, published in 1810, which set out the arguments between the Currency School and the Banking School. The Currency School maintained that under a 'purely metallic standard', any loss of gold to, or influx from, other countries would result immediately and automatically in a decrease or increase in the amount of money in circulation. The resulting rigid control of the money supply would provide the discipline to keep price rises at bay. With a mixed currency of metal and paper, however, this system could not operate satisfactorily, unless it was managed as precisely as if it depended on the amount of gold backing the currency. Any deviation from this principle, it was averred, would lead to inflation.

The Banking School, on the other hand, denied that a purely gold-based currency would operate in the manner claimed for it by the Currency School. Because of hoarding and other uses to which gold could be put, it was far from clear that the amount available to back the currency was as constant as the Currency School claimed it would be. Furthermore, it was contended that the Currency School greatly overestimated the risks involved in expanding paper money. The Banking School believed, on the contrary, that the need for prudence in the process of competitive banking would exercise a necessary restraint on the issue of paper money. This approach would have led to a much more accommodating monetary stance and a lower exchange rate for sterling, but it was not to be. The committee came down in favour of the currency principle, by advocating a return to the gold standard at the 1797 parity, despite the increase in prices which had taken place. The majority concluded that the price rises during the wars had come about because monetary discipline had slipped, and that the only way to secure financial stability in the future was to get the pound back to where it had been previously in terms of its value in relation to gold. The views which prevailed in this report, setting as they did the tone of British financial policy for many years into the future, were to have a profound impact on Britain's economic history to the present day.

Despite the reservations of the minority of the committee, which included David Ricardo (1772–1823), one of the key economic theorists of his time, sterling was restored to its pre-war parity against gold during the years following the end of the Napoleonic Wars. This objective was achieved by methods which have an all-too-familiar ring to them. The money supply was reduced, interest rates were raised, and the pound strengthened against foreign currencies which had mostly left their parities against gold or silver where they were at the end of the Napoleonic Wars. It took six years, from 1815 to 1821, to force wages and prices down sufficiently to enable cash payments in gold at the pre-war parity to be resumed. In consequence, there was a sharp depression as the post-war boom broke, leading to business failures, falling living standards, rising unemployment and great hardship for working people. Opposition culminated in a riot in Manchester in 1819 – Peterloo – which was broken up by a local cavalry force, generating echoes of the battle which had ended the Napoleonic Wars so successfully for Britain only four years previously. Trade unions were made illegal by the repressive Six Acts, passed into law at the end of 1819.[30] The final victory of the Currency School, easily recognised as having views close to those of modern monetarists, was the 1844 Bank Charter Act, which locked the pound into its high value measured in gold, a parity which was only finally abandoned in 1931.

The resulting relatively high cost of producing goods and services in Britain compared with the rest of Europe did not, however, hold back the British economy for long. During the first half of the nineteenth century, Britain was the only country which was industrialising fast. In consequence, the cost of goods produced in Britain fell rapidly compared with output elsewhere in Europe, making them very competitive despite the relatively high gold parity for sterling compared to other currencies inherited from the outcome of the banking controversy. The British economy expanded by 2.8% per annum on average for the whole of the period from 1820 to 1851, when the Great Exhibition was held in London, marking the high peak of British pre-eminence. From 1851 to 1871 the growth rate slowed to 2.3%.[31] Even so, the cumulative increase in wealth and the standard of living was without parallel with anything ever seen in the world before, except in the United States, far away on the other side of the Atlantic and heavily protected by tariffs, but also in Australia and New Zealand where high rates of growth were also being achieved.

With increasing confidence in its industrial capacity, the case for trade liberalisation in Britain appeared to become stronger. The Industrial Revolution had started in Britain behind substantial tariff barriers, themselves a legacy of the mercantilist policies of self-sufficiency against which Adam Smith had preached in *The Wealth of Nations*. As the expanding population pressed on the domestically-produced food supply, however, necessitating increased imports of corn and other foodstuffs, the case for keeping down the cost of living by removing import tariffs and quotas became more appealing. Free trade arguments were also extended to manufactured goods, leading to the trade treaties negotiated in the 1840s and 1850s. By 1860 the total number of dutiable items coming in to Britain had been reduced to 48. By 1882 only 12 imported articles were taxed, and these purely for revenue raising purposes.[32]

Unilateral free trade, however, acts like a revaluation of the currency. It makes imports relatively cheaper than exports. Adopting free trade policies therefore had the same effect as raising the sterling exchange rate, which was already very high. Free trade in consequence also contributed to Britain's undoing as the nineteenth century wore on. All over Europe, but particularly in France, Germany and the Benelux countries, British manufacturing techniques began to be copied. The initial impulse came primarily from the development of railways, as their construction got under way on a substantial scale all over Europe from the 1840s and 1850s onwards. This necessitated not only major developments in civil engineering, but also large investments in production facilities capable of turning out thousands of kilometres of rail, relatively sophisticated rolling stock, and complex signalling equipment. Characteristically, while in Britain all these developments had been financed entirely by the private sector, in France and Germany the state was heavily involved in railway construction from the beginning, underwriting a considerable proportion of the high risks involved. Differing perceptions about the role of the state vis-à-vis the private sector across Europe have a long history.

British production techniques were soon copied not only in

railways but also in virtually all other fields. Other forms of communications were employed, such as canals which already had a long history in Britain. Mass production of textiles followed, particularly initially in north-east France, but soon spreading throughout Europe. Iron and steel output, greatly stimulated by the development of railways, but also providing the basis for the production of metal goods for a wide range of other purposes, began to grow rapidly, particularly in Germany. The output of steel trebled there between 1840 and 1860, and trebled again between 1860 and 1880.[33] The economies of Europe became better able to compete with Britain for other reasons too. Germany was united first loosely under the Zollverein of 1834, and later more tightly under Otto von Bismarck (1815-1898), once Prussia had secured its position of leadership.[34] Everywhere, although much more rapidly in some places than others, there were improvements in education, the legal system, the organisation of the professions and the training of skilled workforces.

A major turning point came in the 1870s, as the worldwide consumer and investment boom, caused by the American Civil War and the Franco-Prussian conflict, collapsed when the wars ended, resulting in a major fall in demand for armaments, and a slowdown in railway building. For the first time, Britain felt the full blast of foreign competition, and the British lead in industrial output became seriously threatened. The value of British exports fell from £256m in 1872 to £192m in 1879. Much of this fall was compensated for in volume terms by lower prices, but not all. The 1872 export figure in money terms was not exceeded again until 1890. In the case of manufactures, the ground lost was not recovered in terms of value until 1903, more than 30 years later.[35] The growth rate of the British economy stabilised at 2.0% per annum for the last quarter of the nineteenth century. From 1870 to 1900 the economy in Germany grew by 125%, the Netherlands by 96%, Britain by 85%, Belgium by 82% and France by 56%.[36]

The sources of increases in output differed between France and Britain, which were falling back, and countries such as Germany which were pulling ahead. In Britain, in particular, more and more investment went abroad. In the slower-growing economies, a rising percentage of investment went into housing and infrastructure, and a relatively low proportion into industry. Total investment as a percentage of GDP in these countries fell or remained static. Where investments were made in industry, more went into widening rather than deepening the industrial structure. In Britain, in particular, there was a vast expansion of the cotton industry and coal mining, both of which were labour intensive, but where large additional productivity gains were difficult to achieve.

In Germany, and to a lesser extent elsewhere on the continent, these trends were reversed. A higher proportion of investment went into new industries, such as the production of dyes and chemicals, sophisticated metal products, and later motor vehicles and electrical goods. The significance of these industries was that the scope for increased output and improved productivity was much greater than in the kind of industries to which Britain, trapped by the strength of sterling within the gold standard system, was moving. The circumstances which had given Britain the advantage in the early part of the nineteenth century were reversed. It was Germany and the Netherlands which now had more competitive exports, and which were less prone to import penetration because of the strength of local manufactures and the protection they enjoyed. Influenced particularly by Friedrich List (1789–1846), whose *Das nationale System der politischen Oekonomie* was published in 1837, the continental economies were much more willing than the British to use tariffs to protect their rising industries. This made sense partly because they were much more self-sufficient in foodstuff production so that free trade had less general attractions. They could therefore concentrate production where the growth prospects were highest, and reinvest productively a greater proportion of their national incomes in their own economies.

The result was that by the start of World War I, much of the gap between the income per head in Britain and the rest of north-west Europe had closed. Whereas in 1850, GDP per head had been twice as high in Britain as in the most advanced parts of the continent of Europe, by 1914 the difference was only about a quarter.[37] Furthermore, in industrial capacity Germany was well ahead of Britain in many respects. German steel output had overtaken Britain's in the 1890s. By 1910, Britain was producing 6.5m tons of steel per year, but Germany was producing 13m.[38] Just before the outbreak of World War I, Germany had twice as many kilometres of rail track as Britain and was generating six times as much electricity.[39] The high value of sterling compared to the currencies of the countries now competing with Britain ensured that a very substantial price was paid for this privilege in the form of slower growth.

Economic power was seeping away from Britain, and with it the capacity of the British to continue dominating the world as had been possible for the previous 100 years. Between 1870 and 1913 the population in Germany grew a third faster than it did in Britain,[40] further strengthening Germany's military position. Rivalry between the great powers increased, and world war, with all its disastrous consequences for the world economy, came closer.

The US economy to World War I

When the first settlers arrived in North America from Europe, they brought with them immeasurable advantages over the indigenous population. The early colonists were by all historical standards exceptionally well endowed with their European legacy when they reached their destination, as indeed were many of those who subsequently followed in their steps. Nevertheless, the life of early settlers in the USA, and for many years subsequently, was tough and arduous. The country was enormous, and communications extremely primitive. Internal transportation was difficult and expensive, and sea-borne traffic provided the only practical solution to the movement of goods and people, producing a strong incentive for the development of efficient sailing ships. The population was overwhelmingly rural. Even as late as 1790, when it totalled about 3.9m, of whom almost 700,000 were slaves, there were only seven towns with a population of over 5,000 and 12 with over 2,500. In these circumstances, manufacturing on anything but the smallest of scales was impractical, because internal transport problems so severely limited the size of the potential market. Almost all US export trade was in raw materials, primarily cotton, tobacco and wheat flour.[41]

The Declaration of Independence in 1776, followed shortly afterwards by the Napoleonic Wars, in which the USA did not directly participate, and then the 1812 war with Britain, produced both opportunities and disadvantages. Trade was disrupted, but domestic manufacturing was encouraged, and exports grew dramatically, if erratically. Overall, the value of exports, which had been $20m in 1790 had grown to $52m by 1815, while imports rose from $24m $85m.[42] Part of the growth in output in the USA was attributable to its rapidly rising population, which had reached 7.2m by 1810 and 9.6m by 1820. The really explosive growth in the number of people living in the USA did not start, however, until about 1830, when the population was almost 13m. By 1860 it was 31m. The peak for immigration during this period was 1854, when 428,000 people moved to the the USA.[43]

As early as 1820, the USA was among the richest countries in the world, judged by GDP per capita. Estimates show the USA a little over 25% below the British living standard of the time, a little under 20% behind the Dutch and Australians, and about on a par with Austria, Belgium, Denmark, France and Sweden. By 1850, Britain was still well ahead of the USA, but the gap was closing.[44] The disruption of the American Civil War held back the USA for a few years, but by 1870, the US growth rate was poised for the rapid increase in output achieved over the period between 1870 and 1913. During the 50 years between 1820 and 1870, the US economy had grown much faster than those on the other side of the Atlantic. Between 1820 and 1850, it grew cumulatively by 4.2% per annum, although the increase in output per head was much lower at 1.3% per annum, close to the British figure for the period of 1.25%. This was now to change. During the 43 years from 1870 to 1913, the US economy achieved a cumulative growth rate of 4.3% per annum. Allowing for compound population growth of 2.1% per annum, US GDP per head rose by 2.2% per annum.[45]

A differential in growth rates either in GDP or GDP per head of 1% or 2% per annum has a huge cumulative effect over a period such as the 43 years between 1870 and 1913. If two economies start at the same size at the beginning of a period this long, one which is growing 2% faster per annum than its rival will be 134%

larger 43 years later. Even if the differential is only 1%, it will be 53% bigger at the end of the period. The results of the differential growth rates which occurred between the USA and most of Europe in the late nineteenth and early twentieth centuries – reflected, of course, in what is happening now between West and East – thus presaged a seismic shift in world power. By 1913, the USA had overtaken Britain in living standards, leaving all the rest of Europe well behind. Only Australia and New Zealand were still ahead, but with much smaller populations and GDPs. By this time, the USA not only had a high GDP per head, but also a large population to go with it. By 1890 the US population was 63m, and by 1913 it was 98m.[46] As a result, the US economy was by then well over twice the size of its nearest rival, Britain, and more than four times that of Germany. Japan, which had grown by a respectable 2.8% per annum during the previous three decades, had an economy only about 13% the size of that of the USA in 1913.[47]

During the latter years of the nineteenth century and the early 1900s, gross domestic investment as a proportion of GDP was much higher in the USA than it was in other countries. It averaged nearly 20% of GDP for the whole period, compared with about 12% for Britain and 15% for France.[48] Achieving a high investment ratio was as important in the nineteenth century as it is now. All these factors helped, but the key figures then, as now, were not so much expansion of the total economy but output per head. As the figures above show, large increases in the population meant that American living standards grew much more slowly than the American economy as a whole during the decades running up to World War I. It is noteworthy that Sweden and Denmark increased their GDP per head faster than the USA over this period.[49]

The overall growth achieved by the USA in the nineteenth century was nevertheless unprecedented. By 1900 the American economy was about 25 times larger than it had been in 1820. By 1980, another 80 years later, by comparison, the increase was to a little over 13 times the 1900 figure.[50] The key period for expansion of the US economy, however, started during the decade before the Civil War when mechanisation and industrialisation really got into their strides. Between 1830 and the beginning of the 1865, manufacturing output increased nearly tenfold, while the population rose to about three times its 1830 figure. In the final decade before the Civil War began, steam engines and machinery output increased by 66%, cotton textiles by 77%, railroad production by 100%, and hosiery goods by 608%. As Reconstruction got under way, and the opportunities for a wide range of new technologies were exploited, improving communications and the quality of manufactures, the economy took off. The US gross stock of machinery and equipment increased by almost 400% between 1870 and 1890, and by 1913 it had nearly trebled again.[51]

It is no coincidence that it was the advent of large-scale increases in industrial output which triggered the rise in the US growth rate. The proportion of US GDP deriving from industry was on a strong upward trend throughout the nineteenth century. It employed 15% of the labour force in 1820, 24% in 1870, and 30% by 1913.[52] The USA also used its investment more efficiently than the average, especially towards the end of the nineteenth and beginning of the twentieth centuries, thereby gaining an important additional advantage.[53] This is a characteristic which the US economy still maintains, although the proportion of the US economy's output derived from manufacturing is now much lower than it was, down to 12.3% in 2014[54] from the 27% average achieved during the post-World War II period.[55]

It is often alleged that a stable financial environment is the key to economic growth, and that low interest rates and low inflation are required to ensure high levels of investment and increases in output. It is hard to square this view of the world with the experience of the US economy in the nineteenth century. For most of this period, the USA had no central bank at all. The charter of the First Bank of the United States expired in 1811, when it was not renewed by the Jeffersonians then in power. The Second Bank of the United States, established in 1816, was wound up shortly after the re-election in 1832 of President Andrew Jackson (1767-1845), who bitterly opposed its existence.[56] Thereafter, until the establishment of the Federal Reserve system in 1913, there was no central control of the US money supply. Credit creation was in the hands of thousands of banks, spread all over the country, many of them poorly run, undercapitalised, prone to speculation, and liable to fail.

It is hardly surprising that, in these circumstances, US interest rates, prices and credit availability gyrated from boom to bust repeatedly during the nineteenth century. The abolition of the Second Bank of the United States in 1833 was followed only four years later by the most serious depression the USA had experienced so far, in some ways a worse crash than in 1929. Prices fell 40% between 1838 and 1843, railroad construction declined by almost 70% and canal building by 90%. Large scale unemployment developed, and serious food riots broke out in New York City. It was not until 1844 that the next upswing started, culminating in the downturn in 1856, which lasted until 1862. This pattern was to be repeated throughout the nineteenth century, accompanied every time there was a fall in economic activity by bank closures, bankruptcies and widespread defaults.[57]

Nor was the price level at all stable during the nineteenth century. Between 1815 and 1850, the wholesale price level fell by 50%, with substantial fluctuations in intervening years. It rose by 50% during the 1860s, peaking in 1866 as a result of the Civil War, with the impact of the Californian gold rush on the money supply causing much of the underlying inflation. Between 1848 and 1858 California produced $550m worth of gold – 45% of world output between 1851 and 1855.[58] After 1870 prices fell until, by the turn of the century, they were 40% lower than they had been in 1870. They then climbed again about 25% during the years to 1913, mainly because the development of the cyanide process for extracting gold in South Africa led to another major increase in the world's monetary base, inflating the money supply and allowing prices to rise.[59]

Since World War II, promoting freer trade has been a major plank of US policy, also in sharp contrast to the high tariff protection promoted by successive administrations during the nineteenth century. Some import duties were imposed partly for revenue-raising purposes, as they were the major source of government income at the time, but industrial protection was also a factor from the beginning. The tariff of 1816 imposed duties of 20% to 25% on manufactured goods and 15% to 20% on raw materials.[60] Thereafter the tariff level fluctuated, with the trade cycle, as always, playing a major role. The depression of 1837, for example, stimulated a new wave of protectionism as American industrialists blamed high unemployment on cheap imported goods. The major shift to a much more protectionist policy came in 1861 with the Morrill Tariff, designed to make the importation of most mass produced goods into the USA completely uneconomic. Import duties were not to be lowered again until 1913, under Woodrow Wilson (1856-1924), although even then they still stood at about 25%. Wool, sugar, iron and steel, however, were added to the free list.[61]

A distinguishing feature of the US economy has always been the low proportion, by international standards, of US GDP involved in foreign trade. Exports averaged about 11.5% of GDP during the period running up to World War I – compared to 13.0% now. Imports ran then at under 8%,[62] compared with 15.2% at present.[63] Part of the reason for these relatively low ratios has always, of course, been the sheer size of the country, and its ability to supply a high proportion of its needs from domestic sources. There is little doubt, however, that in the circumstances of the years up to 1913, the high tariff barrier helped the USA develop its manufacturing industries, unhampered by competition from abroad. Goods which might have been purchased from Europe were produced in the USA. The high level of demand, albeit subject to severe fluctuations, which the unregulated credit and banking system generated, provided opportunities which US manufacturers were quick to seize. Under the gold standard regime, which the USA joined in 1879,[64] when bimetallism was abandoned, it would have been difficult for the USA to have lowered its prices internationally sufficiently to have held off growing import penetration. The competitiveness of European exports at the time is amply demonstrated by the high proportion of their output which the European economies were capable of selling overseas during the nineteenth and early twentieth century. In 1900, about 25% of all British GDP was exported, and about 16% of all of Germany's. Even in 1913, Britain was still exporting twice the value of goods and services supplied by the USA, although its economy was almost 60% smaller.[65]

The lessons to be learnt from the USA's economic history up to 1913 are just as relevant now as they were then. If the economy is to grow fast, advantage needs to be taken of the ability of industry, and particularly manufacturing, to generate high rates of growth of output. By 1870, a quarter of the US GDP came from industry, and by 1913, almost 30%.[66] The increase in productivity in manufacturing, and agriculture, during this period was about 50% higher than it was in the service sector – a ratio which has widened since then.[67] As the proportion of the US economy devoted to manufacturing rose, so did growth increase in the place where it really counts, which is not the size of the national income, but in output per head of the population, determining, as it does, the standard of living.

Lessons from the gold standard era

Between 1820 and 1913, economic output is estimated to have risen in the 56 major economies of the world by just over 300%, or cumulatively by 1.5% per annum. The rise in output per head was 140%, or a little under 1% per year.[68] These were much greater increases than had ever been seen on a wide scale in world history, demonstrating conclusively the immense power of the Industrial Revolution to change the prospects for humanity.

Could these ratios have been larger? Could the techniques used to garner the increased output obtainable from industrialisation have been spread significantly more widely, more intensively, and more quickly than they were? In theory, no doubt they could have been, although there were many practical obstacles. In the first place, it took even the most perspicacious observers, such as Adam Smith, some time to realise what a momentous change in production methods was taking place. Second, the diffusion of knowledge about the Industrial Revolution did in fact spread rapidly, partly because of the popularity and success of *The Wealth of Nations*. Jean Baptiste Say (1767–1832) published his own major work *Traite d'Economie Politique*, refining and extending Smith's work, in France in 1803. Translations into languages other than French increased its influence. There was also a stream of visitors from both home and abroad to British factories, supplemented by the publication of learned and practical journals, and exchanges of personnel and opinions in the relatively liberal world of the time.

The major practical constraints on spreading the use of the new industrial processes, which were then mostly being discovered in Britain, were those which had impeded the Industrial Revolution starting in other countries in the first place. Widely prevailing disparaging attitudes to industry, the disruption caused by wars, particularly the Napoleonic Wars which lasted for nearly a quarter of a century, the lack of stable government and enforceable contract law in many countries, and inadequate capital and credit facilities were major obstacles. Inevitably, also, there was a lengthy catch-up process which had to take place, even when copying of British techniques on a substantial scale began to happen. It took time to formulate plans, to arrange finance, to find and train suitable staff and to make the necessary physical investments even when the will to do so had been established. Nor can an industrial base be created overnight. A process of accumulation has to take place, often with the ability to move ahead depending on previous steps being accomplished successfully. Expansion from a small or almost non-existent base, which cannot be achieved even in the most favoured circumstances at more than a manageable pace, necessarily constrains the size of the total output achievable for a long way ahead.

The more challenging question about the nineteenth century, and indeed the one to follow, was whether, despite all the delays inevitably surrounding the adoption of new ways of organising production, different institutional developments and economic policies might have speeded the process of diffusion and development, particularly since many of the basic constraints inhibiting progress had already been overcome. Could countries such as Britain, which slowed down, have maintained momentum and grown faster? If different economic policies, particularly those concerned with macro-economics, had been adopted, would it have made a major difference?

The history of economic progress set out so far provides a framework for answering this question. This certainly suggests that a number of significant and clearly identifiable policy mistakes were made in Britain. The re-establishment of the pre-Napoleonic Wars parity between sterling and gold in the period following 1815 not only severely depressed output for five or six years, but also, much more seriously, locked Britain into having a relatively high cost base compared to that potentially available in other countries when they started to industrialise. As long as Britain had world markets substantially to itself this was not of crucial significance, but once foreign competition got into its stride, British vulnerability became all too evident. The adoption of free trade then made a bad situation worse, by effectively revaluing sterling still further as Britain lowered tariffs while competitors raised them.

While other countries were able to expand their economies largely unconstrained by foreign competition or balance of payments problems, Britain was unable to do so. The British economy, lacking the stimulus from export-led growth, was therefore the major loser from inappropriate macro-economic policies in the nineteenth century. Why did Britain allow this to happen? Partly, it was because the reasons for Britain's relative decline were not understood, so there was no clearly articulated policy available for reversing it. Economic policy followed the classical precepts laid down by John Stuart Mill (1806-1873). Building on the work of his predecessors in the same tradition, the emphasis was heavily orientated to a minimalist role for the state with low taxation and public expenditure, financial stability in so far as it could be secured by clearly defined central bank operations, free trade, and the maintenance of the gold standard as the underlying stabiliser.

This was a mixture of policies which well suited the growing strength and preponderance of the financial interests in Britain, exemplified pre-eminently by the City of London. In these circumstances there was no place for a determined and well formulated series of policies to keep the British economy on a high growth track, although there was mounting concern about the extent to which Britain was falling behind its competitors. *The Final Report of the Royal Commission on the Depression of Trade and Industry*, published in 1887, is full of agonised concern about the state of the economy.[69]

In the end, however, there was little serious challenge to the conventional views of the time, and the result was that those with accumulated wealth dominated the way the economy was run, as against those striving to create new industries. Sterling was too strong, encouraging imports and discouraging domestic production. Too much investment went abroad. Too few talented people went into industry and commerce. Too many went into the professions, administering the empire acquired almost entirely as a result of Britain's earlier economic pre-eminence, and into academic life, the civil service, the church – anything, if they could avoid it, except industry and trade.

If an effective challenge to the policy status quo was to come from anywhere, it would have had to come from the intellectual world, but it was not to be. The mainstream thinkers and writers of the time, such as John Stuart Mill, amplified and endorsed the classical economic approach, building on a tradition with a heavy emphasis on markets being self-regulating, and the role of the state being as non-intrusive as possible. The doctrines advanced by Thomas Malthus (1766-1834), stressing that increased output of food and other necessities would always encourage an equal increase in the population, thus making improvements in living standards impossible, discouraged efforts to raise them, despite the evidence well within Malthus's lifetime that they were in fact increasing.[70]

Say's Law, propounded by the same Jean Baptiste Say who had publicised *The Wealth of Nations*, held that a deficiency in demand was impossible since the income from the sales of all the goods and services which were produced necessarily generated exactly enough expenditure to purchase all of them. This view, which was not seriously challenged until the advent of John Maynard Keynes (1883-1946), ruled out the possibility of any kind of systematic demand management. The most significant challenge to orthodoxy which did materialise, from Karl Marx (1818-1883), was not designed to make the capitalist system work better, but to get rid of it altogether. The major innovations in economics which the nineteenth century produced, from writers such as Auguste Walras (1801–1866), William Stanley Jevons (1835–1882), Alfred Marshall (1842–1924) and others, were mainly in micro-economics. They were primarily concerned with the formation of prices and marginal utility, rather than macro-economic issues which generated little interest. Britain, and the world in general, paid a heavy price for this trend in intellectual fashion.

2

International Turmoil: 1914 to 1945

World War I began as the result of a network of treaty obligations being called into play following the assassination of Archduke Franz Ferdinand (1863-1914) in Sarajevo on 28th June 1914.[1] Although few had anticipated the outbreak of war, its advent was greeted with a surprising amount of enthusiasm. Huge crowds turned out in Berlin, Paris, Petrograd (St Petersburg), London and Vienna, clamouring for military action.[2] By 1945, all such enthusiasm for war had been spent. Two ruinous conflicts had cost millions of lives, had caused untold damage, and had drastically set back living standards – although there was to be a remarkably rapid recovery after World War II. In the meantime, however, not only had immense human and physical damage been done during the periods of open warfare but also the network of international trading and financial arrangements which had allowed the world economy to function reasonably smoothly during the nineteenth century, and the early years of the twentieth, was catastrophically disrupted by the impact of World War I. The result was a period of great instability and lost opportunities between the wars, as fragile booms in the 1920s collapsed into the worldwide slump of the early 1930s. Thereafter there were sharp divergences as some economies continued to decline while others made remarkable recoveries.

Throughout the period, the record of most of those responsible for economic policy was confused and inadequate. The near universal consensus among political and intellectual leaders up to the outbreak of World War I was that the state should see its role as holding the ring rather than being a major player. Clearly, however, this stance made no sense at all at a time of total war. Within a very short time, therefore, in all the belligerent economies, the proportion of output which went through the government's hands rose dramatically. In Britain it increased from 15% in 1913 to an astonishing 69% in 1917[3], while similar rises were seen in France and Germany. In the USA the peak, at 36% in 1918, was considerably lower, but even so it represented a dramatic change from pre-war days.[4] The outcome was that governments in all the countries involved in fighting the war were presented with problems for which they were singularly ill-prepared. While mobilising to produce vast quantities of guns, ships, aircraft and munitions, and recruiting large numbers of people under arms, was found to be problematic but achievable, securing these objectives without over-stretching and destabilising the economy proved much more difficult. Even in the relatively under-stretched USA, prices rose by about 50% between 1915 and 1918, but inflation was much less there during the war period than it was in other countries. Britain's price level rose nearly 80%, France's doubled, and Germany's increased by 200%.[5]

More than anything else, it was the disruption to the rough balance of competitiveness between the pre-World War I economies which turned out to be the bane of the inter-war period, compounded by the impact of the insistence by the victorious powers of payments of reparations by Germany, the major belligerent on the losing side. World total demand was depressed by the policies pursued by countries such as Britain, which was determined to restore sterling's pre-war gold parity, and willing to go through a period of severe deflation to do so. In Germany, until the advent of the Nazi regime, with very different ideas about how the economy should be run, a similarly cautious attempt was made to follow classical economic remedies, culminating in the cuts to unemployment benefit which, as much as anything else, led to Adolf Hitler (1889-1945) becoming Chancellor in 1933. In the United States, during the 1920s the economy was unconstrained by the balance of payments problems and the apparent need for deflation which afflicted most of Europe. The result was a major boom, culminating in a bout of speculation on an unprecedented scale which left the banking and financial system heavily exposed to a downturn. When this came, the authorities were completely unprepared to deal with it. As elsewhere, vain attempts to balance a rapidly deteriorating fiscal position simply made an already catastrophic situation worse.

While the world's economies were languishing, work was being done by John Maynard Keynes and others which would lead, at least for a while, to much more stable conditions after World War II. The influence of those who realised that Say's Law was not correct, and that it was possible for economies to suffer from insufficient total demand for years on end, however, was only marginal between the wars. Their thinking had some impact in Britain, Sweden and the USA, particularly on some of those involved in the New Deal, but only to a limited degree. Keynes' major influence on policy was to come later, as the institutions for the post-World War II period were established, although he also had a substantial impact on the way in which World War II was financed in Britain.

By the end of World War II, therefore, much had been learnt about how to control and finance total mobilisation, and inflation in all the main belligerent countries was much less than it had been during World War I at least during the early wartime years. Prices nevertheless rose steeply in those countries which were defeated and occupied during the war, and in those which were eventually on the losing side as the war ended. At the same time, a number of major advances had also been made in thinking about how to structure the post-war world, laying the foundation for the great advances in living standards achieved in much of the world during the 1950s and 1960s. The period from the 1970s onwards, however, as world growth rates declined sharply, showed that still more needed to be done to develop policies which would combine reasonable rates of economic growth with other economic objectives, particularly fairly low rates of inflation.

The period from 1914 to 1945 is therefore an exceptionally interesting and important one, both in terms of the impact it had on economic and political history and in the development of ideas. Much was lost in terms of damage, foreshortened lives, unemployment, output foregone and in the production of destructive military equipment, but important ground was gained in better understanding some of the key requirements for improved economic management.

Europe's disastrous years

Turning back to 1914, World War I was a catastrophe for Europe in every way. There was huge loss of life and immense material destruction. Even worse than this, the relatively stable and secure social and economic systems which had been developed during the nineteenth century, which had stood Europe and the world as a whole in good stead, were disrupted, dislocated and dismembered. It took the passage of three decades and another world war before anything resembling the peace, prosperity and security of pre-World War I Europe would be re-established.

Approximately 10m people lost their lives in Europe prematurely as a result of World War I,[6] and a substantial additional number, harder to quantify, in the influenza epidemics which struck down a weakened population in the immediate aftermath of the war. The damage done to towns and factories, although much less than in World War II, was still considerable. The national incomes of the countries of Western Europe fell precipitously between the period just before World War I started and the early years after it ended, when the demand for war-orientated production fell away. France's industrial production dropped by over 40% between 1913 and 1919, caused partly by the disruption and damage caused by the war, and partly by the post-war slump.[7] It was 1927 before German GDP rose again to its 1913 level.[8] Britain did not do so badly, with the GDP staying more or less constant during the war, although it fell heavily, by about 20%, immediately the war finished.[9]

Economic instability in Europe was greatly compounded by the Treaty of Versailles, negotiated between the powers which had won the war and the humiliated Germans. The Americans had not come into the war until 1917, and insisted on the large debts run up by Britain and France for war supplies being repaid. Britain and France, in turn, looked to Germany to make huge reparations, partly to pay the Americans and partly on their own account. None of these arrangements, negotiated by political leaders under immense pressure from electorates much more interested in settling old scores than in facing up to new realities, bore any relationship to the ability of the Germans to make these payments. Leaving aside the extent to which the German economy was already languishing as a result of the damage done to it by the war, the only feasible way for the Germans to pay the reparation bill was to run a very large export surplus. In the fragile state of the world economy in the 1920s, no country was prepared to tolerate a large German trade surplus, even if it could have been achieved. Payment of reparations on the scale demanded, whatever its electoral appeal, or the requirements of the USA to see debts to it settled, was never therefore a remotely realistic prospect.

Attempts to extract reparations, however, compounded with post-war political and economic disruption, caused havoc in Germany. The government was unable to produce sufficient revenue through the tax system to meet the obligations it had undertaken to fulfil. It therefore resorted to the printing press to create the money it was unable to raise in any other way. The result was the German inflation of 1923, which ended in hyper-inflation and the total collapse in the value of the currency.[10] The Reichsmark had already lost two-thirds of its value during World War I.[11] Now all those with savings in cash lost everything. This experience understandably scarred the German attitude to inflation and monetary rectitude, with reverberations which are still felt today.

Gradually, however, towards the end of the 1920s, some measure of normality began to reassert itself. There was a significant recovery in France, where industrial output doubled between the post-war low of 1921 and 1928, although even in 1928 it was only 10% higher than it had been in 1913.[12] Industrial production also rose in the late 1920s in Germany, peaking in 1929 at about 20% higher than it had been in 1913, while Germany's GDP grew cumulatively between 1925 and 1929 by a respectable 2.9% per annum.[13] In Germany's case in particular, however, the recovery was fragile. It depended heavily on large loans flowing in from abroad, especially from the United States, to enable reparation payment to continue at the scaled-down rate agreed by the Young Plan in 1929, replacing the much harsher 1924 Dawes Plan. Nevertheless, in the late 1920s, Germany's unemployment was falling and living standards were slowly increasing.

Britain remained depressed, mainly because of a repetition of the same process which had taken place after the Napoleonic Wars. The link between the pound and gold had been suspended on the outbreak of World War I, and the pressure on the economy during the war had led to considerable price inflation. Nevertheless, on the recommendation of the Cunliffe Committee, in 1918 it was decided to restore the gold value of the pound to the same parity, $4.86, as it had enjoyed in 1914. Attaining this objective meant forcing down costs in Britain, attempted by imposing severely deflationary policies. The reductions achieved, particularly in labour costs, were nothing like sufficient, however, to restore Britain to a competitive position at the target parity. As a result, Britain spent the whole of the 1920s in an all too wearisomely familiar position, suffering from a combination of lack of competitiveness at home and abroad, leading inevitably to domestic deflation and slow growth in output and living standards.

Europe therefore appeared to be very poorly placed to weather the depression which followed, beginning with the collapse of the US stock market in 1929. The most immediate effect of the American slump on Europe was that the flow of loans from the USA to Germany dried up, plunging the German economy into a crisis of the same order of magnitude as had overcome the United States. Between 1929 and 1932, German GDP fell by almost a quarter. Industrial production dropped by nearly 40%.[14] Unemployment, which already stood at 9.3% in 1929, increased to over 30% of the labour force by 1932.[15] During this year it averaged 5.5m, peaking at 6m. In Britain, GDP fell, but by not so much as in the USA and Germany. Industrial production dropped by 5%, but unemployment, which was already 7.3% in 1929, rose to 15.6% in 1932.[16] Similar patterns to those seen in Britain were to be found in France and the Benelux countries. Mussolini's policy in Italy of keeping the lira at as high a parity as possible, mirroring British ambitions, ensured that the Italian economy suffered similar disadvantages, although the proportion of Italian GDP involved in foreign trade was much lower than in Britain.

The crucially important lessons to be learnt from the 1930s derive from the different ways in which the major economies in Europe, particularly Germany, France and Britain, reacted to the slump which overtook all of them at the same time. In Germany, the collapse of the economy, coming as it did on top of the trauma of World War I, the vindictiveness of the Versailles settlement, particularly the reparations clauses, the political instability of the Weimar regime, and the hyperinflation of 1923, provoked a wholly counter-productive response from the Brüning government. In July 1931, and again in the summer of 1932, the amount and duration of unemployment compensation was reduced. Instead of attempting to reflate the economy, Chancellor Heinrich Brüning (1885-1970), supported by the SDP opposition, cut wages and benefits. This made the economic situation worse, precipitating the German banking crisis of July 1931, which followed the Austrian Kreditanstalt collapse two months earlier.[17] The desperate attempts by democratic, well-meaning politicians to maintain financial respectability – putting the interest of finance above those of working people – were their undoing, and that of the whole of Europe as the Nazis came to power. This mistake, on top of all the others, provided Hitler and his associates with their opportunity to take over the government of Germany in 1933.

The economic policies pursued by the new Nazi regime, however disastrous in leading Europe into World War II, and however much racist and fascist policies are to be deplored, were nevertheless remarkably successful in economic terms. Unemployment, which stood at over 30% in 1932, was reduced by 1938 to just over 2% of the working population.[18] Over the same period, industrial production rose by more than 120%, a cumulative increase of 14% per annum. The gross national product increased by 65%, a cumulative increase of nearly 9% a year.[19] A substantial proportion of the increased output was devoted to armaments, but by no means all. Military expenditure, which had been 3.2% of GDP in 1933, rose to 9.6% in 1937. It then almost doubled to 18.1%, but only as late as 1938.[20] Between 1932 and 1938 consumers' expenditure rose by almost a quarter.[21] Nor were these achievements bought at the expense of high levels of inflation. The price level was very stable in Germany in the 1930s. Consumer prices rose by a total of only 7% between the arrival of the Nazi regime in 1933 and the outbreak of war in 1939.[22]

How were these results achieved? Some of the outcomes could only have been accomplished by a non-democratic regime, with access to total power. In particular, the pressure exerted to hold down wage increases, and the policies imposed to restrict trade, so as to increase Germany's capacity to supply all its essential needs internally, would have been difficult for any democratic government to implement. Unquestionably, these policies also led to increasing distortions in the economy, with a price which would have to be paid sooner or later. All the same, there was plenty of increased new output available with which to pay these costs.

The expansion of the economy was made possible partly as a result of vast increases in expenditures by the state, which nearly trebled between 1933 and 1938.[23] An increasingly high proportion of these were spent on rearmament as the decade wore on, but during the earlier years most of it went on civil expenditure, such as building a road system far superior to anything seen before, although this clearly also had significant military potential. A substantial proportion of the rest of the rise in output, however, went on increasing the German standard of living. Much of the initial expenditure was financed by borrowing on a large scale, some of it through bonds, but much of it from the banking system. There was a large expansion in the money supply. Rising tax revenues, flowing from the greatly increased scale of economic activity and falling welfare costs, however, kept the finances of the regime relatively easily in bounds, which was partly why inflationary pressures were subdued.

In Britain, the initial reaction to the advent of the slump was much in line with the economic policies previously pursued. The Labour chancellor of the exchequer, Philip Snowden (1864-1937), tried to persuade his reluctant cabinet colleagues that the only solution to the financial crisis overwhelming the country was to maintain a balanced budget by implementing the same sorts of cuts in expenditure which had been the undoing of the Brüning government in Germany. Eventually, there was a revolt when the overwhelming majority of the Labour Members of Parliament ceased supporting the government, refusing to back any more cuts. They preferred to go into opposition, allowing a National

Government to be formed with the support of the Conservative opposition.

The policies then implemented were a complete break from those previously in play. Sterling was allowed to be driven off its gold parity and to fall in value by 24% against all other major currencies and by 31% against the dollar.[24] Far from the government then making efforts to restore the previous parity, as it had after the Napoleonic Wars and World War I, presaging the same mistaken response time after time to exchange rate falls in the future, policy was dedicated to ensuring that the new lower parity was retained. An Exchange Equalisation Account was established, with resources of 5% of the gross national product, to keep the pound at its new competitive level. There was a very substantial expansion in the money supply, which increased by 15% between 1931 and 1932, before rising a further 19% during the first half of 1933.[25] Interest rates fell to almost zero. In 1933 three-month Treasury bonds paid an average interest rate of just under 0.6%.[26] Protection, including a 15% tariff on manufactured goods,[27] was added to reinforce the protective effects of the reduction in the exchange rate, adding significantly to the effective size of the devaluation. A recent study showed that the result was the creation of some 80,000 jobs in Lancashire alone.[28]

In Britain, as in Germany, the results were dramatic and positive. Far from living standards falling, as almost all commentators had confidently predicted would happen, they started to rise rapidly. Industrial production also increased substantially, if not as fast as in Germany. In the five years to 1937, manufacturing output rose by 48% to 38% above the 1929 peak.[29] Unemployment fell sharply, as the number of people in work quickly increased. Over the period between 1931 and 1937, the number of those in work rose from 18.7m to 21.4m as 2.7m new jobs were created, half of them in manufacturing.[30] Unemployment fell from 3.3m to 1.8m. The poor business prospects in the previous decade had left Britain bereft of much investment in the most modern technologies. Now the ground was quickly made up, with new industrial capacity employing the latest technical developments, as was also happening in Germany. Nor was inflation a problem. Contrary to all conventional wisdom, the price level fell heavily, partly reflecting the slump in world prices, until 1933 after which it began a slow rise.[31] The British economy grew faster during the five years between 1932 and 1937 – at a cumulative rate of 4.6% per annum[32] – than for any other five-year period in its history, showing clearly how effective a radical expansionist policy could be, against what appeared to be the most unpromising background.

Towards the end of the 1930s, the growth in the British economy began to slacken off, despite increased expenditure on armaments, which was a delayed response to the increasing threat from Germany. The reason was largely a further round of exchange rate changes. The Americans had devalued the dollar by 41% in 1934. In 1936 they were followed by the Gold Bloc countries, France, Switzerland, Belgium and the Netherlands, which had hitherto been in the doldrums with low growth and high levels of unemployment as a result of their over-valued currencies.[33] Incredibly, in the light of the experience of the previous few years, instead of devaluing with them to keep sterling competitive, the British agreed to support the new currency alignments with the Exchange Equalisation Account. The competitiveness which had enabled the British economy to recover so quickly from the slump was thereby thrown away. In 1948, the Economic Commission for Europe estimated that sterling was as overvalued in 1938 as it had been in 1929.[34]

The French experience during the 1930s was the mirror image of that of Britain. Until 1936, when, under the Popular Front government headed by Leon Blum (1872-1950), deflationary policies were at last abated, France, along with the other Gold Bloc countries, stayed on the gold exchange standard. French refusal to devalue depressed the economy further and further, producing the inevitable consequences. French GDP dropped steadily in real terms almost every year from 1930 to 1936, falling a total of 17% over these six years. Industrial production fell by a quarter. Investment slumped. Unemployment rose continually.[35]

A few telling statistics summarise what happened. French crude steel production fell from 9.7m tons in 1929 to 6.1m tons in 1938. In Germany, over the same period, it rose from 16.2m to 22.7m tons. France produced 254,000 cars and commercial vehicles in

1929 and 227,000 in 1938. In Germany output went from 128,000 to 338,000. British crude steel production rose from 9.8m tons in 1929 to 10.6m in 1938, while vehicle output went up from 239,000 to 445,000.[36] These figures show with crystal clarity how much the French economy weakened compared to that of Britain and particularly Germany over this critical period. Although other factors were of course involved, the results of the battles of 1940, during the early part of World War II, were to a very significant extent determined by whether or not the combatant countries had adopted policies during the previous decade which provided them with the industrial capacity to manufacture the aircraft, guns, tanks and other armaments they so urgently needed once the fighting started.

The contrast between the three largest economies in Europe in the 1930s could hardly have been more marked – between the relatively successful results, at least in economic terms, achieved by Germany and Britain, and the disastrously poor outcome in France and the other Gold Bloc countries. These lessons are highly material today. The really interesting exemplar is the British experience, at least until 1936, combining democracy with recovery. Thereafter, reverting to type, the huge advantage of a competitive exchange rate, rapid growth and falling unemployment enjoyed by Britain for the middle years of the 1930s was gratuitously thrown away. 1931 to 1937, however, showed what could be done by a democracy faced with daunting economic problems when the right policies were chosen. Expanding the money supply, reducing interest rates and establishing the exchange rate at a competitive level were the keys to success. Creating conditions where exports could boom, the home market could be recaptured from foreign suppliers, and where industry could flourish, all had an enormously positive impact on the country's economic performance.

Boom and slump in the USA

It was not until 1917, three years after World War I broke out in 1914, that the USA became directly involved in the war as a belligerent. By 1918 the US economy had grown by almost 16% compared to 1913.[37]

While the 1920s saw most European economies recovering from deep post-war slumps, leaving their populations with significantly lower GDP per head than they had enjoyed before the war, the US economy soon began to surge ahead. Recovering quickly from a brief post-war setback in 1919–21, during most of the remaining 1920s a major and sustained boom developed. Between 1921 and 1929, the US economy grew by 45%, achieving a cumulative 4.8% rate of growth per annum during these eight years.[38]

From 1920 to 1929, industrial output climbed by nearly 50%, while the number of people employed to achieve this increase in output hardly altered. This reflected an enormous increase in manufacturing productivity, which rose cumulatively by nearly 5% per annum as factories were automated.[39] The use of electricity in industry rose dramatically – by 70% between 1923 and 1929.[40] Living standards increased by 30%, although those on already high incomes gained much more than those further down the income distribution. Investment as a percentage of GDP rose from 12.2% in 1921 to 17.6% in 1928. Meanwhile, the price level remained remarkably stable, consumer prices being on average slightly lower in 1928 than they were in 1921.[41]

The confidence engendered by such economic success was reflected not only in an almost tripling of consumer credit during the 1920s, but also on the stock market. A bull market began to build in 1924. It surged ahead with only minor setbacks for the next five years. The Dow-Jones Industrial Average, whose high was 120 in 1924, reached 167 in 1926, soared to 300 in 1928, and peaked at 381 on 3rd September 1929, a level not to be exceeded for another quarter of a century. Speculative fever reigned in a largely unregulated market. Much of the increase in the value of stocks was financed by increasingly risky but lucrative loans. As the boom gathered strength, those buying shares often had to put up only as little as 10% of the cost themselves, the balance being provided as 'brokers' loans'. Initially, these were provided by banks, but later increasingly by corporations, which found the potential returns irresistible, resulting in many of the major American companies investing more and more of their resources in speculation rather than productive plant and equipment. Brokers' loans, which had totalled about $1bn during the early years of the decade, had risen to $3.5bn by the end of 1927, $6bn by January 1929 and reached $8.5bn by October 1929. The huge demand for such loans forced the interest rate on them up and up. By the time the stock market peaked in the late summer of 1929, 12% interest rates were not uncommon at a time when there was no inflation.[42]

The initial falls from the stock market peak were modest, but by late October 1929, confidence was draining away. A wave of panic on 24th October was followed by 'Black Friday', 25th October, and a frenzy of selling on 29th October 1929. In the first half-hour that day, losses ran at over $2bn and by the end of the day they were $10bn, as the Dow-Jones fell 30 points, reducing the value of quoted stocks by 11.5%. Worse was to follow. Despite periodic rallies, the market moved inexorably downwards, until by July 1932, the Dow-Jones stood at 41, nearly 90% below its 381 peak. United States Steel shares fell from 262 to 22, General Motors dropped from 73 to eight, and Montgomery Ward plummeted from 138 to four.[43]

The collapse of prices on the stock exchanges had a devastating effect on the rest of the economy. The huge sums which had been lost caused a wave of bank failures from coast to coast, dragging down countless businesses with them. As both consumer and industrial confidence evaporated, sources of credit dried up, and demand disappeared for many of the goods and services which the US economy was amply capable of producing. Between 1929 and 1933, US GDP fell by 30%. Industrial output went down by nearly half in just three years from 1929 to 1932. By 1933, a quarter of the American labour force was out of work. Nearly 13m people had no job.[44]

The condition of the economy reached its nadir in 1933. Meanwhile, in 1932, Franklin D. Roosevelt (1882–1945) had ousted the hapless Herbert Hoover (1874–1964) as president in a landslide vote, initiating a New Deal for the American people, designed to tackle the slump. The policies implemented by the incoming Democrat administration fell into two main parts. The first was a substantial increase in the role of the state. More financial help was provided to those hardest hit by unemployment. The Federal Emergency Relief Act provided $500m in direct grants to states and municipalities. New agencies were established, some of them designed to act in a counter-cyclical way, increasing demand by using the borrowing power of the state to provide funding. The Tennessee Valley Authority provided regional energy and flood control. The National Recovery Administration assisted with industrial revitalisation. The Agricultural Adjustment Administration had as its goal the regeneration of the weakened farming sector of the economy. The result of these initiatives was probably as much in terms of increasing confidence that something was being done by the federal government to improve conditions than in their direct impact, although expenditure on these schemes no doubt had some reflationary impact.[45]

Much more significant in terms of causing the economy to revive were other steps taken on the macro-economic front. In 1934, the dollar was devalued by 41%, adding to the substantial protection for American industry which had already been achieved by the Smoot-Hawley tariff in 1930, a major step towards the economic nationalism which was one of the curses of the 1930s. One of the Roosevelt administration's early steps had been to stabilise the financial system by declaring a bank holiday, and then allowing the Treasury, under emergency legislation, to verify the soundness of individual banks before allowing them to reopen. Ten days later half of them, holding 90% of all deposits, were back in operation. The result was that thenceforth deposits exceeded withdrawals, as confidence in the banking system was restored, thus increasing the availability of credit. The Fed also encouraged recovery by allowing the money supply to rise as the economy picked up. M1 rose from just under $20bn in 1933 to a little less than $30bn in 1936, generating a major increase in the underlying credit base.[46]

The result was that by 1936 the US economy was in considerably better shape than it had been three years earlier. In these three years, real GDP grew by 32%, while unemployment fell by nearly a third, from 25% to 17%. Industrial output rebounded, growing 50%.[47] Corporate net income moved from being $2bn in deficit to $5bn in surplus.[48] There was little change in the consumer price level.[49] Despite these striking achievements, Roosevelt, who, notwithstanding all the New Deal rhetoric, had never felt wholly comfortable with borrowing to spend, became alarmed by the fiscal deficit, which reached $3.5bn in 1936. As a result, he ordered a cutback in federal spending.[50] This coincided with both a reduction in the competitiveness of US exports as the Gold Bloc countries devalued, and the deflationary impact of the promised new social security tax, another part of the New Deal, which was introduced at the same time. The consequence was a sharp recession. GDP fell by 4% between 1937 and 1938, industrial output fell back nearly a third, and unemployment rose from 14.3% to 19%.[51]

By then, however, the start of World War II was imminent, transforming the prospects for the US economy. Although the USA did not become a belligerent until December 1941, following the Japanese attack at Pearl Harbor, the lend-lease arrangements agreed with the Allied powers at the start of the European war rapidly provided a massive stimulus to US output. Between 1939 and 1944, US GDP grew by an astonishing 75%, a compound rate of almost 12%. Over the same period, industrial output increased by over 150%, while the number of people employed in manufacturing rose from 10.3m to 17.3m, an increase of just under 70%. The difference between these two percentages reflected a huge further advance in manufacturing productivity, which rose cumulatively by some 7% per annum. Prices increased by an average of less than 5% a year, a far better outcome than had been achieved during World War I.[52] By the end of World War II, the USA was therefore in an extraordinarily strong position vis-à-vis the rest of the world. Most developed countries had suffered invasion and defeat at some stage in the war, and in consequence their economies had been severely disrupted, and in some cases devastated. Between 1939 and 1946, Japanese GDP fell by almost half, and Germany's by just over 50%. Even countries such as Britain, which had avoided invasion and had finished on the winning side, did nothing like as well as the USA. The British economy grew by only 10% between 1939 and 1946.[53] No wonder that in 1945 the US economy looked supreme.

Keynes and demand management

The major contribution made by John Maynard Keynes to economic thought was his perception that demand and supply would not always be in balance at a level which kept the economy with more or less full employment, as Say's Law had claimed would be the case. On the contrary, Keynes maintained, while the money spent by the nation on consumption always creates an equivalent income flow for producers, there is no reason why the same should be true for that proportion of its income which the nation saves. The corresponding expenditure in this case is by companies and the state on investment. There is no reason why, *ex ante*, these should be the same. If there is more *ex ante* saving in the economy than expenditure on investment, there will be an overall shortfall in demand, which will lead to deflation and unemployment. Furthermore, if, as economic conditions become more depressed, precautionary savings rise, while investment falls as profitable opportunities decrease, the result may be an increasingly intense depression. As an accounting identity, investment and savings, or more strictly speaking investment and borrowing, have ex post to be identical in size.[54] It might well be the case, however, that equilibrium between them would be found at a level which left the economy as a whole heavily short of the total level of demand to keep everyone in employment, with a reasonable rate of growth being achieved.

The classical economist's response to the problem of unemployment had been to deny that it could exist, except in the case of workers changing jobs or being out of work because of poor fits between skills and job opportunities, unless wages were too high or too rigid. The solution, if unemployment appeared, was therefore to ensure that wages fell until everyone was priced back into a job. A further important contribution from Keynes was to point out that this was not correct, but a fallacy of composition. What might be true of individual workers was not true of all the labour force taken together. If employers generally lowered wages at a time of unemployment, total purchasing power – aggregate effective demand – would diminish *pari passu* with the diminished wages, thus worsening the deflationary problem.[55]

Nor was it true, Keynes maintained, that lowering interest rates would necessarily improve the prospects for investment, to provide a sufficient stimulus to pull the economy out of a depression. Worse still, lowering interest rates might increase savings, thus further aggravating the imbalance, as savers felt they needed larger cash investments to offset the lower returns which they were likely to receive. The only solution was for the state to assume a much more active role, to make up for the deficiency in demand in the private sector. If the economy was operating at below full employment, the state should offset the excess saving in relation to investment by borrowing itself, and spending the money to increase overall demand.

Keynes also had strong views about the role of the exchange rate on the performance of the economy. He had railed against Winston Churchill (1874-1965) when, as chancellor of the exchequer, he had in 1925 returned Britain to the pre-World War I gold parity, realigning sterling with the US dollar at \$4.86 to the pound.[56] Speaking nearly 20 years later for the Coalition government in the Bretton Woods debate in the House of Lords on 23rd May 1944, the then Lord Keynes[57] said:

> We are determined that, in future, the external value of sterling shall conform to its internal value, as set by our domestic policies, and not the other way round. In other words, we abjure the instruments of Bank Rate and credit contraction operating to increase unemployment as a means of forcing our domestic economy into line with external factors.[58]

Unfortunately, however, Keynes died in 1946, and British exchange rate policy soon regressed back to the norm – keeping sterling as strong as possible on the foreign exchanges, in line with the perennial conventional wisdom which still very largely prevails.

Not only did Keynes, nevertheless, have great influence on the way in which domestic policy operated in the post-World War II period, he was also heavily involved, with the Americans, for whom Harry Dexter White (1892-1948) took the lead, in designing the architecture for the post-World War II international settlement. Planning started in 1942 and culminated in the Bretton Woods agreement of 1944. Common ground between the British and Americans was their jointly perceived need to avoid both competitive trade restrictions and floating exchange rates, both of which, as inter-war experience had shown, could be manipulated to secure unilateral advantage at heavy multilateral expense, if used in a 'beggar-thy-neighbour' fashion.[59] Floating exchange rates were also believed to encourage inflation, by allowing politicians an easy escape from overheating their economies, to enhance their popularity. There was more difficulty in securing a consensus over the timing as to when liberalisation of trade – let alone capital movements – should take place. It was agreed that some barriers would be required to short-term capital movements, at least in the immediate post-war period, but the Americans were also keen that trade restrictions should be removed as quickly as possible. The problem was that, with trade barriers removed, the demand from Europe and elsewhere for US exports was far higher than their dollar earnings could meet. The 'dollar gap', which manifested itself for some years after the end of the war, showed that British caution was well justified.

Buttressed by the establishment of the International Monetary Fund (IMF), to deal with short-term international financing needs, and the World Bank, to manage longer-term development loans, and, in 1946, by the General Agreement on Tariffs and Trade (GATT), the Bretton Woods system, as it finally emerged, had a number of key characteristics. The centrepiece was agreement that exchange rates in future should be fixed, with all participating countries having to establish a par value for their currencies in terms of either gold or the US dollar. These par values could only be changed to correct a 'fundamental disequilibrium' in their balance of payments. Each country was expected to hold reserves to support its fixed exchange rate, which could be supplemented by the Fund's resources. Agreement was reached on procedures for the liberalisation of world trade by the removal of trade barriers and the progressive lowering of tariffs.[60]

The period of high growth and relative stability in the 1950s and 1960s which followed the setting up of the Bretton Woods system, once the initial dislocations of the immediate post-war period had been overcome, was unquestionably impressive, and a vast improvement on the record of the inter-war period. Between 1950 and 1970 the world economy grew by 157% compared to 97%

between 1913 and 1950.[61] Nevertheless, the arrangements agreed suffered from deficiencies, which were to become increasingly evident as the years wore on. The major problem was that they contained no built-in mechanism for stopping economies which started doing better than the average from accumulating greater and greater competitive advantage. Under the gold standard, any country which accumulated a balance of payments surplus automatically had its monetary base expanded by the influx of gold. This tended to push up its price level, redressing, at least in part, the balance with its competitors. Under Bretton Woods, no such mechanism operated. The onus for adjustment therefore tended to fall almost wholly on the less competitive countries, forcing them into deflation to protect their balance of payments position, or to devaluation. There was no corresponding pressure on the more successful economies to share their competitive advantage with others by revaluing their currencies.

The result was that countries such as Britain, whose exchange rate soon after the war was evidently much too high, had no easy way of securing international agreement to getting it down to a more realistic level. Germany and Japan, on the contrary, whose exchange rates had been fixed at artificially low levels after the war, were in a strong position to resist revaluing them. Towards the end of the Bretton Woods era, the USA also began to suffer from the same malaise – increasing foreign payments weakness – as Britain, in more acute form, had experienced almost continuously since 1945. During the Bretton Woods negotiations, such was the relative strength of the US economy at the time that it probably never occurred to the Americans that they would ever find themselves in this position. When they did, it culminated in the devaluation of the dollar in 1971, and the break-up of the system of fixed exchange rates shortly afterwards.

The consequence of this bias in the system was that countries with competitive exports and strong balance of payments positions could grow very fast, while those which were less competitive were held back by slow-growing exports, rising import penetration and balance of payments constraints. The result may have been to hold back overall growth from being as high as it could have been, but nevertheless not by much as during most of the immediate post-World War II period only a small number of countries, primarily Britain, were adversely affected. Between 1950 and 1970 the cumulative expansion in the world economy averaged 4.9%.[62] The driving force was a combination of Keynesian policies at national level and relatively minor disequilibria in trading competitiveness between the major trading nations internationally, allowing nearly all economies to expand rapidly with full employment. With comparatively low welfare dependency levels, as a result of almost all families having breadwinners, most countries had easily containable pressures on their taxation and expenditure systems, helping to keep inflation at bay.

As long as these conditions held, rapid growth could continue. When the Bretton Woods system broke up, however, the world economy began to perform much more poorly. Deprived of the restrictions and discipline within which world leaders had been used to working for a quarter of a century, there was initially, in the early 1970s, an unsustainable boom, fuelled by monetary laxity now that the Bretton Woods constraints no longer exerted their previous restraining influence. This was followed by a long period during which most of the world's major economies began to grow significantly more slowly, to exhibit much higher levels of unemployment, and to suffer far more severely than previously from inflation. As we shall see, new policy ideas were forthcoming in the move in intellectual fashion towards monetarism, provided by Milton Friedman (1912-2006) and his associate, Anna Jacobson Schwartz (b. 1915), in their seminal book, *A Monetary History of the United States, 1867–1960*, published in 1963. Although the ideas in this work proved to be exceptionally appealing to many people, they also turned out to be disappointingly ineffective at dealing with the fundamental objectives with which most people think that economic policy ought to be concerned, particularly in western countries. Between 1973 and 1992, the cumulative rise in world output slowed significantly, falling from 4.9% to 3.5% per annum, and to just under 2.9% in industrialised countries[63] at the same time as their performance on unemployment and inflation also deteriorated markedly. Nor has the record for recent years been much better. Inflation has fallen, but in many countries in the West there is little sign of unemployment diminishing. Between 1992 and 2015, world annual growth was 3.2% per annum but only 1.5% a year in advanced economies.[64]

The world therefore still urgently needs a framework of international economic policies which will enable the dynamism of the 1950s and 1960s throughout the industrialised world to be recovered, but which can be made to operate without the fixed exchange rate regime which in the end undermined the Bretton Woods system. The history since the dollar devaluation in 1971 shows how much was lost because no adequate replacement was available to carry the Keynesian legacy forward when the Bretton Woods construct, which worked better than anything the world had ever seen previously, reached the end of the period when it was viable.

3

Post-World War II

World War II was an even worse disaster for the world in terms of loss of life and material destruction than World War I. Many more people were killed as a result of the hostilities. The increased destructiveness of the weapons used, particularly those involved with aerial bombardment, caused far more damage to railways, houses and factories than had occurred during World War I.

Of the major European economies, Germany was by far the worst affected. Constant bombing by day and night for the last half of the war had reduced most German cities to ruins. Coal production, which had totalled 400m tons in 1939, fell to just under 60m tons in 1945. Crude steel production, which had been nearly 24m tons in 1939, fell to almost nothing by the end of the war.[1] The currency collapsed again, and many transactions were conducted by barter, or by using cigarettes as a temporary substitute for money. During the period immediately after the war, not only was there a desperate scarcity of industrial raw materials of all kinds, but there was also a serious food shortage. The German standard of living plummeted to a fraction of its pre-war level, as the German people eked out a living as best they could amid their shattered country.

France, too, suffered severely during the war, but not as badly as Germany. French GDP fell 17% in real terms between 1938 and 1946, and industrial production by about the same amount. Britain did a good deal better. British industrial output grew by about 5% between 1938 and 1946, while total GDP rose 16%.[2] Paradoxically, however, the British emerged from the war in many ways much worse prepared for the peace than continental countries, almost all of which had suffered defeat at some stage during the preceding years. Britain's world pretensions were still intact, whereas those of the continental countries were greatly reduced. Germany, in particular, was allowed no more than token defence forces, whereas Britain still had millions of its citizens under arms, deployed all over the world. Britain had also run up substantial debts with supplier countries during the war, despite the large quantities of materiel provided by the USA, much of it shipped across the Atlantic without payment being required. Although substantial quantities of British foreign investments had been sold during the war to pay for supplies, large debts remained. Paying off the so-called Sterling Balances – debts, denominated in sterling, run up during World War II mainly to Commonwealth countries – was a major commitment for Britain, unmatched by any comparable obligations undertaken by the Germans or French.

The post-World War II settlement for Europe, after some initial aberrations, was generally a great deal more reasonable and considerate than the provisions of the Versailles Treaty after World War I. The Americans, in particular, showed outstanding generosity with Marshall Aid, which, peaking at 3% of US GDP, poured into the economies of Western Europe, underpinning the recovery which was beginning to take place. Of course, Marshall Aid also served the interest of the USA by supporting the creation of demand in economies with which the USA wanted to trade. There was also a political dimension. By improving living standards, it was intended to reduce the appeal of socialism and communism in Europe. It was thus both a very generous policy but also one which had clearly perceived benefits to the USA.

Currency reform in Germany in the summer of 1948 was followed by a substantial and, as it turned out, largely unnecessary 20% devaluation in 1949. In the same year, an excellent harvest did much to solve the food shortage, suddenly leaving West Germany in an extraordinarily competitive position. Even though manufacturing in 1948 was still at only half its pre-war level, and output per head was even lower as a result of the large influx of refugees from the east, over the next 15 months production rose 57% to 87% of the 1936 level. Exports more than doubled from 19% to 43% of the pre-war figure.[3]

The French economy also emerged from the immediate post-war period in a much more competitive position than it had been in before the war, and began to expand rapidly. Starting from a higher base than the Germans, increases in output were still impressive. The French economy grew by 42% between 1946 and 1950, and while some of this increase reflected recovery from the dislocations of the war years, much of the rest of it resulted from heavy investment in new industrial facilities triggered, as in Germany, by rapidly rising exports and home demand.[4] In Italy and the Benelux countries, too, there was a much swifter recovery from the war than had been predicted. Growth in exports and industrial output surged ahead, as all the erstwhile devastated economies in Europe began to recover much more quickly than the British and Americans had thought they would. By contrast, the British economy, whose wartime output peaked in 1943, did not regain this level of performance until 10 years later, in 1953.[5]

The British, in particular, were left heavily exposed by the rapidly increasing competitiveness of the continental economies, combined with war debts, world-wide defence obligations, and major commitments on the domestic front to the creation of the Welfare State by the Labour government elected in 1945. The loss of income from foreign investments, caused by sales of assets to pay for war supplies, meant that Britain had to cover a much higher proportion of its import costs than previously by export sales. This proved to be an impossible task during the early years after the war, despite strenuous efforts by the government. Britain was caught in a double pincer. On the one hand, there was a big dollar gap, caused by a major balance of payments deficit between Britain and the USA. On the other hand, British exports were unable to hold their own against competition from the reviving export industries of Europe. The British dollar gap problem was largely solved by the devaluation of sterling in 1949 from $4.03 to $2.80, but as much of the rest of Europe devalued at the same time, the continental producers retained their competitive edge vis-à-vis British exporters.[6]

The British problem was worsened by the outbreak of the Korean War in June 1950. British efforts to maintain its coveted – if not wholly reciprocated – special relationship with the USA led to Britain embarking on a major rearmament drive, pre-empting industrial resources away from exports, and adding to inflationary pressures. The economies on the continent of Western Europe, on the contrary, were largely immune from these commitments, and continued to expand both their domestic and foreign markets.

The continental European economies were thus poised for the enormous expansion in output which they achieved in the 1950s and the following decade. Driven by highly competitive exports, and aided by high levels of investment and modest rates of inflation, between 1950 and 1960, the French economy grew by 56%, Italy's by 80% and West Germany's by 115%. The British achieved a much more modest 30%. France's industrial output over the same period grew by 89%, Italy's by 131%, and West Germany's by 148%, while Britain's grew by only 28%.[7] Significantly, this was a lower percentage than the growth in the British economy as a whole, presaging problems which would be shared by the other erstwhile successful economies in future decades.

The results of the differential performance of the major economies in Europe during the 1950s and 1960s was a massive shift in their relative rankings, reflected in share of world trade, income per head and, not least, in self-esteem and self-confidence. Britain, which in 1945 had seemed to be much the most successful country in Europe, gradually began to have increasing doubts about its economic strength and its military and diplomatic position in the world. The continental economies, on the other hand, began to see each other in an increasingly favourable light, as the traumas of World War II faded in peoples' memories. Discussions about some sharing of trans-national sovereignty had started early after the end of the war, culminating in the Treaty of Paris in 1951 which established the European Coal and Steel Community. Now seemed the time to embark on a more substantial and far-reaching venture.

European recovery and the Common Market

It is difficult to exaggerate the extent to which the history of Europe since World War II has been dominated by the determination of the generations which had lived through two devastating wars to make sure such a calamity never occurred again. This has been the source from which all the post-war supra-national institutions in Europe have sprung, though inevitably, once in place, the organisations which had been established developed a momentum of their own. The key issue, from an economic standpoint, is the impact which this integration had on the achievement of growth, full employment and manageable rates of inflation.

The European Coal and Steel Community (ECSC) was the first major consequence of the vision of Jean Monnet (1888-1979) and his associates of a Europe not only at peace with itself, but bound together by increasingly integrationist and federal arrangements. From the beginning, it was made clear that the intention was not just to link the countries of Europe together by expanding the commercial bonds between them, but to build supra-national political structures which might eventually become the framework for a United States of Europe. The rise in power of the USA and the Soviet Union, and the divisions of Europe into East and West, made it look prudent to create a European political entity as a counter-balance to the other superpowers. Furthermore, despite the successful rate at which the continental West European economies were growing, they were still divided from each other by remarkably high tariff barriers. Most of these countries had long histories of protectionism but, in the light of inter-war experience, accepted that there were powerful arguments in favour of freer trade, with the creation of a customs union as a first step towards closer integration.

Britain was offered membership of the ECSC, but rejected it. The ECSC was set up to support production, research and development and the restructuring needs of the coal and steel industries in the countries which participated in its establishment – the same six countries which subsequently came together initially to form the Common Market. It fulfilled its function as a supra-national body, exhibiting for the first time the willingness of the participating states to give up some sovereignty for a common purpose, but in other ways it was less successful. The ECSC was essentially a cartel, whose primary function was to keep prices up to assist its members. Like all such cartels, the benefits to its constituents in enhanced revenues were clear enough. The cost to everyone else in the countries covered by ECSC, in the form of higher prices for coal and steel than might otherwise have prevailed, were not so obvious. The benefits to the coal and steel industries were bought at the expense of all their customers, some of whom, competing in international markets, were severely disadvantaged by higher raw material and energy costs.

Nevertheless, the experiment with ECSC was sufficiently promising to encourage the participating countries to convene the Messina Conference in 1955. The main agenda was to consider integration on a more comprehensive scale. The outcome was the Treaty of Rome, signed in 1957, which brought the Common Market into being on 1st January 1958. The Treaty's immediate objective was to establish a customs union, although the preamble to the Treaty spoke of those setting up the customs union being 'determined to establish the foundations of an ever closer union among the European peoples'.[8] There is no doubt that many of those involved saw the Treaty of Rome as the first step towards a much more substantial political goal.

Britain, much the largest and most important European economy not included among the original Six, was asked to participate at Messina. The British, still sufficiently confident in their world role, the Commonwealth and their supposed special relationship with the Americans, declined to join the new organisation. An alternative British proposal, to set up an industrial free trade area in Europe without the political overtones of the Common Market and without the Common Agricultural Policy regime, was decisively rejected by the Common Market founders. They were not interested in just an economic union. As with so many of the decisions taken in Europe, which shaped the way the European Community developed, Britain's rejection of membership was taken largely on political grounds, with little thought being given to the economic consequences. In this respect the British mirrored their counterparts in Germany, France, Italy and the Benelux countries. The motivation for setting up the Common Market was almost entirely political, as was Britain's refusal to join. In both cases, the economic arguments were treated as secondary and subordinate – a potent and very unhappy precedent for the future.

In fact, the case for setting up a customs union in Europe was never as clear-cut as its proponents claimed it was. Nevertheless, a plausible justification could be made for it, on the grounds that the conditions required for the advantages to outweigh the disadvantages might, on balance, be fulfilled. The Treaty of Rome did not, however, just establish a customs union. It also set up a number of other subsidiary organisations, of which the most significant was the Common Agricultural Policy, which was part of a deal between France and Germany. France was only willing to provide duty free access to German goods in its heavily protected market if French agriculture was protected from world competition.

The Treaty of Rome stipulated that the tariffs between the economies of the Common Market at the beginning were to fall to zero over a transitional period of 10 years, starting in 1959 and ending in 1969, while a Common External Tariff was established. In fact, the abolition of internal tariffs was completed eighteen months ahead of schedule in 1968.[9] One way of testing whether the formation of this tariff free zone was in the best interests of the constituent countries is by comparing their growth rates during the period before and after its establishment. Table 3.1 shows the comparative figures for the seven-year period prior to the start of the Common Market, and for six years after it came into being.

Table 3.1: Growth in the original member countries of the Common Market for the 15 years spanning its establishment in 1958

| | 1950-57 | | 1958-64 | |
	Total % increase	% increase per year	Total % increase	% increase per year
France	38	4.8	46	5.5
Germany	78	8.6	48	5.8
Italy	53	6.2	59	5.9
Belgium & Luxembourg	24	3.1	39	4.8
The Netherlands	38	4.8	44	5.3
Average of the original six countries	54	6.3	47	5.7

Source: Derived from OECD National Accounts.

There was a small fall in the growth rate for all the six countries taken together. Most did better in the earlier than the later period, at the expense of the German annual average growth rate which fell from 8.6% to 5.8%. Yet the most significant major influence on the relative competitiveness of the Six over the 15 years covered by the figures were the double devaluations of the French franc at the end of the 1950s. These reduced the parity of the franc against the Deutsche Mark by a quarter, following five smaller devaluations of the franc which had taken place since 1949, evening up the competitiveness of the French and German economies, particularly in relation to their differing inflation rates. Thus the early success of the Common Market can be traced to a significant extent to the exchange rate flexibility which enabled all the constituent countries to grow at similar rates. They each preserved a broadly equal level of competitiveness, even if their inflation rates differed, without some countries running into balance of payments problems vis-à-vis others. Maintaining these conditions was one of the vital keys that was thrown away in the 1970s, when attempts began to be made to lock Community currency parities together.

During the same periods as those in Table 3.1, the British economy had grown respectively by 20% and 29%, with average annual growth rates over each of the two periods of 2.6% and 3.7%,[10] about half the average achieved by the Six. The contrast between the performance of the British economy and the Common Market countries was all too striking, provoking the first application for membership by Britain in 1961. This was rebuffed by Charles de Gaulle in 1962. A second British application in 1967 fared no better with the General, whose distrust of British attitudes and intentions remained undiminished.

The logic, as opposed to the emotion, behind Britain's membership application was, however, not easy to follow. It was widely assumed that by joining a union of fast expanding countries, Britain's growth rate would automatically be lifted to something closer to the average of those to whom it was attaching itself. Exactly how or why this should happen was not explained. Critics of Britain's application remained concerned that the root problem behind Britain's slow growth rate, which was its lack of competitiveness, would be exacerbated rather than improved by exposing Britain to more competition inside the customs union. Between 1963 and 1973, the total Common Market GDP rose by 58%, a cumulative annual growth rate of 4.7%, whereas the British GDP, protected by significant tariffs, had grown by only 39%, or 3.3% per annum.[11] These sceptical arguments failed to win the day, however, leading to the third, and this time successful, membership application by Britain in 1970. The European Free Trade Area, comprising Britain, Ireland, Switzerland, Denmark, Sweden, Finland, Austria and Norway, established in 1960, had failed to provide the dynamism which Britain sought. Britain became a Community member at the beginning of 1973, bringing with it Ireland and Denmark, both major British trading partners, but not Norway which opted to remain outside the Community.

Up to 1973, therefore, the Common Market had been able to maintain most of the momentum established during the post-World War II recovery period. The growth rate had slowed a little since 1957, but not much, and there had also been some convergence in economic performance. Unemployment throughout the years to 1973 was very low, averaging little more than 2% over the whole period in all Common Market countries. Inflation varied somewhat from economy to economy in the Community, but was maintained at an average of a little less than 4%.[12] Pride in the achievements of the last quarter of a century was understandable and considerable. An enormous increase in wealth and living standards had been accomplished. At the same time, generous welfare systems had been established, progress had been made towards making post-tax income distribution more equal, and vast improvements had been made in housing and education. Political stability seemed assured. Few people, therefore, foresaw the scale and nature of the problems which were about to unfold.

US experience post-World War II

The years immediately following the end of World War II saw a substantial slackening of demand on the US economy as government procurement for the war effort fell away, and US GDP fell over 17% between 1944 and 1947. Unemployment rose from 1.2% to 3.9% and the peak wartime level of output achieved by the US economy in 1944 was not regained until 1951.[13] The US economy was, nevertheless, in an extremely strong position after 1945. Partly because of the dominant position in which it found itself in the post-war period, however, the USA was faced with a number of problems which tended to sap rather than reinforce its growth performance in the decades to follow.

First, its victorious position left it with heavy international commitments, which greatly increased US unilateral transfers abroad. The most substantial of these was expenditure on major military presences in Europe, the Far East and elsewhere, whose cost increased sharply with the advent of the Cold War. An additional peak was caused by the Korean War which broke out in June 1950. Significant sums were also paid out to various international programmes, not least Marshall Aid.

Aid programmes also went some way towards helping to deal with the second problem with which the USA had to contend, which concerned trade imbalances. Although there was a large potential demand for US exports, which should have helped to boost the US economy, during the immediate post-World War II period the rest of the world was extremely short of dollars with which to pay for them. Marshall Aid helped fill the gap, not only by assisting recovering economies directly with aid on soft terms, but also by providing them with disbursements in dollars, which they in turn could use to buy American goods and services. There was still, however, a substantial 'dollar gap' which could only be filled when the recovering economies had got themselves into a strong enough position to trade on equal terms with the USA. This was a prerequisite for the achievement of one of the major US policy goals in the immediate post-war period, which was to see artificial barriers to trade and international payments removed, allowing the world to return to something like nineteenth-century conditions as opposed to those of the inter-war period. Although, as we have seen, American tariffs in the period running up to World War I were very high, the US authorities now recognised that, in their own interests as well as those of the world as a whole, protectionism was not the way ahead. Freer trade and multilateral payments were not, however, achievable unless all the economies concerned could participate on manageable terms.

These considerations led to the third problem, which in the long term proved to be the most serious. After the war, the victorious Allied powers were anxious that the defeated nations should not indefinitely require succour and subsidy. Greatly underestimating their erstwhile enemies' capacity for revival, the Allies therefore took active steps to ensure that the economies of the countries which had lost the war should have some chance of speedy recovery by providing them with exceptionally competitive parities for their currencies. This affected not only the German Deutsche Mark, following the currency reforms of 1948 and the DM devaluation of 1949, but also the yen, where similar financial reforms carried out at the same time by the administration of General Douglas MacArthur (1880-1964) in Japan, provided the Japanese economy with an exceptionally competitive cost base.

Germany and Japan, therefore, soon began to surge ahead with remarkably rapid recoveries. At the same time, other developed nations which had been overrun during the war also began to perform much better than they had done previously. Some of this performance was due to recovery from the wartime devastation, but other causes were almost certainly important. Nearly all the leaders of these countries exhibited a new determination to run their economies more successfully, learning from the mistakes of the inter-war period, fortified by the doctrines of Keynes and his associates. Old elites were swept away, discredited by wartime failure or collaboration, leaving the field free for fresh talent, which was widely available because of the strength of the education and training traditions in many continental countries. Opportunities opened up by rapid growth in the post-war recovery period sucked able people into those parts of the economy where the scope for productivity gains was greatest, in manufacturing and exporting. As a result, strong and influential social and political groupings were established, determined to safeguard industrial and trading interests. The absence of the benefits from this kind of upheaval was a major reason why during the 1950s and 1960s the US economy grew more slowly, at 3.6% per annum, than those of either continental Europe and Japan, or that of the world as a whole which grew at 4.8% a year during this period.[14]

Again, it is important to remember that the impact of differential growth rates, which may seem small viewed a year at a time, has a huge compound effect over any reasonably long span of years. During the 20 years between 1950 and 1970, the ratio between the size of the British economy at the end of this period compared to the beginning was 1.7, for the USA it was 2.0, for the West European economies it was 2.6, and for Japan it was 6.8. Allowing for population growth, the disparities in the changes of living standards caused by these differences in growth rates were even more marked. By 1970, another massive alteration in the distribution of world economic power had taken place. Whereas up to 1945, however, the underlying trend had been to increase the relative strength of the US economy vis-à-vis the rest of the world, for all of the first quarter of a century after World War II the USA was in relative decline, a trend which has continued since.

During the late 1960s the prospects for the American economy began rapidly to darken. A major cause of these upsets was the combination during the late 1960s of escalating expenditure on the Vietnam War with the rapidly rising costs of implementing the Great Society programme, which the Democrat president, Lyndon Johnson (1908-1973), had close to his heart. Successive reports from the military in charge in Vietnam, particularly General William Westmoreland (1914-2005), each suggesting that a further comparatively modest increase in expenditure would move the outcome of the war decisively in the USA's favour, had turned out to be false. As a result, the cost of the war had steadily mounted. Total defence expenditure rose from $51bn in 1964 to $82bn in 1968, an increase as a proportion of GDP from an already high 7.4% to 9.4%.[15] The Great Society programme was both a cherished big government Democrat initiative in its own right, and a response to the civil rights campaigns of the 1960s, which in turn had drawn in other disadvantaged groups. Its cost, however, was also high. Expenditure on income support, social security, welfare, veterans' benefits and family assistance, which had been $38bn in 1964, had risen by 1968 to $63bn, an increase from 5.7% of GDP to 6.9%.[16] The combined cost of the war and rising social expenditure therefore involved an increase in expenditure of 2.6% of GDP in three years.

A shift of this magnitude might not have been a problem if taxation had been raised to pay for it, but this did not happen. Federal receipts as a proportion of GDP stayed the same between 1964 and 1968 at 17.6%.[17] The result was highly reflationary as government expenditure rose rapidly, financed largely by borrowing from the banking system, generating a fiscal deficit which peaked at $25bn in 1968. This occurred at a time when the US economy was already booming, although, very significantly, private fixed investment as a proportion of US GDP never rose during the 1960s to above a little over 15%,[18] a very low figure by international standards. By the end of the 1960s, the average age of US plant was 18 years, compared to 12 in West Germany and 10 in Japan.[19] The overall result was that the economy became progressively more overheated, and its output less internationally competitive. Consumer price inflation, which had averaged 1.3% per annum between 1960 and 1965, reached 5.7% in 1970.[20] The surplus on trade in goods and services achieved every year since 1945, shrank to $91m in 1969 and moved into a heavy deficit in the 1970s.[21] Imports of motor vehicles and parts alone rose from $0.9bn in 1965 to $5.9bn in 1970, a real increase of nearly 450%, while over the same five years, imports of consumer goods, excluding vehicles, rose from $3.3bn to $7.4bn, almost doubling in real terms, allowing for inflation.[22]

When President Richard Nixon (1913-1994) took over the White House in early 1969, he therefore faced an increasingly difficult economic situation. The Vietnam War was wound down, and government expenditure cut, but inflation persisted, despite rising unemployment. The wage and price control programme, introduced by the new president, helped to bring the rate of increase in the consumer price index down from 5.7% in 1970 to 3.2% in 1972, but at the cost of unemployment rising to 5.6% by 1972,[23] up from 3.5% in 1969.[24]

Meanwhile on the external front, the situation was also deteriorating. Having moved back into surplus in 1970, the balance of trade showed a $1bn deficit in 1971, to be followed by $5bn in 1972.[25] It became clear that the dollar was seriously overvalued. The result was a conference, held in 1971 at the Smithsonian Institution in Washington DC, at which the USA announced that the link between the dollar and gold, which had underpinned the Bretton Woods system, could no longer be kept in place. The dollar was then devalued, and the Bretton Woods fixed exchange regime broke up. With the dollar no longer available as an anchor reserve currency, all the major currencies in the world began to float against each other.

By 1972, the dollar had fallen 16% against the yen, 13% against the Deutsche Mark, 4% against the pound sterling and around 10% against most other currencies.[26] As a result, by 1973 the US balance of trade showed signs of recovery. The absence of exchange rate constraints for the first time for decades, however, left policymakers throughout the world without familiar landmarks to guide them. Shorn of accustomed restraints, most countries began to reflate simultaneously. Credit controls were relaxed, and the money supply greatly increased, partly fuelled by an increasing pool of euro-dollars – cash balances held outside the USA by American companies and individuals – themselves the product of the US deficit. World output soared, growing 6.7% in 1973 alone.[27] The impact on commodity markets was dramatic. After years of falling prices, caused by excess capacity, demand suddenly exceeded supply. The prices of many raw materials doubled or trebled. Then, in 1973, the Yom Kippur War broke out between Israel and the surrounding Arab States. It ended with a resounding victory for the Israelis, but at the cost of the West seriously alienating the Arab States, many of them major suppliers of oil to the western nations, particularly the USA, which had supported Israel during the conflict. Shortly afterwards OPEC, the oil producers' cartel, raised the price of oil from around $2.50 to $10 per barrel.[28]

The consequences of all these events for the developed world were disastrous. The increased cost of oil, although it only represented about 2% of the West's GDP, presented oil importers with a new and highly unwelcome blow to their balance of payments. Almost all tried to shift the incidence elsewhere by a process of competitive deflation. At the same time, the quadrupled price of oil, accompanied by the doubling and trebling of the cost of other commodity imports, greatly increased inflationary pressures. Growth rates tumbled, and unemployment rose all over the world, as inflation moved to unprecedented levels. Mirroring similar developments in other advanced countries, the US economy, far from growing, shrank by 0.6% in 1974 and 0.4% in 1975. Unemployment rose to 8.5% in 1975.[29] while the year on year increase in the consumer price level peaked at nearly 11% in 1974.[30]

The severe economic difficulties and disruption facing the whole world – not just the USA – in the mid-1970s did not, however, only affect rates of inflation, growth and unemployment. They also had a profound effect on the intellectual climate. The consensus around the ideas of Keynes and his associates, which appeared to have guided world economic policy so successfully in the 1950s and 1960s, was shattered. Demand management did not appear to provide any satisfactory solutions to the problems faced by those confronted with the severely unstable conditions, particularly unprecedently high peace-time inflation, with which they now had to cope. Into the vacuum thus created, moved an old economic doctrine in a new guise, to take the place of discredited Keynesianism. Monetarism arrived on the scene in the USA and elsewhere as the intellectual underpinning of economic policy formation in a world which had lost fixed exchange rates and the discipline they provided as the anchors for taking decisions.

Mixed fortunes in Japan

The countries in Asia comprised the largest part of the world economy in 1820, with nearly 70% of the world's population and nearly 60% of its GDP.[31] At this time, there was not a huge disparity in income levels between different countries in the region. By 1992, however, GDP per head in Japan was over six times the level achieved in China, more than 14 times that in India, and 27 that in Bangladesh.[32] How did the Japanese manage to secure this achievement?

The turning point came with the arrival of the US Navy in Tokyo Bay in 1853, forcing an end to the policy pursued in Japan for more than two centuries of almost total isolation. In the 1630s the new Tokugawa shogunate, established at Edo, now Tokyo, had prohibited all travel abroad. All foreigners were expelled, except for a small colony of Dutch East India Company traders on Deshima Island, near Nagasaki, who were allowed to receive one ship a year from Indonesia. Christianity, introduced previously by St Francis Xavier (1506-1552), was suppressed.[33] When the Americans arrived, therefore, the Japanese economy was in an exceptionally backward condition, with living standards roughly on a par with those found in Europe in the Late Middle Ages.

While the economy was undeveloped, however, Japanese political and social institutions were considerably more flexible and robust than might have been expected. The Japanese were therefore able to respond far more positively to the challenge presented by western intruders than had happened elsewhere in the East. This was partly because the Japanese had always borrowed important elements of the Chinese and Korean civilisations, and were therefore not ashamed to copy a western model which had demonstrated its superior technology so dramatically.[34] The process which followed was that trade concessions were extracted by the Americans, and extended to the French, Dutch, Russians and British, and treaties were forced on Japan in 1854 which restricted its commercial and fiscal autonomy. The Tokugawa shogunate, humiliated by the challenge from abroad, was overthrown in 1867, and Emperor Mutsuhito (1852-1912) assumed full powers, adopted the title Meiji, which means 'enlightened rule', and launched a policy of swift westernisation.[35]

The results were dramatic. Within a remarkably short period the previous rigid stratification of society was abolished. Land could be bought and sold freely. Primary education became compulsory, and new textbooks were written with a western orientation. Large numbers of students went abroad to receive technical and higher education. Tariffs were fixed at no more than 5%, so that the economy was open to western imports. The Japanese Army and Navy were reformed and rearmed using western technology. The government then set out on a programme of economic development, much of it with a heavy military orientation, which had no parallel elsewhere in Asia, though not so dissimilar to developments elsewhere in the world where militaristic regimes were in control.[36]

The result was a steady expansion of the Japanese economy, which grew at a cumulative rate of 1.4% per annum between 1870 and 1885, accelerating to 3.1% between 1885 and 1900, and then slowing to 2.5% between 1900 and 1913. World War I saw the Japanese economy growing rapidly, and by 1919, Japanese GDP was over 40% more than it had been in 1913. After a sharp post-war recession, the economy continued to expand during the inter-war period, checked only by a comparatively minor drop of 7% between 1929 and 1930. As in Germany, the advent of a militaristic regime, determined to drive the economy forward, produced a much higher growth rate. Between 1930 and the entry of the Japanese into World War II at Pearl Harbor in 1941, Japan's economy grew at a cumulative rate of 5.4% per annum.[37] By then GDP per head in Japan was approaching the level of the poorer West European countries, though it was still only half the level in Germany and 40% of that in Britain at the time.[38] Close to half of all employment in Japan – 43% – was still in agriculture, forestry and fishing.[39]

While Japanese military ventures, including, during the 1930s, the invasion and occupation of Manchuria and parts of China, followed, in 1940, by French Indo-China, had helped to stimulate the economy, World War II was a total disaster for Japan, as it was, to a similar extent, for Germany. Between 1941 and 1945, Japanese GDP fell by more than half.[40] By 1946, industrial production was down to 20% of its 1941 level, and steel production had fallen 92%. Two thirds of its large cotton textile capacity had been destroyed.[41] In 1945, Japan – before long to be the car maker for the world – produced a total of 8,200 cars and commercial vehicles.[42] Leaving aside the damage done by atomic weapons in Hiroshima and Nagasaki, American bombing raids had left all major Japanese cities in ruins. Inflation was rampant. The Japanese were humiliated and destitute.

When the American occupation, headed by General MacArthur, began, its major objectives were first to reform Japanese political institutions, to extirpate the militaristic legacy which had caused so much harm, and secondly to get the economy back on its feet, and to stop it being a drain on the American taxpayer. The main problem, apart from general distress, was to get exports moving again, so that the country would be able to pay for the food and raw materials it needed, which in the immediate post-war period had been provided only through the Allied occupation forces, financed largely by the USA. The solution adopted was a reform of the currency, fixing the yen in 1948 at 360 to the dollar as part of the Dodge Line financial measures.[43] As post-war recovery set in, this left the cost base in Japan, measured by international standards, at an exceptionally low level, exactly as happened in Germany.

The response in Japan was very similar to what it was among all the developed countries which had been defeated at one stage or another during World War II. All found themselves, in varying degrees in the same competitive position, as the victorious Allies hugely underestimated the capacity of vanquished nations to recover. Talent poured into industry, as major opportunities opened up to make fortunes on world markets. Japanese sales abroad began to soar. By 1973, Japanese merchandise exports were 27 times as high in volume terms as they had been in 1950. Germany's by contrast were 15 times as high, the USA's four times, and Britain's 2.4 times.[44] In 1950, Japan's share of world trade was 1.3%. In 1973 it was 16.4%.[45] Nothing shows more clearly than these figures that the history of the world, especially since the trade liberalisation that has taken place since 1945, is largely written in export competitiveness, and the alignment of exchange rates which either makes astounding success possible if the parity is favourable, or inhibits it if it is not.

Initially, Japanese post-war exports consisted mostly of comparatively simple goods in all of which Japan had an enormous price advantage because the costs of production, measured internationally, were so low. Japan had a long history of textile manufacturing and metal working. Newer industries, such as those involving the use of plastics, where the technology was comparatively simple, were quick and easy to establish. As had happened in the nineteenth century, however, the Japanese were not content to see their role solely as the producers of cheap goods. The economy rapidly developed a formidable capacity for moving up-market and for making its own capital goods, as well as expanding its heavy industries in steel and shipbuilding, and its oil refining and electricity generating capacity. Crude steel production, which had been 557,000 tons in 1946, reached almost 120m tons by 1973. By then, Japan was generating over 20 times as much electricity as at the end of World War II. Perhaps the most outstanding success story of all was to be found in the motor vehicle industry. Starting from the 8,200 units of all kind produced in 1945, by 1973 Japanese manufacturers produced over 7m vehicles, and by 1983, more than 11m.[46] Riding on the massive growth in exports, which averaged a cumulative increase of over 15% per annum between 1950 and 1973, the Japanese economy grew extremely rapidly. Having only exceeded its 1943 peak wartime output for the first time in 1953, by 1973 it was 7.6 times the size it had been in 1950, after a cumulative average growth rate throughout these 23 years of 9.2%.[47] The comparatively low increase in the population – just over 1.1% per annum between 1950 and 1973 – avoided much dilution of the increase in GDP, so that GDP per head also rose strongly, by 8.0% per annum throughout this period. By 1973, Japanese living standards were on a par with those in Britain, and not far behind those in most of Western Europe – a massive change from the position which had prevailed a quarter of a century earlier.[48]

There is a vast literature about the reasons for the remarkable achievements of the Japanese economy, especially during the period up to 1973 when its growth rate was at its highest. Undoubtedly, a number of factors played an important role. All the countries defeated at various stages in World War II had a resurgence once the war ended, as older leaders became discredited, and new opportunities opened up for those, hungry for success, who replaced them. All of them had well educated, well trained and experienced labour forces. The disruption caused by such large-scale warfare as had taken place during the first half of the twentieth century left a substantial legacy of inventions and technical possibilities to be exploited, and the Japanese were well placed to take advantage of these opportunities. Other characteristics more specifically orientated to institutions and culture in Japan have also been cited. The homogeneity, discipline and national pride of the Japanese people undoubtedly helped to generate a focused work ethic. Some have argued that the consensual Confucian tradition may also have assisted. The heavily protected domestic market generated massive savings which produced a large pool of investible funds available to the export sector.

By far the strongest argument that none of these special factors was fundamentally the cause of Japanese success, however, lies in the fact that their alleged influence evaporated as soon as the Japanese economy lost the real reason for its rapid growth, which was its undervalued exchange rate. Until 1971, this stayed at 360 yen to the US dollar.[49] Because the Japanese export drive was so successful, and the amount of investment in production available for the world market was so high, Japanese export prices rose during the 1950s and 1960s by barely 1% a year,[50] despite relatively high domestic inflation. This averaged 5.2% per annum between 1950 and 1973[51], incidentally showing how low rates of domestic price rises are difficult to combine with very high growth rates, and certainly not necessary for fast growth to be achieved. The result was that Japanese exports became more and more competitive, thus fuelling the next stage of their expansion. Although, immediately post the 1971 move towards floating rates, the nominal value of the yen strengthened against the dollar by some 20%, followed by a slow further hardening of the yen, the competitiveness of Japanese exports continued to increase.[52]

The turning point came in the mid-1980s, when the yen suddenly strengthened against the dollar as the exchange rate moved from 238 yen per dollar in 1985 to 168 in 1986 and 145 in 1987, strongly assisted by the 1985 Plaza Accord, an international agreement to drive down the value of the dollar and the Deutsche Mark against the Japanese currency . After staying roughly stable until 1990, the yen nevertheless moved up again, peaking at just under 100 in 1995, before weakening to 131 in 1998.[53] The reason for the hardening of the yen was the huge balance of payments surplus which the Japanese started to accumulate from the early 1980s onwards, after decades when the Japanese current account had been in rough balance. There was a massive surplus on merchandise account, which reached over $44bn in 1984, and which averaged almost $90bn per annum in the late 1980s, partly offset by a deficit on services, but increased by a rising net income from investments abroad. Overall, the current account surplus run up by the Japanese economy between 1984 and 1994 totalled a staggering $932bn.[54]

The effect on the volume of Japanese exports as a result of the strengthening yen at the beginning of the 1990s was immediate. The price in yen which Japanese exporters could charge the rest of the world fell by about 20%, putting a severe strain on their previously buoyant profitability. The increase in volume of exports slowed to a crawl. Between 1973 and 1985, the cumulative annual rise had been 8.6%. From 1985 to 1994 it was 2.0%.[55] As the stimulus to the economy from exports died down, so did the overall growth rate, but only after a period of speculative boom in the 'bubble economy' of the late 1980s. This kept GDP rising between 1985 and 1991 at an average of 4.4% per annum, but no longer on the sustainable basis which had applied previously when exports had been growing faster than GDP. The result was that when the boom broke, Japanese banks were left holding massive uncovered debts, and the economy stalled. In 2000, Japanese GDP was only 10.4% higher than it had been in 1991.[56] Expenditure on investment, previously another major growth component, was the same in 1997 as it had been six years earlier.[57] The first decade and a half of the twenty-first century was no better, with growth averaging barely 1% per annum.[58] All the efforts made to reflate the economy and to get it growing again – exacerbated by the overhang of non-performing debt still left over from the 1980s bubble – foundered on the fact that the value of the yen, propped up by all the well-known difficulties of selling into the Japanese market, was far too high.

The major mistake made by the Japanese was to allow their huge balance of payments surplus to accumulate in the 1980s. Every country's surplus has to be matched by corresponding deficits somewhere else, and the rest of the world choked on the success of Japanese exporters, unrequited by sufficient imports to keep Japan's current account in reasonable balance. It may have seemed a good idea to MITI at the time to promote the myriad ways in which the Japanese discouraged imports, thus allowing their surprisingly inefficient non-export-orientated part of their economy to remain protected, but the price eventually paid for this error was extremely heavy.

In the end, therefore, there is nothing that cannot be explained about the Japanese economy. It was only an extreme example of the impact which an exceptionally low cost basis can achieve, followed by this huge advantage being lost as a result of policy mistakes being made which caused the currency massively to appreciate. As with the leaders of so many other countries, however, those in Japan appear never to have fully understood or appreciated the fundamental underlying reasons for the success over which they presided. If they had, it seems hard to believe that they would have allowed the conditions which were so important to the economy for which they were responsible to melt away so pointlessly and as damagingly as they did.

The USSR and the command economies

By far the largest departure from the organic way in which most of the world's economies have grown was the deliberate attempt to get rid of the capitalist system undertaken by the successful revolutionaries in Russia in 1917, and their successors in subsequent regimes devoted to running their economies on non-market lines. While the writings of Karl Marx had been the basis on which communist beliefs were founded, Marx had little to say about how economies were to be run when the revolutions he advocated had taken place. Lenin (1870–1924) and his associates and successors therefore had to formulate policies as they went along, without much of a blueprint from which to work, other than the general objective of eliminating as much private ownership as they could, while getting the economy to grow as fast as possible with a crash programme of industrialisation.

The Russian economy which the Communists inherited had expanded substantially during the late nineteenth and early twentieth centuries, with growth rates of 2.0% per annum between 1870 and 1900 and a rather more impressive 3.2% per annum between 1900 and 1913.[59] Mostly as a result of state initiatives, by the start of World War I, there was a reasonably extensive railway system,[60] and some heavy industry. The standard of living in Russia was, however, well below the level of most of the rest of Europe, although slightly above that of Japan.[61] The Russian economy was severely disrupted by World War I, and there was heavy loss of life. Another 10m died in the course of the revolution, civil war and attacks on the new regime from western powers, fearful of what the successful replacement of capitalism might presage. As a result, it was 1930 before the Soviet economy recovered the same level of output as it had enjoyed in 1913,[62] providing its rulers with a poor, backward and fractured economic base on which to build.

Although initially relatively liberal, during its New Economic Policy phase, the Soviet regime soon toughened its stance. Lenin died in 1924, to be succeeded by Joseph Stalin (1879–1953), who introduced the system of five year plans, the first two of which covered the period from 1928 to 1939. Heavy and light industries were developed, and agriculture collectivised. The country began to be transformed as industrialisation proceeded and the urban population quickly doubled.[63] The cost, however, was prodigious not only in human terms, as millions died in the Ukraine and Kazakhstan famines of 1932–4 and in political purges and liquidations, but also in economic terms as state policies drove down the current standard of living to enable more and more resources to be mobilised for investment in the future.

The result was that the Soviet economy grew during the 1930s relatively quickly, but, as a result of high capital to output ratios, much more slowly than would have been achieved if western standards of return on the use of capital had been attained. Between 1928 and 1940, Soviet output rose by an estimated 81%, with an average per annum growth rate of 5.1%.[64] Thereafter, although until 1941 the USSR had staved off being involved in World War II as a result of the non- aggression pact negotiated with Germany in 1939, once the German invasion began in June 1941, the USSR was subjected to four traumatic years of carnage and physical damage. About 25m Soviet citizens are believed to have lost their lives as a result of the German invasion,[65] and the damage done to the area occupied by Axis forces was immense. As a result, in spite of huge continuing investment in new production facilities, the output of the Soviet economy was over 20% lower in 1946 than it had been in 1940.[66]

The post-World War II period, however, saw a steady increase in output, which rose every year until the end of the 1950s at an average rate between 1947 and 1958 estimated at 7.3%, a considerably higher pace than was being achieved anywhere else except in Japan and Germany.[67] This began to cause mounting concern in the West, particularly in the USA, whose growth rate was barely half that of the Soviet economy, prompting Nikita Khrushchev (1894-1971), by then leader of the Soviet Union, to promise while in the USA in 1959 that the USSR would shortly overtake the American standard of living.[68] This threat, however, gradually, became emptier. As the years wore on, it became increasingly clear that, although the Soviet economy had responded reasonably well to large investments in basic industries, running a consumer-orientated economy was much more difficult to manage without a market framework within which to do it.

Although, after Stalin's influence had worn off and following Khrushchev's speech in 1956 denouncing his excesses, valiant attempts were made to get the Soviet economy to produce more consumer goods of reasonable quality, the results were remarkably unsuccessful. The Soviet economy continued to have a high proportion of its GDP devoted to investment, but the growth rate in the economy slowed, and consumers remained dissatisfied. Between 1959 and 1973 the Soviet economy grew at a still more than respectable estimated 4.9% per annum, but thereafter, during the era presided over by Leonid Brezhnev (1906-1982), growth slowed to 1.9% per annum.[69] During the whole of the period between 1973 and 1989, before the USSR began to disintegrate, GDP per head in the Soviet Union increased at a cumulative rate of less than 1% per annum.[70] Allowing for the military build-up which was taking place, the disposable income for the average Soviet citizen stopped rising after 1973, stabilised, of course, at a far lower level than in the USA, where nevertheless a remarkably similar stagnant real income phenomenon was to be found among large sections of the population.

Unquestionably, part of the reason for the relatively poor performance in the later years of the USSR was the exceptionally heavy military burden which the economy had to bear, particularly from the mid-1960s onwards when the Cold War intensified.[71] After making all allowances for this, however, the root problem with the system proved to be the impossibility of running a more and more complex economy on the basis of central plans, with market signals largely suppressed. This led not only to the rate of growth slowing down, but to more and more serious problems of resource allocation, as their appropriation became ever more complicated, reducing the real value to the final consumer of the goods and services which were produced.

The problems of the Soviet economy were mirrored in varying degrees of intensity among all the East European countries which had been obliged to adopt command economies at the behest of the USSR after the installation of communist regimes following the Soviet occupation after World War II. A particularly interesting example was the German Democratic Republic (DDR), which was long regarded as being the most successful of the Soviet satellites. Prior to reunification, western estimates of East German per capita GDP levels had put them at about three-quarters of those in the Federal Republic and about two-thirds of those in the USA. When in 1990 the Berlin Wall came down, however, and East and West Germany were reunited, these estimates were found to be about 50% too high. The actual East German level of GDP per head was only about two-thirds of what it had been thought to be, confirming strongly the deep-rooted inefficiency of even a comparatively well run command economy, and emphasising the weaknesses in economic performance from which the erstwhile USSR had suffered.[72]

It was therefore hardly surprising that the process of integrating the two parts of Germany together was found to be far more difficult and expensive than had been previously envisaged. Part of the problem was the well-meaning but actually very damaging undertaking by Helmut Kohl (b. 1930) to provide parity between the Ost Mark and the Deutsche Mark which, at a stroke, made almost all of the former DDR's output grossly overpriced and uncompetitive. Meanwhile, the condition of even those parts of the DDR's economy which were thought to be performing reasonably well generated requirements for massive remedial expenditure. The concentration on production at all costs in East Germany had left environmental considerations well down the order of priorities. The result was pollution over large areas on a scale which those used to western-style regulation found hard to comprehend. The quality of the goods which were being produced, having never been exposed to competitive pressures, was far below world standards, apart from the fact that they were now, in addition, very expensive. The legacy of command economies for those who lived in them and the states which succeeded them has not, therefore, been an easy one. Wrenching transitions were required, tending to be more pronounced for those economies longest exposed to communism. Between 1990 and 1992 alone Russian GDP fell by over 30%.[73] The weaknesses of the command economy approach lay exposed for all to see.

Yet a sense of balance is required. Some of the post-1989 transition problems were made much worse than they needed to be by policy errors such as parity between the DM and the Ost-Mark in Germany. In the longer term, the record of the Soviet economy and its satellites had some points in its favour. Although achieved at very high cost, the growth rates for long periods were greater than those attained elsewhere in the world. For much of the time, they were also steadier. While the western world plunged into depression post-1929, the Soviet economy grew every year from 1928 onwards, except for a minor 1% fall in 1932.[74] The command economies also provided employment for virtually everyone, although at a heavy cost in the efficiency with which the labour force was used. These achievements, combined with the Soviet ability to expand without assistance from outside, were sufficient to attract partial copying by many third world countries, once they had gained independence after World War II. There was no problem about maintaining a high level of demand in command economies or – however expensively – in achieving high levels of investment. The difficulties, which in the end overwhelmed them, were those of allocation of scarce resources and quality of output.

The Third World

While the main emphasis so far has been on those countries which began to industrialise earliest, and which therefore now have the highest standards of living, most of the world's population has lived elsewhere. In 2014, out of a world population of 7.3bn, just under 20% of the world's inhabitants lived in fully developed parts of the world.[75] In 1992, the average income per head among the then remaining 76% of humanity, measured in 1990 US dollars, was $2,173, compared to $19,175 for the industrialised countries.[76]

The developing and undeveloped nations of the world are not, however, by any means homogeneous either in the absolute standards of living which they have managed or in their growth records during the previous decades. The broad picture, according to Purchasing Power Parity figures for 2015 compiled by the CIA is that the standard of living in Latin America is a little above the world average of $15,546, with Chile at $22,370 and Peru at $12,529. In Asian countries, the spread is much wider. Singapore ($85,382) and Hong Kong ($56,924) were well above average EU levels, Japan ($37,322), and South Korea ($34,549) about the same, while others, such as Thailand ($16,340), China ($14,450) and Indonesia ($11,058) were much lower, with India ($6,101), Pakistan ($5,011) Bangladesh ($3,340) and Myanmar ($5,250) lower still. The income levels in Africa were both lower than in Asia, and even more skewed. South Africa ($13,179) had a relatively high average figure, masking very large income differentials within its boundaries, but other major African countries had GDP per head at little more than 10% of western levels at best, with Nigeria at $6,004, shading down to desperate poverty in Liberia ($835) and Zaire ($784), where the average income for the whole population was barely more than $2 per day.[77]

As to the growth records leading up to where they are now, the Latin American economies had all started developing fairly early. By 1913 their average living standards were a little less than half those in the western industrialised economies. By 1950, mainly because they were not involved to any significant extent in either of the world wars, they were at just over half the western level. Thereafter, they continued to perform more or less on a par in terms of growth rates with the more advanced economies, helped by the boost provided to some of them by the discovery and exploitation of large oil deposits. Between 1950 and 1973, the combined cumulative average growth rate for Latin America was 5.3% per annum. Between 1973 and 1992, it was 2.8% and since then to 2005 it has been 3.2%.[78] High growth rates in the population, however, meant that the expansion of the South American economies was not matched by corresponding increases in living standards, which grew much less than those in the western world – cumulatively at over 1% per annum more slowly.[79]

In Asia, the growth record has been much more impressive, with an overall cumulative average growth rate of 6.0% between 1950 and 1973, 5.1% between 1973 and 1992, and 8.1%[80] between 1992 and 2015, starting from a base position which, in 1950, showed GDP per head to be on average not much more than one-tenth of its level in the West. As the population growth rate was markedly lower than in South America, living standards rose correspondingly more quickly – cumulatively by 3.8% for the first period, 3.2% in the second[81] and 6.5% in the third.[82] A point of considerable significance, however, is that while Japanese per annum growth slowed up dramatically from about 1990 onwards, most of the rest of the major Asian economies did better in the third period than the first two. The improved performance included much better results between 1992 and 2015 from Pakistan at 4.1% cumulative growth per annum, 5.6% for Bangladesh, 5.5% for Malaysia, 6.9% for India and 9.6% for China. These figures illustrate all too graphically how rapidly economic power is moving from the West to the East. The average cumulative growth rate across the whole of the developed world between 1992 and 2010 was 2.0%.[83]

In 1950, the average standard of living in Africa was a little higher than in Asia,[84] and between 1950 and 1973, the overall growth record in Africa, at a cumulative 4.4% was only a little below the world average of 4.9%.[85] The period 1973 to 1992, however, showed the growth rate slowing to 2.8% a year. The major problem in Africa was not so much the slow increase in GDP but the very high birth rate – leading to population growth of 2.4% per year in the earlier period and 2.9% in the second.[86] The result was a 2.0% per annum increase in living standards between 1950 and 1973, but a fall of 0.1% a year between 1973 and 1992.[87] Between 1992 and 2015, the growth rate rose to 3.4%, accelerating in the 2000s as exploitation of Africa's natural resources gathered pace. The very high birth rate in Africa, however, meant that the rise in living standards has still been very low.[88]

There are some important lessons to be gained from the experiences during the last 50 years of the developing and less developed countries covered in this brief survey. Unquestionably, some of the poor results achieved were the consequence of maladministration, corruption, warfare and instability, which no economic policies, however well-conceived, are capable of overcoming. Leaving these factors aside, however, a number of patterns can be detected.

First, the Soviet model of forced industrialisation turned out to be an extremely poor one. Not only did it lead to large-scale waste and misallocation of resources, but the bureaucratisation and industrial favouritism which it encouraged militated against opening up the economies adopting this approach to the stimulus of international competition. The results were high import tariffs, exchange controls and restrictions on capital movements, designed to protect indigenous industries, often owned by the state or by those associated with its political leaders. Economies which adopted such policies tended to suffer from the need to service the costs of large-scale borrowing to finance investments, many of which both achieved little or no financial return, and failed to produce world class goods and services. The inefficient and uncompetitive export sectors which were the consequence were unable to launch themselves successfully on world markets. Most countries which once modelled themselves at least in part on the USSR have now long since ceased doing so, and their economic performance, although sometimes offset by other factors, has improved accordingly.

Second, there are a number of social policies which clearly favour fast growth and rising living standards. The more successful economies have tended to be those with high literacy rates and good technical training, rather than those, such as India, which have been inclined to concentrate resources on university education at the expense of the wider population. In the mid-1990s, 38% of men and 66% of women in India were still illiterate, compared to 16% and 38% respectively in China, and 9% overall in Taiwan, with much more difficult kanji-based writing to learn.[89] It is also evident that countries which have reliable legal systems, well-regulated financial sectors, successfully planned infrastructures and fair and impartial tax systems, ought to have an edge on those which lack them, although it is easy enough to find examples of countries which have prospered without these advantages. None of these requirements, desirable though they may, appear to be a sine qua non of economic success.

Third, rising populations have clearly been a major factor in increasing the size of many of the world's economies, but the dilution of GDP caused by there being more and more people among whom it has to be shared, has held back living standards in many countries, especially in Africa and some parts of East Asia, where the population is rising most rapidly. By far the most effective way to slow down population growth is to raise living standards, but this generates a difficult chicken and egg problem if increasing GDP is being heavily diluted by population growth. The time when the richer parts of the world can afford to ignore the need to provide more direct and indirect assistance, particularly better trading opportunities, to help deal with this issue, however, may be shorter than many people realise.

Fourth, the strongest link between those economies which have achieved high growth rates, as against those which have not, is exactly the same for poorer countries as it is for richer ones. The most important requirement is a competitive export sector, which sucks in talent and investment to where they can be most productively employed, enables a cumulative increase in foreign sales to be accomplished, and thence fuels sustainable high rates of growth in the economy as a whole. It is growth in exports which drives expansion generally, as can easily be seen from the statistics.[90] It is countries whose exports, and particularly whose merchandise sales abroad, grow faster than the world average whose economies expand most rapidly, and vice versa. From Chile to South Korea, from Turkey to China, the record is the same.

When using appropriate macro-economic policies to achieve the desired end, therefore, the crucial policy variable to get right is the cost base for internationally tradable goods and services. If this is low enough to generate a buoyant export market, it is not too difficult to get a variety of complementary economic policy elements to work successfully. If the cost base is too high, however, no supplementary mixture of policies will offset this major obstacle. The inevitable result will be relative if not absolute stagnation, as scarce talent is concentrated more and more heavily in sectors of the economy which have comparatively little to contribute in terms of competitiveness and growth.

4

Monetarism and Neo-Liberalism

As the certainties of the Bretton Woods world crumbled away in the early 1970s, intellectual fashions in economics moved decisively away from the Keynesian orthodoxy of the previous quarter of a century. Despite the objections of no less than 364 British economists, who wrote to the *The Times* in 1981 stating that there was 'no basis in economic theory or supporting evidence' for the policy the government was then pursuing, monetarism became the theoretical and practical discipline to which the vast majority of those involved in economic affairs, both in the academic and policy making worlds, began to subscribe. It is no coincidence, however, that the prevalence of monetarism – and the neo-liberal orthodoxy into which monetarism morphed – has been most significant in economies which were already growing slowly. This is because these sorts of doctrines are inclined to receive their most sympathetic hearing among political and intellectual leaders who are at the helm of economies where finance is much more dominant than manufacturing industry. There are interlocking reasons why this is so. It is partly that monetarist prescriptions lead to slow growth, and partly that the cultural attitudes, which breed a proclivity for them, flourish especially strongly in economies with relatively poor growth records.

This has been particularly the case in the Anglo-Saxon countries, the USA and Britain, but by no means exclusively so. Similar ideas have also managed to get their grip on the European Union, leading to the determination, exemplified in the provisions of the 1992 Maastricht Treaty, to put monetary stability before prosperity. The loss of confidence in Keynesian policies after the rising inflation and international dislocation of the early 1970s caused policy shifts in a monetarist direction particularly in Germany and France. This change in intellectual fashion, as much as anything else, was responsible for the EU switching from being one of the world's fasters growing regions into becoming an area of exceptionally slow increase in output, accompanied by painfully high levels of unemployment. Countries which have given monetarist prescriptions less priority, on the other hand, both in Europe and elsewhere, continued to grow apace. Norway, a prime example, outside the European Union but admittedly greatly assisted by oil, achieved the highest rate of GDP per head within the OECD between 1973 and 1992, just ahead of Japan, increasing the population's living standards by 71%. The Norwegians succeeded in combining this achievement with one of the better OECD records on inflation, with an unemployment rate barely one-third of the then EU average.[1] Over the same period Britain and the USA, both countries strongly influenced by monetarist ideas, achieved GDP per head increases period of only 31% and 26% respectively. The EU as a whole chalked up 41%.[2]

Monetarist prescriptions, stripped of their theorising and rhetoric, are familiar to anyone who knows the preconceptions of most of those who make their living out of finance or those with old money fortunes to protect. Their hallmarks are relatively tight money, high interest and the consequently uncompetitive exchange rates which slow down productive enterprise, and make it harder to sell abroad and easier to import, discriminating against manufacturing investment and draining the talent out of industry. Monetarist ideas, and the devotion to balanced budgets and financial conservatism which was its predecessor, harking back to nineteenth-century classical economics, have never been far below the surface, especially in the USA or Britain. This is why, post-1973, and especially in the 1980s, macro-economic conditions prevailed in both countries, and subsequently in most of the rest of the western world, which were almost wholly responsible for the low growth and productivity increases of the subsequent quarter of a century. They were also directly responsible for the huge widening of incomes there has been over the last 25 years, with which the attenuation of manufacturing capacity, itself a direct result of monetarist policies, is heavily bound up.

These are familiar themes and it is therefore worth exploring why a combination of self-interest and social attitudes should produce an environment where monetarist ideas can take strong hold even if they are weak in intellectual coherence and undermined by prescriptive inadequacies, and have such damaging consequences. Why should mature, stable, slow growing economies be particularly prone to producing a climate of opinion where such ideas can flourish?

The answer is that the implications of monetarist policies are far from unattractive to large sections of the population, especially in slow growing economies where lenders tend to be in a strong position and borrowers in a weak one. Those who have achieved success in finance rather than manufacturing tend to move into positions of influence and political power. As they do so, the monetarist doctrines which appeal to people with financial backgrounds become increasingly predominant. The attitudes of those whose business is lending money, who have an obvious stake in high interest rates and scarcity of the commodity they control, become politically significant, not least because their opinions have a self-fulfilling quality. If there is great fear that losing their confidence will lead to a run on the currency, this places those in a position to keep the parity up by their decisions in a very powerful role. Those whose incomes depend on high interest rates – pensioners and many others – are also naturally inclined to support a policy which seems so obviously in their favour. Bankers, financiers and wealth holders are the immediate beneficiaries of the deflationary policies which follow, buttressed by those who can see no further ahead than obtaining the immediate benefits from low cost imports and cheap holidays abroad. The losers are those engaged in manufacturing and selling internationally tradable goods and services.

When the economy grows slowly, the power and influence of finance increases against that of industry. This is partly a result of the process of accumulation of capital wealth, much of which tends to be invested abroad rather than at home, because slow growth in the domestic economy creates better opportunities overseas. This was the story of Britain in the nineteenth century, the United States for a long period post-World War II, Japan from the 1980s onwards and now China is moving in the same direction. This process produces profound effects on social attitudes and political power, particularly if these conditions prevail for a long period of time, as they have in most of the slow growing industrialised countries.

If the economy is run with relatively tight money, and high interest and exchange rates, the inevitable consequence is to produce adverse trading conditions for all output exposed to international competition. Adequate returns on investment are much harder to achieve. It becomes increasingly difficult to pay the going wage or salary rates for the calibre of employees required for success in world markets. Of course there will always be exceptionally efficient companies, or even industries, such as, for many years, pharmaceuticals, and nowadays motor vehicle production, in Britain which buck the trend. They are not, however, enough. It is the average which counts, and here the results are impossible to dismiss. The profitability of large sections of manufacturing in the western world has become insufficient for it to be worthwhile for them to continue in business. This is why the proportion of GDP derived from manufacturing has fallen so precipitately in most western economies over the last four decades. It explains, for example, why in 2015 China produced 804m tons of crude steel compared to 166m tons in the whole of the EU and 79m in the USA.[3] In the same year, China produced 24.5m vehicles, Japan – the world leader in the 1970s, '80s and '90s – 9.3m and, the USA – the world leader before Japan took over – 12.1m, up from no more than 7.7m in 2010.[4] The same trends affected swathes of other industries in many other developed economies. Meanwhile, in countries which gave their industrial base a better deal, fortunes were made in manufacturing, and the rest of the economy struggled to keep up.

The most able graduates from western universities nowadays go decreasingly into industry. The easiest money and most glittering careers beckon in the professions, in finance and in the media. The academic world, politics and government service look increasingly more attractive, and for those bent on a career in mainstream business, distribution or retailing generally offer more security and better prospects than manufacturing. If the most able people choose not to go into industry, but instead become lawyers or bankers or television personalities, the educational system responds accordingly. The subjects orientated to those engaged in making and selling are downgraded in importance compared to those required for other careers. Practical science falls in status compared to the arts. Commercial studies come to be regarded as second-rate options compared to professional qualifications. Practical subjects, such as engineering, become perceived as less glamorous and attractive – and potentially less lucrative – than the humanities. In the USA, from the mid-1980s to the early 1990s, when an extreme example of monetarist policies was in full flight, there was a precipitate fall in freshman enrolments from the mid-1980s to the early 1990s in subjects where employment prospects had been adversely affected, particularly by the blood-letting of manufacturing which took place at the time. Those planning to pursue business studies fell from 21% of the total in 1980 to 14% by 2009 and the proportion choosing engineering from 11.2% to 9.7%, while those studying Arts and Humanities rose from 10.5% to 13.3%.[5] These figures provide clear evidence as to how quickly and profoundly the educational system then becomes part of cultural conditioning, as peer pressure, career prospects and the priority and prestige accorded to different subjects, determine where the nation's talent is attracted to go.

A significant consequence of the social bias which runs through the whole of this process is that it determines the background of people most likely to reach the peak of their careers running major companies, especially in manufacturing. An interesting contrast between countries such as the USA and Britain, which have grown slowly, and those economies which have grown fastest, is that quite different people tend to become CEOs. In slow growing economies, chief executives are often professional people such as lawyers and accountants. Where the economy is growing fast, they tend to be engineers and salesmen. No doubt both cause and effect are operating here. If the most able people in the commercial field are in the professions, they will finish up at the top of big companies, where their particular talents will be especially in demand to deal with powerful financial interests. In fast growing economies, where exporting is highly profitable, and where financial considerations are consequently less immediately pressing, engineers and salesmen tend to hold the top positions. It is hardly surprising that companies which are run by accountants and lawyers are particularly concerned with financial results, while those controlled by salesmen and engineers are more orientated to markets and products.

Nor is the low status of industry only a financial or social matter. It also has a large impact on the political weight of manufacturing interests as against those of other parts of the economy. Exercising political power requires talent, takes time and costs money. All are in increasingly short supply particularly in American and British industry, and the results are clear to see. Few Members of Congress or Parliament have any significant hands-on manufacturing experience. The role models to whom the younger generation looks up are nowadays not usually those running manufacturing industries. Those in law practice, accountancy, the media and – at least until recently – investment banking look more impressive and secure. In these circumstances it is small wonder that economic ideas which promote finance over manufacturing tend to find favour. It does not follow, however, that these ideas are well founded. Still less is it true that they are in the best long-term interests of the economy as a whole, or even of those in the financial community itself. In the end, those concerned with finance depend as much as everyone else on the performance of the underlying economy, and in particular on its capacity to hold its own in world markets.

Monetarist theory and practice

Although monetarism in its more formulaic forms has now largely gone out of fashion, much of the ways of thinking which it promoted – and which still underlie the heavily pro-market, neo-liberal approach which has superseded it – are still very widely prevalent. Despite monetarism's deficiencies, it provides much of the intellectual hinterland for most of West's political establishment's view on economic and financial affairs.

This view of the world has been underpinned by the thinking of a number of key figures, not least those of Professor Friedrich

Hayek (1899-1992) and other Chicago associates, who had always had serious reservations about the Keynesian revolution. Monetarist ideas, in their standard form, would not have become accepted as widely as they were, however, without the theoretical and statistical underpinning provided by Milton Friedman and his associate, Anna Jacobson Schwartz, in their seminal book, *A Monetary History of the United States, 1867–1960*, published in 1963. In this book, they made three important claims which had a major impact on economic thinking all over the world. First, they said that there was a clear association between the total amount of money in circulation and changes in money incomes and prices, but not economic activity, until approximately two years later. Changes in the money supply therefore affected the price level, but not, except perhaps for a short period of time, the level of output in the real economy. Second, these relationships had proved to be stable over a long period. Third, changes, and particularly increases in the money supply, had generally occurred as a result of events which were independent of the needs of the economy. In consequence they added to inflation without raising the level of economic activity.

The attractive simplicity of these propositions is easily recognised. The essence of the monetarist case is that increases in prices and wages not mirrored by productivity increases can be held in check by nothing more complicated than the apparently simple process of controlling the amount of money in circulation. Ideally, a condition of zero inflation is achieved when the increase in the money supply equals the rise in output in the economy. Since both wages and prices can only go up if extra money to finance them is made available, rises in either cannot occur unless more money is provided. Thus as long as the government is seen to be giving sufficient priority to controlling the money supply, everyone will realise that it is in his or her interest to exercise restraint, reducing the rate of inflation to whatever level is deemed acceptable.

These prescriptions attracted much support to the monetarist banner, although it had always been clear that its intellectual underpinning had severe deficiencies. To start with, the theory begged the fundamental question as to the appropriate way to measure the money stock when so many different ways of determining it were available. It was, in any event, well known that the ratio between the stock of money, however defined, and the volume of transactions could vary widely, as the so called 'velocity of circulation' altered. In addition, there has been widespread criticism of the methodology used by Friedman and Schwartz in their analysis of the relationship between money and prices in the USA, indicating that the statistical basis from which their conclusions were drawn was not nearly as sound as they claimed it was.[6]

As with so much else in economics, there is a major feedback problem with much of the monetarist position, making it difficult to distinguish between cause and effect. It may be true that over a long period the total amount of money in circulation bears a close relationship to the total value of the economy's output. It does not follow, however, that the money supply determines the money value of GDP, and hence the rate of inflation. It may well be, instead, that the total amount of money in circulation is a function of the need for sufficient finance to accommodate transactions. If this is so, then an increase in the money supply may well accompany an increase in inflation caused by some other event, simply to provide this accommodation. It need not necessarily be the cause of rising prices at all.

Common sense tells us that changes in the money supply are only one of a number of relevant factors determining rises or falls in inflation. Monetarists, however, rejected this proposition, alleging that all alterations in the rate of price increases are caused by changes in the money supply some two years previously. They also claimed that the future course of inflation could be guided within narrow limits by controlling the money stock. Empirical evidence demonstrates that this contention is far too precise, and greatly overstates the predictive accuracy of monetarist theories.

For this amount of fine tuning to be possible, an unequivocal definition of money is required. It is one thing to recognise a situation where clearly far too much money, or, more accurately, too much credit is being created. Monetarists are right in saying that if credit is so cheap and so readily available that it is easy to speculate on asset inflation, or the economy is getting overheated by excess demand financed by excessive credit creation, then the money supply is too large. This is a broad quantitative judgement. It is quite another matter to state that small alterations in the money supply generate correspondingly exact changes in the rate of inflation. Yet this is the claim which monetarists put forward.

This claim is implausible for a number of reasons. One is the difficulty in defining accurately what is money and what is not. Notes and coins are clearly 'money', but where should the line be drawn thereafter? What kinds of bank facilities and money market instruments should also be included or excluded? Many different measures are available in every country, depending on what is put in and what is left out. None of them has been found anywhere to have had a strikingly close correlation with subsequent changes in the rate of inflation for any length of time. Often, different measures of the money supply move in different directions. This is very damaging evidence against propositions which are supposed to be precise in their formulation and impact.

Another major problem for monetarists, referred to above, is that there can be no constant ratio between the amount of money in circulation, however defined, and the aggregate value of transactions, because the rate at which money circulates can, and does, vary widely over time. The 'velocity of circulation', which is the ratio between the GDP and the money supply, is far from constant. In the USA the M3 velocity fell 17% between 1970 and 1986, but by 1996 it had risen 22% compared to 10 years earlier. It has been exceptionally volatile in Britain, where it rose by 7% between 1964 and 1970, and by a further 28% between 1970 and 1974, only to fall by 26% between 1974 and 1979.[7] Other countries, such as the Netherlands and Greece, have also had large changes in the velocity of circulation, particularly during the 1970s.[8] More recently there have been huge increases in the money supply in relation to GDP, implying very substantial reductions in the velocity of circulation. In the USA, for example, M2, one of the widely used money supply measures, rose 79%[9] between 2000 and 2010 while the economy grew in money terms by no more than 49%.[10]

Some of these movements were caused by changes in monetary policy, but a substantial proportion, especially recently, have had nothing to do with the government. They have been the results of radical changes to the financial environment, caused by the effects of deregulation on credit creation, and the growth of new financial instruments, such as derivatives. Variations like this make it impossible to believe in the rigid relationship that monetarism requires. In fact, the statistical record everywhere on the money supply and inflation shows what one would expect if there was very little causation at all at work. Except in extreme circumstances of gross over-creation of money and credit, changes in the money supply have had little or no impact on the rate of inflation. The need to provide enough money to finance all the transactions taking place has, over the long term, proved to be much more important a determinant of the money supply than attempts to restrict it to control inflation, although some countries have certainly had tighter monetary policies than others. In the short term, there is no systematic evidence that changes in the money supply affect subsequent inflation rates with any precision at all.

It is not surprising, therefore, that the predictions of monetarists about future levels of inflation, based on trends in the money supply, have turned out to be no better, and often worse, than those of other people who have used more eclectic, common-sense methods. Monetarists have not kept their predictions, however, solely to the future rate of inflation. There are three other areas of economic policy where their ideas have had a decisive effect on practical policy over the last 40 years, shaping the way in which governments of all political persuasions in the UK and elsewhere have approached economic policy formation. These are to do with unemployment, interest rates and exchange rates. Pure monetarism may have faded from fashion but it has left a very powerful and durable legacy in these key policy areas.

The monetarist – now shading into the neo-liberal – view of unemployment is that there is a 'natural' rate which cannot be avoided, set essentially by supply-side rigidities. Any attempt to reduce unemployment below this level by reflation will necessarily increase wage rates and then the price level. This will leave those in employment no better off than they were before, while the increased demand, having been absorbed by higher prices, will result in the same number of people being employed as previously. Increasing demand only pushes up the rate of inflation. It will not raise either output or the number of people in work.

At some point, as pressure on the available labour force increases and the number of those unemployed falls, there is no doubt that a bidding up process will take place, and wages and salaries will rise. This is an altogether different matter, however, from postulating that unemployment levels like those seen over much of the developed world since the 1980s are required to keep inflation at bay. Nor is it plausible that supply side rigidities are the major constraint on getting unemployment down. There is no evidence that these rigidities are significantly greater now than they were in the 1950s and 1960s, and on balance they are almost certainly less. If, during the whole of these two decades, it was possible to combine high rates of economic growth with low levels of unemployment, while inflation remained reasonably stable at an acceptable level, why should we believe that it is impossible now for these conditions to prevail again?

Monetarism also had a considerable influence on interest rates, particularly during the 1980s. The tight control of the money supply which monetarists advocate then could only be achieved if interest rates were used to balance a relatively low supply of money against the demand for credit which has to be choked off by raising the price of money. This requirement was made to seem less harsh by suggesting that a positive rate of interest would always be required to enable lenders to continue providing money to borrowers. It was alleged that any attempt to lower interest rates to encourage expansion would fail as lenders withdraw from the market until the premium they required above the inflation rate reappeared.

Yet again, we have a proposition much more strongly based on assertion than on evidence, especially in the light of recent experience. For years on end, in many countries, real interest rates paid to savers have been negative, sometimes even before tax. Lenders, of course, have never regarded negative interest rates as fair, and frequently complain bitterly when they occur. There is, however, little that they can do about them. Their ability to withdraw from the market is generally limited. It is undoubtedly the case, however, that high positive rates of interest are a discouragement to investment, partly directly, but much more importantly, because of their influence on driving up the exchange rate.

This is particularly paradoxical in relation to the third major impact of monetarist ideas on practical issues, which has been on exchange rate policy. Monetarists have always argued that no policy for improving an economy's competitiveness by devaluation will work, because the inflationary effects of a depreciation will automatically raise the domestic price level back to where it was in international terms. This will leave the devaluing country with no more competitiveness than it had before, but with a real extra inflationary problem with which it will have to contend. This proposition, which is still widely believed, is one which it is easy to test against historical experience. There have been large numbers of substantial exchange rate changes over the last few decades, providing plenty of empirical data against which to assess the validity of this monetarist assertion. The evidence, as is amply demonstrated by Table 4.1, is overwhelmingly against it. There is example after example to be found of devaluations failing to produce sufficient excess inflation, if any, to wipe out the competitive advantage initially gained. On the contrary, there is ample evidence indicating that exactly the opposite effect has been the experience in a wide variety of different economies. Those which have devalued have tended to perform progressively better, as their manufacturing sectors expanded, and the internationally tradable goods and services which they produced became cumulatively more competitive.

Countries which have gained an initial price advantage therefore tend to forge ahead, with increasingly competitive import-saving and exporting sectors. Rapidly growing efficiency in the sectors of their economies involved in international trading gains them higher shares in world trade, providing them with platforms for further expansion. High productivity growth generates conditions which may even allow them, with good management, to experience less domestic inflation than their more sluggish competitors. In practice, monetarist policies have had pronounced effects on the exchange rates of the countries where they have been most effectively imposed, but invariably their impact has been to push them up.

Table 4.1: Exchange rate changes, consumer prices, the real wage, GDP, industrial output and employment

	Year	Consumer prices	Wage rates	Real wage change	GDP change	Industrial output change	Unemployment per cent
Britain - 31% devaluation against	1930	−6.0	−0.7	5.3	−0.7	−1.4	11.2
the dollar and 24% against all	1931	−5.7	−2.1	3.6	−5.1	−3.6	15.1
currencies in 1931	1932	−3.3	−1.7	1.6	0.8	0.3	15.6
	1933	0.0	−0.1	−0.1	2.9	4.0	14.1
	1934	0.0	1.5	1.5	6.6	5.5	11.9
France - 27% devaluation against	1956	2.0	9.7	7.7	5.1	9.4	1.1
all currenties in 1957/58	1957	3.5	8.2	4.7	6.0	8.3	0.8
	1958	15.1	12.3	−2.8	2.5	4.5	0.9
	1959	6.2	6.8	0.6	2.9	3.3	1.3
	1960	3.5	6.3	2.8	7.0	10.1	1.2
	1961	3.3	9.6	6.3	5.5	4.8	1.1
USA - 28% devaluation against	1984	4.3	4.0	−0.3	6.2	11.3	7.4
all currencies over 1985/87	1985	3.6	3.9	0.3	3.2	2.0	7.1
	1986	1.9	2.0	0.1	2.9	1.0	6.9
	1987	3.7	1.8	−1.9	3.1	3.7	6.1
	1988	4.0	2.8	−1.2	3.9	5.3	5.4
	1989	5.0	2.9	−2.1	2.5	2.6	5.2
Japan - 47% revaluation against	1989	2.3	3.1	0.8	4.8	5.8	2.3
all currencies over 1990/94	1990	3.1	3.8	0.7	4.8	4.1	2.1
	1991	3.3	3.4	0.1	4.3	1.8	2.1
	1992	1.7	2.1	0.4	1.4	−6.1	2.2
	1993	1.3	2.1	0.8	0.1	−4.6	2.5
	1994	0.7	2.3	1.6	0.6	0.7	2.9
Italy - 20% devaluation against	1990	6.4	7.3	0.9	2.1	−0.6	9.1
all currencies over 1990/93	1991	6.3	9.8	3.5	1.3	−2.2	8.6
	1992	5.2	5.4	0.2	0.9	−0.6	9.0
	1993	4.5	3.8	−0.7	−1.2	−2.9	10.3
	1994	4.0	3.5	−0.5	2.2	5.6	11.4
	1995	5.4	3.1	−2.3	2.9	5.4	11.9
Finland - 24% devaluation against	1990	6.1	9.4	3.3	0.0	−0.1	3.5
all currencies over 1991/93	1991	4.1	6.4	2.3	−7.1	−9.7	7.6
	1992	2.6	3.8	1.2	−3.6	2.2	13.0
	1993	2.1	3.7	1.6	−1.6	5.5	17.5
	1994	1.1	7.4	6.3	4.5	10.5	17.4
	1995	1.0	4.7	3.7	5.1	7.8	16.2
Spain - 18% devaluation against	1991	5.9	8.2	2.3	2.3	−0.7	16.3
all currencies over 1992/94	1992	5.9	7.7	1.8	0.7	−3.2	18.5
	1993	4.6	6.8	2.2	−1.2	−4.4	22.8
	1994	4.7	4.5	−0.2	2.1	7.5	24.1
	1995	4.7	4.8	0.1	2.8	4.7	22.9
	1996	3.6	4.8	1.2	2.2	−0.7	22.2
Britain – 19% devaluation against	1990	9.5	9.7	0.2	0.6	−0.4	6.8
all currencies in 1992	1991	5.9	7.8	1.9	−1.5	−3.3	8.4
	1992	3.7	11.3	7.6	0.1	0.3	9.7
	1993	1.6	3.2	1.6	2.3	2.2	10.3
	1994	2.4	3.6	1.2	4.4	5.4	9.6
	1995	3.5	3.1	−0.4	2.8	1.7	8.6
Argentina – 72% devaluation against	2000	−1.1	1.2	3.3	−0.8	−0.3	14.7
all currencies early 2002	2001	25.9	−2.6	−23.3	−4.4	−7.6	18.1
	2002	13.4	1.9	−11.5	−10.9	−10.5	17.5
	2003	4.4	22.0	17.6	8.8	16.2	16.8
	2004	9.6	23.3	13.7	9.0	10.7	13.6
	2005	10.9	22.8	11.9	9.2	8.5	8.7
Iceland – 50% devaluation against	2005	4.0	6.3	2.3	7.2	12.4	2.6
all currencies 2007/2009	2006	6.7	8.8	2.1	4.7	16.8	2.9
	2007	5.1	9.8	4.7	6.0	0.7	2.3
	2008	12.7	8.5	−4.2	1.2	35.5	3.0
	2009	12.0	3.0	−9.0	−6.6	3.8	7.2
	2010	5.4	6.1	0.7	−4.0	10.6	7.6
	2011	4.0	7.1	3.1	2.6	13.5	7.0

All figures are year on year percentage changes except for Unemployment. Sources: Economic Statistics 1900-1983 by Thelma Liesner. London: *The Economist* 1985. IMF *International Financial Statistics Yearbooks, Eurostatistics* and British, Argentine and Icelandic official statistics and International Labour Organisation tables.

The economies concerned then suffer the worst of all worlds – an all too familiar mixture of unimpressive growth, low increases in output to absorb wage and salary increases, and sometimes higher price inflation than their more favoured competitors.

Monetarist theories start by appearing simple and straightforward, but end by being long on complication and assertion, and short on predictive and practical prescriptive qualities. They pander to the prejudice of those who would like to believe their conclusions. They lack convincing explanations about the transmission mechanisms between what they claim are the causes of economic events, and the effects which they declare will necessarily follow. Where they can be tested against empirical results, the predictions their theories produce generally fail to achieve levels of accuracy which make them worthwhile. This is why monetarism in its purer forms is no longer fashionable.

Monetarist theories have nevertheless reinforced everywhere all the prejudices widely held in favour of the cautious financial conservatism, which monetarism so accurately reflects, and in this key respect, monetarist ideas still have a very powerful influence on current policy-making. By allowing themselves to be persuaded by these misguided doctrines, it becomes all too easy for those responsible for running the nation's affairs to acquiesce in accepting levels of low growth and under-unemployment which would never have been tolerated if everyone had realised how unnecessary they were. The result has been that policies which should have been rejected have continued to be accepted, although they failed to work. Because expectations have been lowered, the deflationary consequences of high interest rates, restrictive monetary policies and overvalued exchange rates, have not caused the outcry that might have been expected, and which they deserved.

Slow growth in Europe

During the period from its establishment in 1958 until 1973, the average rate of growth among the Common Market countries was 5.1%, the mean level of unemployment was little more than 2%, and the average rate of inflation was 3.9%. For the 20 years from

1973 to 1993 the growth rate averaged 2.1%, and the inflation rate 7.0%.[11] The rate of unemployment fluctuated over the period, but overall it was much higher than it had been previously. The average registered unemployment level across the whole of the European Union during the 1980s and 1990s averaged close to 10%, an almost fivefold increase.[12] Even then, the claimant count, which this figure represents, substantially underestimates the total number of people who would like to work if they had the opportunity to do so at a reasonable wage.[13] What went wrong? If the whole world had plunged to a much lower growth rate after 1973, it would be plausible to argue that the experience of the western world was part of a universal trend. Although there was a fall elsewhere, however, it was much smaller than in the West. The growth rate in the whole of the rest of the world dropped from 5.1% in 1959-1973 to 3.4% between 1973 and 1992 and then averaged 3.5% per annum from 1992 to 2015.[14]

Three major developments were mainly responsible for the substantial sea change to the fortunes of the Community economies in the 1970s. The first was the oil crisis, caused by OPEC's quadrupling of the price of crude oil, following the breakdown of the Bretton Woods system and the 1973 Yom Kippur War. The second was the change in intellectual fashion towards a much harder-line version of economic theory and doctrine, as monetarist ideas replaced Keynesian thinking among large sections of those responsible for running economic policy in the Community countries. The third was the political initiatives taken within the Community, intended to lead to closer integration by linking the currencies of the constituent economies together first in the Currency Snake, then the Exchange Rate Mechanism, and finally with full Monetary Union.

The effect of the quadrupling of oil prices in 1974[15] on the economies of Europe, none of which at that time was producing any significant quantity of oil, was to shift about 2% of their GDPs away from their own populations to those of the oil exporting countries. With good management, and a well-co-ordinated response, this should not have been an impossibly difficult situation to contain. The problem was that the oil shock came on top of other causes of instability, including, in some countries, a crisis in the banking system as the early 1970s boom broke, and in all countries the main strain was taken on the balance of payments. The result was that everyone reined in at once, trying to shift the trade balance problems elsewhere. Growth rates fell back sharply as deflationary policies were implemented everywhere. Indeed, the economies then comprising the Common Market collectively saw no growth in either 1974 or 1975, before resuming a much slower growth trajectory than had previously prevailed.[16]

If the real world events of the oil price hike and the breaking boom were the immediate causes of the deflationary policies which checked Community growth in the mid-1970s, the willingness of the authorities to persevere with them was greatly reinforced by the spread of monetarist doctrines. This second change in direction occurred largely in response to the pressing need to bring inflation down from the dangerous heights to which it had risen in some countries during the mid-1970s. Britain's year on year inflation peaked at 24%, France's at 14%, Italy's at 19%, and Germany's at a much more modest 7%.[17]

Monetarist ideas had a particularly strong appeal in certain powerful quarters. The Bundesbank had always had a strong anti-inflation tradition, harking back to the German hyperinflation of 1923. Understandably it welcomed ideas which reinforced its collective view of monetary priorities. Nearly all Europe's central bankers followed the highly respected Bundesbank's lead. As monetarist ideas also became very much the fashion in academic circles, these convictions were reflected in the tone of an endless succession of newspaper articles, popularising monetarist ideas – and their neo-liberal derivatives – to a wider audience. Despite their intellectual weaknesses, which were apparent from the beginning, monetarist ideas were extraordinarily successful in implanting themselves right across Western Europe as the norm which few people were willing to challenge.

The third and probably most significant long-term influence on Community policies, however, has been the drive to achieve further integration by locking the Community currencies together and thus losing the flexibility which exchange rate changes provide when competitiveness diverged. The first steps were taken a little over 10 years after the Common Market had been established. In March 1970, the Council of Ministers set up a high-level group to prepare plans for full economic and monetary union, rather than just a customs union, among the original six member countries. The chairman was Pierre Werner (1913-2002), then prime minister and minister of finance of Luxembourg, who gave his name to the report which was produced within a few months. The report concentrated on the two principal routes which might be chosen to achieve the convergence required to make monetary union a viable proposition. This involved an uneasy marriage of Keynesian and monetarist approaches. Nevertheless, in March 1971 the Council of Ministers accepted the broad thrust of the Werner Report, and agreed that, as a first step towards its implementation, the exchange rates of the member currencies should be maintained within 0.6% of each other from 15 June 1971 onwards.

The start date for the Werner proposals came at an awkward time, though this is not an excuse for their subsequent abandonment. In May 1971 the dollar crisis began, leading to the break-up of Bretton Woods at the Smithsonian Conference, and abandonment of the existing IMF exchange rate bands. Major fluctuations in the European rates meant that that the new narrow bands for what came to be called the Snake were difficult to establish. A European Monetary Co-operation Fund was set up, operated by the central banks, to keep market rates within 1.125% either side of the central parities. In view of their impending Community membership, Britain, Denmark and Eire joined the new arrangements, as well as the original Six.

The life of the Snake, however, was relatively brief. Speculative fever in the international money markets switched from the dollar, after its Smithsonian devaluation, to attacking sterling. Within six weeks of joining, the British authorities were forced to abandon attempts to maintain the agreed parity for the pound, which dropped out of the Snake, taking the Irish punt with it. Six months later, in January 1973, the Italian government abandoned its commitment to keeping the lira within the required limits and withdrew. A year afterwards, in January 1974, the French followed suit. The franc rejoined the Snake in July 1975, but the second attempt to keep to the agreed parity lasted no longer than the first. In March 1976 it left permanently. In less than four years, therefore, three of the four major Community currencies had abandoned their efforts to keep up with the stability and low inflation rate of the Deutsche Mark. The Snake had been reduced to a Deutsche Mark zone embracing, apart from Germany, only the Benelux countries and Denmark. This first major attempt to bring together all the Community currencies had failed. Phase two of the Werner plan, the originally proposed move to monetary union, was quietly forgotten.[18]

It might have been thought that lessons would be learnt from this experience, so that similar problems could be avoided in future. It was not a convincing explanation for the failure of the Snake to say that its demise occurred because the time at which its regime was introduced was difficult and turbulent. If the Snake was worth having at all, it ought to have been more useful in times of stress than in easier conditions. The political pressures for resuming attempts to lock Community currencies together, however, proved stronger than the arguments from experience. At the initiative of the Commission's president, Roy (subsequent Lord) Jenkins (1920-2003), within three years, at Summit Meetings in Copenhagen and Bremen, monetary union was back again at the top of the Community agenda.[19]

The main argument put forward for monetary union on this occasion was that the full benefits of the Community's customs union could not be achieved in an environment of exchange rate instability and uncertainty. It was alleged that fluctuating rates were damaging to trade and steady economic growth. While this may have seemed an appealing argument, there was no evidence that it was correct. Indeed, a number of studies, including a particularly extensive one carried out by the Bank of England, had shown that any disruption caused by exchange rate movements had little, if any, effect on growth rates, incidentally reconfirmed by a recent World Trade Organisation study.[20] The fact that the Common Market countries had been growing up to then at unprecedented rates without having their currencies locked together was ignored. It was also alleged that floating exchange rates were inherently inflationary. Again, however, no concrete evidence was produced to show that this argument was well-founded and, as demonstrated elsewhere in this book, there is ample evidence to show that in most cases it is false. Nevertheless, in 1979, the Snake was reborn as the Exchange Rate Mechanism (ERM), as part of a new European Monetary System (EMS).[21] When it began operations in March 1979, the new EMS had at its disposal a substantially more potent battery of weapons to deploy against the markets than were available at the time of the Snake.

The first phase had two main objectives. The primary task was to achieve a high degree of stability in the exchange rates of the participating currencies. The second was to secure convergence in the performance of the constituent economies. Both proved difficult to achieve. In the decade following its inception, there were 12 realignments of one or more of the central rates, caused by widely different experience with inflation and competitiveness among the constituent economies. Over this period the central rate of the strongest currency, the Deutsche Mark, appreciated by 18%, while the weakest, the lira, fell by 29%. The combined impact of these changes was that the parity of the lira at the end of the decade vis-à-vis the Deutsche Mark was 50% of its value at the beginning. The effect of the ERM was not to stop exchange rate changes occurring, but merely – at great cost – to delay them. Nor was any greater success achieved on convergence. Living standards across the whole Community did not become significantly more equal, although the Irish economy, with a standard of living well below the EEC average, grew considerably more rapidly than the rest. Nor did variables such as inflation rates come together. For example, in 1981, the consumer price index increased by 6% in Germany, 13% in France and 18% in Italy.[22]

These variations in inflation rates highlighted the basic problem with the Snake and ERM, which was that for nearly all the period in which they were in operation, Germany's low price increases and consequent export competitiveness made it extremely difficult for the other countries in the exchange rate systems to remain able to compete with the Germans. As their trade balances deteriorated, they were faced with the familiar choice of deflation or devaluation.

With the latter being ruled out, except in extreme circumstances, they had to deflate. As about half of all Germany's exports went to other Community countries during the ERM period,[23] the consequence was that its main export markets were depressed, pulling down the German growth rate. As a result, the whole of the Community's economy slowed down. Table 4.2 shows the figures. Against a long-term background of falling growth rates, each time the Community currencies were locked together, the performance of all the participating countries deteriorated – more quickly in the period of the Snake, and more slowly under the ERM – an ominous portent for the Single Currency were proposals for its implementation to be realised.[24]

Table 4.2: Growth in the EEC during the 'currency snake' and Exchange Rate Mechanism (ERM) periods

Year	Totals all countries except Germany		Germany alone		Totals all countries including Germany			Comments on growth rates
	GDP in 1985 US$	annual % growth	GDP in 1985 US$	annual % Growth	GDP in 1985 US	Annual % growth		
1966	664		377		1,041			1950-69
1967	700	5.4	376	−0.3	1,076	3.4		average
1968	737	5.3	396	5.5	1,133	5.3		5.5%
1969	785	6.6	426	7.5	1,211	6.9	SNAKE	snake
1970	827	5.4	447	5.0	1,274	5.3	SNAKE	period
1971	856	3.5	461	3.1	1,317	3.3	SNAKE	average
1972	888	3.7	481	4.3	1,368	3.9	SNAKE	3.7%
1973	940	5.8	504	4.8	1,443	5.5	SNAKE	fall from
1974	974	3.7	505	0.2	1,479	2.5	SNAKE	6.9% to
1975	963	−1.1	498	−1.3	1,461	−1.2	SNAKE	−1.2%
1976	1,014	5.3	525	5.3	1,539	5.3		1976-1979
1977	1,046	3.1	540	2.8	1,586	3.0		average
1978	1,070	2.4	556	3.0	1,626	2.6		3.6%
1979	1,123	4.9	579	4.2	1,703	4.7	ERM	
1980	1,041	−7.3	585	1.0	1,627	−4.5	ERM	
1981	1,157	11.1	586	0.1	1,743	7.1	ERM	ERM
1982	1,170	1.2	580	−0.9	1,751	0.5	ERM	period
1983	1,182	1.0	590	1.8	1,772	1.2	REM	average
1984	1,209	2.3	607	2.8	1,816	2.5	ERM	2.1%
1985	1,236	2.2	619	2.0	1,855	2.2	ERM	
1986	1,268	2.6	634	2.3	1,906	2.5	ERM	ERM
1987	1,298	2.3	643	1.5	1,941	2.1	ERM	period
1988	1,349	3.9	667	3.7	2.016	3.9	ERM	fall from
1989	1,395	3.5	691	3.6	2,087	3.5	ERM	4.7% to
1990	1,432	2.6	731	5.7	2,163	3.7	ERM	−1.0%
1991	1,449	1.2	764	4.5	2,213	2.3	ERM	
1992	1,467	1.3	776	1.6	2,243	1.4	ERM	
1993	1,459	−0.6	761	−1.9	2,220	−1.0	ERM	
1994	1,483	1.6	782	2.8	2,265	2.0		1993-1997
1995	1,522	2.6	792	1.2	2,313	2.1		average
1996	1,546	1.6	802	1.3	2,348	1.5		2.0%
1997	1,584	2.4	820	2.2	2,403	2.4		

Sources: Table 7 on pages 120 and 121 in *National Accounts 1960-1992*. Paris, OECD, 1994 and Table 0101 in *Eurostatistics 11/95 and 4/00*. Luxembourg: The European Community, 1995 and 1999.

And, indeed, notwithstanding these problems, further moves were afoot to proceed to full monetary union. The drafters of the 1986 Single European Act had succeeded in having the achievement of monetary union embodied in the Treaty in which the Act was incorporated as a specific commitment, with a target date of 1992. In 1988 Jacques Delors (b. 1925), the then president of the Commission, persuaded the Council of Ministers to give him the task of 'studying and proposing concrete stages leading towards economic and monetary union'. While these proposals were being considered, and embodied in the 1992 Maastricht Treaty, which set out the programme for moves to a single European currency, the ERM began to run into serious difficulties. During the summer of 1992, market pressure began to attack the weaker members of the ERM, leading to the devaluation of the lira. In September 1992 a wave of speculation against sterling swept the pound out of the ERM. The franc's parity with the Deutsche Mark only just survived, as a result of massive intervention by the Bundesbank. Finally, the pressure built up against the whole ERM system to a point where it became no longer possible to hold it together. In August 1993, the narrow bands were abandoned, and fluctuations of up to 15% either side of the central rate against the ECU were allowed to take their place. Meanwhile, notwithstanding these developments and, indeed, largely to counter them, preparations went ahead for full monetary union.

Neo-liberal policies in the USA

In the USA, the problems to be faced towards the end of the twentieth century were significantly different from those in most of Europe, although the intellectual background to the way they were tackled had much in common.

Compared to many other countries the USA weathered the 1970s reasonably well. Years of small reductions in output in 1970, 1974 and 1975 were offset by substantial growth in other years, producing erratic but, nevertheless, in the circumstances of the time, a tolerably satisfactory outcome. Real GDP growth averaged 3.2% per annum for the decade, a little below the 3.8% average for all the developed countries in the OECD.[25] The reduction in the dollar's post-Smithsonian parity, augmented by the USA's better than average performance on inflation, gave those parts of the American economy exposed to international trade an increasing edge. As a result, exports of goods and services, net of inflation, rose cumulatively by 7.3% per annum, compared to total imports which only increased at a compound rate of 4.9%.[26]

Unfortunately, however, this reasonably good performance was eventually undermined by adverse movements in the US trade balance, caused by a combination of increased costs and import volumes. In particular, during the 1970s the price of oil rose hugely, with a further major price increase in 1979 following the earlier one in 1973.[27] By 1980, the USA was spending $79bn a year on oil imports, compared with only $3bn in 1970.[28] As a result, combined with much larger imports of other goods such as cars, the balance of trade in goods and services began an alarming deterioration. In the late 1970s, a further rapid increase in the value of oil imports began to swamp the deteriorating surplus earned on manufactures. From 1976 onwards, the USA has had a trade deficit every single year.[29]

To maintain a high rate of growth in the 1980s, the USA therefore urgently needed a considerably more competitive exchange rate. By increasing the country's exports of manufactured goods, it would have been possible to offset the heavy burden across the exchanges occasioned by the extra cost of oil imports. Unfortunately, exactly the opposite policy was put into operation. Under the incoming administration of President Ronald Reagan (1911-2004), heavily influenced by monetarist ideas, interest rates were raised sharply. The US Treasury Bills rate, which had fallen to just under 5% during the boom years of the late 1970s, averaged over 14% in 1981.[30] The inevitable result was that the dollar soared on the foreign exchanges. With 1973 equalling 100 as the base, and thus already allowing for the 10% post-Smithsonian devaluation, the trade weighted value of the US dollar had fallen to 89 by 1979. This trend was then dramatically reversed – a classic example, incidentally of the ability of policy decisions to change the exchange rate. By 1982 the index had reached 108, and by 1985 it was 123. In six years, the dollar had sustained a real appreciation of 38%.[31] As a result, the

USA's growth in GDP during the 1980s fell back to a cumulative 2.8% per annum. Because the population was growing fast, GDP per head grew at only 1.8% per annum.[32]

Predictably, the proportion of US GDP derived from manufacturing fell heavily. Between 1980 and 1993, it dropped from 21% of GDP to 17%, a relative reduction of just under a fifth.[33] The number of people employed in manufacturing occupations also fell slightly in absolute numbers, but much more steeply as a proportion of the total labour force. Of those in employment, the proportion working in manufacturing dropped from 22% to barely 16%.[34] The problem was then the familiar one, which is that productivity increases are much more difficult to secure across the board in the service sector of the economy than they are in manufacturing. The decline in industrial output as a proportion of GDP thus contributed directly and heavily to the low growth in overall productivity which was such a key negative characteristic of this period in American economic history. Reflecting the decline in manufacturing, and the incidence of the policies pursued by the Reagan and Bush administrations on the growth rate, both the US savings and investment ratios fell heavily too, dropping from about 20% in 1980 to under 15% by 1993.[35]

Between 1980 and 1993, the first full year of the Clinton presidency, the economy grew cumulatively by 2.7% per annum, and GDP per head rose on average by 1.4% a year,[36] yet none of these benefits worked their way through to the average worker in terms of compensation per hour. On the contrary, across the board average earnings per hour fell. For the whole American economy, in real terms, income per hour peaked in 1973, at $8.55 measured in constant 1982 dollars. By 1998 it was only $7.75. Thus, over the 25 years between 1973 and 1998, earnings per hour for the average American dropped in real terms by a staggering 9%.[37] Against the background of the steady rise in real earnings per hour in the US economy in the 1950s and 1960s of a little under 2% per annum – about 18% per decade[38] – who, predicting in 1973 a fall for the next quarter of a century, would have been given a hearing?

The decline in real hourly earnings, barely offset by a higher labour force participation rate and longer working hours, and aggravated by a tougher line being taken on social security payments, caused the distribution of pre-tax income to become much more uneven. Up to 1980, the proportion of aggregate income going to the bottom 40% of income earners had been roughly stable at about 17%. By 1993 it was 14%. For the bottom quintile, the drop was even more precipitate, from 5.3% to 4.1%, making the whole of this vast swathe of the American population – well over 50m people – about 8% worse off on average in 1993 than they had been in 1980.[39] Meanwhile, at the other end of the spectrum, those in the top 5% of income earners saw their share of total incomes rise between 1980 and 1993 from 15% of the total to 20%.[40] As a result, their total incomes increased in real terms by about two-thirds.

Post-tax, the distribution of income became even more uneven, as tax rates on the rich were cut. The theory behind this was that the government revenues ought to increase if tax rates were lowered, both because there would be less incentive for avoidance and because lower tax rates would stimulate more enterprise and hence more revenues. The 'Laffer Curve' approach to tax policy – one of the more egregious elements of the 'supply-side' economic policies fashionable at the time – never came near improving the overall federal collection rate. It certainly served its purpose, however, in justifying lower tax payments rates for the rich. The result was one of the reasons why the US fiscal deficit began to widen.

The other major reason for the deterioration in the federal government's finances was a vast increase on defence outlays. The result was that the overall government's fiscal stance, including both federal and state levels, which had been $34bn in surplus in 1979, plunged into deficit, reaching a negative $109bn by 1983. Hardly surprisingly, an immediate repercussion from the deterioration in the fiscal balance was a large increase in the value of outstanding federal debt. In 1980, the gross federal debt had been $906bn, representing 33% of GDP. By 1993, it was $4,409bn, equivalent to 67% of GDP, and still rising in money terms, though stabilising as a percentage of GDP.[41]

One of the consequences of the heavy increase in military spending during the Reagan years was that a higher proportion of the relatively weakening US industrial base was drawn into defence work, exacerbating problems on the trade balance, which also hugely deteriorated over the same period. By 1980, the total US foreign payment position was still in balance, with the surplus on investment income offsetting a $19bn deficit on goods and services. From then onwards, the position went from bad to worse. By 1984 the trade deficit was $109bn, and by 1987 it was $153bn.[42] Most of this huge deterioration was the result of a catastrophic turn round in trade in manufactured goods. Even as late as 1980, the USA had a reasonably healthy $12bn surplus in trade on manufactured goods, but by 1984 this had turned into a deficit of $93bn, and $126bn by 1988.[43]

There is an inexorable accounting identity which applies to foreign trade. Any deficit on current account has to be made up by exactly corresponding capital borrowing. To pay for the multi-billion dollar deficits which accumulated, the USA therefore had to become a major net borrower from abroad, and a major net seller of investment assets to foreigners. The result was a drastic change from the USA being by far the world's largest creditor, to it being much its biggest debtor. In 1980 the USA's net international investment position was a positive $392bn. By 1993 it was a negative $503bn.[44]

During the middle years of the 1989-1993 George Bush (b. 1924) regime, the economy had faltered, growing by only 1.2% in 1990, and contracting by almost 1% in 1991.[45] No doubt this contributed to the Republican defeat in 1992, although by then the economy was starting to pick up again. The economy inherited by the new President, Bill Clinton (b. 1946), therefore brought with it all the structural imbalances which the monetarist era had wrought upon it, combined with considerable room for bouncing back from the shallow depression in 1990 and 1991.

Over the period between the spring of 1993, when the Clinton administration took over, and the end of 1998, there were some positive signs, but not nearly enough to counteract the impact of the Reagan and Bush policies on the American economy. Between 1992 and 1998 the growth rate nevertheless averaged a compound 3.2% per annum, which was a good deal better than the 2.6% achieved between 1980 and 1992.[46] The Clinton record on the federal deficit was also much better than those of his two immediate predecessors. A combination of contained expenditure and rising tax revenues reduced the deficit, which had peaked at $290bn in 1992, to $22bn in 1997, with a balanced budget projected for 1999 and subsequent years. The gross Federal debt at the end of 1998 was $5,478.7bn,[47] however, and the interest charges on this large sum were an additional drain on the government's current resources.

By far the largest and fundamental problem facing the Clinton administration at the end of this presidency was the foreign payment balance, for which the strengthening of the US currency vis-à-vis the rest of the world bore a heavy responsibility. The trade weighted value of the dollar rose from an index of 87 in 1992 to 98 in 1998.[48] A combination of devaluations in the Far East and the weakening of most of the major currencies in Europe had left the dollar dangerously exposed. The US economy, despite its travails, may still have seemed immensely powerful, but the borrowing required to finance a deficit on this scale was beginning to look daunting. The net investment income from US investments abroad and foreign investments in the USA, which used to buttress the US foreign payments position, turned negative for the first time in 1997.[49] The scene had been set for the problems of imbalance to be faced by the US economy once the unsustainable boom of the early 2000s broke in 2008.

The Tiger economies

A remarkable phenomenon in the second half of the twentieth century was the growth rates achieved by the so called Tiger economies: Hong Kong, Singapore, South Korea and Taiwan. Table 4.3 sets out the cumulative growth rates they achieved, their increases in population and the rises in GDP per head – a close proxy for living standards – which they managed to secure for their populations.

A number of key points stand out from these statistics. First, the rapid growth which all these economies achieved towards the end of the twentieth century was not a new development. All of them were growing fast from the period starting immediately after the disruption caused by World War II had abated. Second, although there was some slowdown in their growth rates after 1973, it was comparatively modest. This contrasts with the sudden break from relatively fast growth to a consistently much slower pace among the advanced industrialised economies, including, a little later, Japan. Whatever caused these major countries to grow more slowly evidently did not have proportionately the same effect on the Tiger economies. Third – a rather different point – as they became very much better off than they had been previously, they continued to grow fast. It is often alleged that economic growth becomes much more difficult to achieve the higher the level of GDP per head. This was not true of the Tigers, and if they avoided this happening, it is not clear why other economies should not be able to do the same.

Table 4.3: Growth statistics for the Tiger economies.

	Cumulative percentage growth in gross domestic product per annum			
	1913-1950	1950-1973	1973-1990	1990-2010
Hong Kong	n/a	9.2	7.6	4.0
Singapore	n/a	7.8	7.4	6.8
South Korea	1.7	7.6	8.5	5.3
Taiwan	2.7	9.3	8.0	5.1
	Cumulative Percentage Growth in Population per Annum			
	1913-1950	1950-1973	1973-1990	1990-2010
Hong Kong	n/a	3.5	1.8	0.1
Singapore	n/a	2.8	2.0	2.3
South Korea	1.9	2.2	1.4	0.1
Taiwan	2.7	3.0	1.6	0.1
	Cumulative Percentage Growth in GDP per Head of the Population			
	1913-1950	1950-1973	1973-1990	1990-2010
Hong Kong	n/a	5.7	5.8	3.9
Singapore	n/a	5.0	5.4	4.5
South Korea	−0.2	5.4	7.1	5.2
Taiwan	0.0	6.3	6.4	5.0

Sources: Tables D-1e and F-4 in *Monitoring the World Economy 1820-1992* by Angus Maddison. Paris: OECD, 1995; Country Table Pages in *International Financial Statistics* Washington DC: IMF 2010 and 2011; and Tables 1-1a and 2-2 in T*aiwan Statistical Yearbook 2011*.

The major reason why the performance of the Tiger economies was not greatly noticed until the last quarter of the twentieth century is that even as late as 1973, their combined GDPs only represented 1.2% of world output. By 1990, this ratio had more than doubled to 2.7%.[50] Even more impressive was the impact of these four economies on world trade. In 1973 their total manufactured exports (including re-exports in the cases of Hong Kong and Singapore) were 3.8%

of the world total. By 1994, they were 12.9%.[51] Over one-eighth of world trade in manufactured products was being achieved by four countries containing in total only 1.4% of the world's population.[52]

It is indeed this astonishing export achievement which provides the immediate explanation of the success of the Tigers. Between 1950 and 1992 the volume of South Korea's merchandise exports rose cumulatively by 17% per annum, while Taiwan's rose by 16%, compared to 8.5% for the world as a whole.[53] The competitiveness of their exports made their products extremely attractive to buyers all over the world. The opportunities thus created, as always happens in similar circumstances, sucked talent and resources into sectors of the economy where they could be most productively employed. Hardly surprisingly, all the Tiger economies, with the huge investment opportunities which fast growth opened up, had high proportions of their national incomes devoted to investment, generally averaging 30% or more.[54] As a result industrial output soared, and with it productivity. In South Korea, for example, between 1968 and 1997, industrial output increased cumulatively by an average of 13.4% per annum, while productivity in these sectors of the South Korean economy rose by 8.3% a year.[55] Nor was it just the Tiger economies which were following this pattern. In 1970, 4% of manufacturing output was in East Asia. By 1995 it was 11%, while over the same period the proportion in the industrialised countries fell from 88% to 80%.[56] In 1994, 43% of South Korea's GDP came from industry, for example, and 38% of GDP was used for gross domestic investment,[57] roughly twice the ratios for the USA at the time.

The reason why the Tiger economies were able to begin their very rapid growth rates was because each of them, for a variety of reasons, found themselves in the same situation as the other fast growing economies after the recovery period following World War II. Each had a highly competitive export sector, from which all else flowed. This is not to deny that hard work, discipline, access to world markets, good primary education, reasonably competent government and all the other characteristics of most successful economies were not important to the Tiger economies. Of course they were. The overwhelming significance of the export competitiveness factor, however, was that it provided the environment where all the other characteristics of the Tiger economies could flourish and be used to best advantage.

In a number of key respects, the rapid growth which they achieved also made it much easier for them to accomplish a number of other social and political objectives which most people would think were desirable. Unemployment rates were very low throughout the period, with all the benefits this brings. Jobs were readily available for anyone who wanted to work. The dependency ratio – that is the ratio between number of people not working, and therefore reliant on the value added of others who were – was therefore relatively low, which kept down the need for high levels of government taxation and expenditure. Money spent on education and training was seldom wasted, as most people who went through courses to improve their skills could easily find jobs thereafter. The impact of rapid growth on the distribution of income was also different from what is frequently supposed.

Much has been said about the supposedly inexorable rise in inequality that has taken place since the 1980s, but this was not generally the Tiger economy experience. It is also often thought that fast growth leads to incomes becoming more widely dispersed but, again, this is not what the figures show. The fast growing Asian economies have generally had more, not less, even distributions of income than is common in western industrialised economies. If the pre-tax per capita income of the top decile is taken as a ratio of that of the bottom two deciles, studies carried out around 1970 showed the ratio to be 7.6 for South Korea, 7.5 for Japan, 10.5 for Germany and the Netherlands and 14.9 for the USA. Only Sweden at 8.1 and Britain at 9.1 got close to the Asian ratios, though Australia came in 7.2.[58] The distribution of income has widened substantially in the West over the last four decades, especially post-tax, whereas it has stayed roughly constant in most of Asia.[59]

Reflected in the relatively even distribution of income in the Tiger economies are other benefits. Almost everyone is literate. Life chances have been reasonably equal, thus helping to reduce social tensions, and to produce more cohesive societies. All of them have avoided the high crime rates, especially those involving various forms of theft, which have become a problem in the West. They all have low infant mortality rates, high standards of public health and long life expectancies, generally in the mid-seventies.[60]

Should the Tiger economies therefore become models for the rest of the world to follow? To some extent, the answer may be that they should, but in other respects, unfortunately the figures do not stack up. As with Japan during a similar phase of post-World War II development, and now China, the problem with the Tiger economies is that they achieved their huge success by cornering more than their fair share of those economic activities which generate high productivity increases, and hence fast rates of economic growth. Their high concentration on industrial output, where rapid increases in output per head are easiest to secure, have been bought partly at the expense of other economies. These particularly included Britain and the USA, and much of continental Europe. By letting their cost bases become too high, all these areas laid themselves open to becoming net importers of manufactured goods.

The solution to this problem, however, is not, at least as far as this can be avoided, to slow down the progress of the Tigers. It is to ensure that there is enough demand generally, especially in the western world, for industrial output to flourish in the same way as it has not only in the Tiger economies, but also round much of the rest of the Pacific Rim. To achieve this goal, however, some significant rebalancing as to where manufacturing is concentrated will inevitably be required.

5

World Imbalances

The period between 2000 and 2008, may very well, in retrospect, turn out to be viewed as the last few years during which western economies appeared to be doing reasonably well before the storm to come. On the surface at least in the USA and Europe, economic performance seemed to be satisfactory and relatively stable, as the US economy, helped by rapid rises in the value of housing, recovered from the dot.com boom and bust of the late 1990s. Some at least of the economies in southern Europe grew strongly on the strength of low Eurozone interest rates. Consumer price inflation everywhere was low, averaging 2.3% in the USA and 2.1% in Europe, although some countries had much lower price increases than others.[1]

In many countries property values, based on historically low interest rates, increased markedly in value, making everyone who owned property feel richer. Between 2002 and 2007, average house prices rose 90% in the UK,[2] and by over 200% between 1997 and 2007 in Ireland.[3] Stock exchanges recovered strongly. In the USA, the Dow Jones Industrial Average almost doubled between 2002 and 2007,[4] with similar increases seen in Europe. The euro, having been originally established in 1998 as its constituent currencies were locked together, and having become the currency in day to day use throughout the Eurozone in 2001, got off to what looked like a good start. Living standards rose too, although averages could be misleading. A very high proportion of increased GDP everywhere, but particularly in the USA went to the already well off, leaving those not so fortunately placed on the income scales deriving considerably less benefit from the overall growth rates which remained positive throughout the western world.[5] Between 2000 to

2007 US GDP grew by 17.8% and the EU's by 19.8%.[6] The West, therefore, did not appear to most people to be under serious threat.

This apparently benevolent state of affairs, however, belied reality in two crucial closely related developments, one internal and the other external. The internal problem was that the prosperity which was thought by most people to be on a sustainable basis was in fact largely founded on the creation of a huge amount of debt owed by people living within the western world, some of whom were never creditworthy enough to have taken on the scale of the liabilities with which they encumbered themselves. The external problem was that many, although not all western countries, were running increasingly large external payments deficits. This meant that both their citizens internally and their economies as a whole externally were living beyond their means while at the same time getting cumulatively more in debt to those countries in the world, particularly China, Taiwan, Germany, Holland and Switzerland, which were running large balance of payments surpluses.[7]

As long as those who are advancing credit are reasonably confident that the individuals, companies and countries to which they are lending money are going to be able to pay it back – or at the very least are going to be able to service the interest charges involved – mounting debt may appear to be sustainable. The root problem for the western world was that from 2008 onwards, confidence that this requirement would continue to apply began to evaporate. The first major breach came as it became clear that sub-prime housing debt in the USA was nothing like as secure an asset as had been assumed, notwithstanding the role of the credit rating agencies in claiming that, packaged up into consolidated units, it was. As it became obvious that large number of financial institutions were unsure of the value of the assets they held, inter-bank transactions started to freeze up, culminating in the collapse of Lehman Brothers, a major US investment bank, on 15th September 2008.[8] The dangers of contagion spreading were averted, at least for the time being, by a concerted international effort to provide liquidity to the West's major banks, but only at the cost of creating more debt. Furthermore, as confidence in the future drained away, more threats to the banks' balance sheets emerged, not least in the form of property loans in many countries, particularly the USA, the UK, Ireland and Spain, which it was increasingly clear were no longer covered in value by the assets which secured them.

As western economies began falteringly to recover from the big falls in GDP which many of them sustained as a result of the 2008 crisis, new threats began to emerge. In Europe, it became increasingly clear that the Eurozone had major structural faults. Although on the surface these appeared among the weaker economies to be liquidity or solvency problems, the root malaise from which they all suffered was lack of competitiveness. This is a classic exchange rate over-valuation problem of exactly the kind which within a similar time scale had sunk the Snake and the Exchange Rate Mechanism. Just as had happened before when attempts had been made to lock EU currencies together, Germany in particular succeeded in containing costs and thus developing increased export competitiveness far more effectively than less disciplined countries such as not only Greece, Ireland and Portugal but much larger ones such as Spain and Italy, and even Belgium and France. As all the weaker Eurozone members reined in their economies to reduce their deficits and the rate at which they were accumulating debt, Germany's exports faltered because more than half of them went to other EU countries and over a third to other Eurozone economies.[9] Again, exactly as had happened with the Snake and the ERM, the growth rate for the whole of the Single Currency area contracted until, during all the period from 2008 to now, near stagnation has been reached. Meanwhile the strength of the euro on foreign exchanges, buoyed up by Germany's stellar export performance, made it increasingly difficult for the struggling economies in the south of Europe to compete effectively in world markets.

In the USA, different problems materialised, although all related to the same fundamental competitiveness and debt disequilibria which had become the West's hallmark. Mirroring the USA's huge payments deficit, post 2008 there was a massive federal fiscal shortfall combined with falling house prices and high and rising unemployment. Clearly something had to be done about the government deficit but it proved impossible to get any reasonable agreement about the way ahead which both the Democrats and

Republicans could support. While the Democrats were desperate to see measures taken to reflate the flagging economy and to reduce unemployment, the size of the deficit made this appear to be an increasingly dangerous option, mirrored in the USA losing its AAA credit rating from Standard and Poor's in August 2011.[10] At the same time the Republicans, encouraged by their intransigent Tea Party wing, refused to support any tax increases, even those which involved closing loopholes in already agreed tax measures. Buckling under the strain of an increasingly uncertain future, the markets both sides of the Atlantic took fright at the crash although since then, buttressed by huge quantities of Quantitative Easing, there has been a strong recovery in asset prices though not, unfortunately matched by corresponding increases in GDP.

The danger began to loom that the whole of the western world was failing to get a grip on the fundamental reasons for the malaise which has overtaken it. The future, instead of providing even modest growth would, it increasingly appeared, be one of near stagnation, causing most people – although not those who were already rich – to receive little or no increase in their real incomes year after year. The result was increased social tension and a general drift away of support from traditional centre parties to those offering a more populist range of policies.

Surpluses and deficits

The fundamental problem with the world economy at present is that there are trade imbalances which cannot be financed with any reasonable expectation that the debts involved are ever going to be repaid, at least at face value. This situation has arisen mainly because most global trade is in manufactured goods and some countries, mainly because they have very competitive exchange rates, have sequestered much more than their fair share of manufacturing capacity, while others – including most western countries – have allowed the reverse conditions to develop. As a result, all the economies with weak manufacturing sectors suffer in varying degrees from chronic balance of payments difficulties. The scale of the problems involved is exhibited both by how large the imbalances are, their current trends, and what is happening to the debts which are accumulating as a result of them.

Table 5.1a sets out the current account balance of payments position of most of the world's major economies in 2014, the latest year for which all the figures are available, to provide a snapshot of what has been happening. Each country's balance of payments position is made up of four components, these being the deficit or surplus on trade in goods, trade in services, income and transfers. A very clear picture emerges. There were – and are – some countries with chronic very large surpluses and others with equally substantial year-after-year deficits. As an accounting identity – a recurrent theme – all current account deficits have in aggregate to be matched by exactly equal and opposite capital movements. Some of these take the form of asset acquisitions in either individual or portfolio form. Most, however, are financed by debt. This is why the enormous country asset and liability imbalances shown in Table 5.1b have been allowed to accumulate.

Table 5.1a: Current account balances, selected countries, 2014, ranked in order of overall current account balances. All financial figures are in billions of US dollars unless otherwise indicated

	Overall current account balance	Total GDP in local currency	Exchange rate against the US dollar	Total GDP in US dollars	Current account surplus/ deficit (-) as % GDP
Germany	281.3	2,904	0.824	3,525	8.0
China	277.4	64,080	6.119	10,472	2.6
South Korea	84.4	1,486,079	1,099	1,352	6.2
Netherlands	83.5	663	0.824	805	10.4
Saudi Arabia*	73.8	2,827	3.750	754	9.8
Switzerland	61.5	648	0.989	656	9.4
Singapore*	53.5	390	1.321	295	18.1
Italy	38.5	1,616	0.824	1,962	2.0
Japan	36.0	489,623	120.640	4,059	0.9
Spain	12.8	1,058	0.824	1,284	1.0
Russia	5.8	71,406	56.258	1,269	0.5
Greece	−4.9	178	0.824	216	−2.3
France	−27.5	2,141	0.919	2,331	−1.2
India	−27.5	124,882	63.332	1,972	−1.4
Brazil	−104.2	5,521	2.656	2,079	−5.0
United Kingdom	−151.9	1,791	1.561	2,796	−5.4
United States	−389.5	17,348	1.000	17,348	−2.2

Source: Country tables in International Financial Statistics Yearbook 2016. Washington DC: IMF, 2016

Table 5.1b: Total assets minus total liabilities, selected countries, ranked in order of net balances to GDP. All figures are in US dollars and are for 2014.

	Total assets	Total liabilities	Net balance	GDP	Ratio net assets to GDP
Singapore	2,991	2,413	578	308	1.88
Switzerland	4,264	3,575	689	708	0.97
Japan	7,812	4,799	3,013	4,045	0.74
Germany	9,295	7,844	1,451	3,220	0.45
China	6,438	4,836	1,602	10,290	0.16
Russia	1,249	959	290	1,860	0.16
South Korea	1,082	994	88	1,314	0.07
United Kingdom	14,539	14,857	–317	2,955	–0.11
India	493	855	–362	2,047	–0.18
France	7,863	8,371	–508	2,375	–0.21
Italy	2,674	3,228	–554	1,793	–0.31
United States	24,596	31,615	–7,019	17,348	–0.40
Brazil	765	1,565	–800	1,658	–0.48
Spain	1,852	3,060	–1,208	1,173	–1.03
Ireland	4,535	4,776	–241	210	–1.15
Greece	279	549	–270	197	–1.37

Source: Country Tables in International Financial Statistics. Washington DC: IMF, 2016.

This situation has arisen as a result of foreign payments surpluses and deficits being allowed to continue by the main countries involved for year after year. The sums involved are huge. Between the start of 2000 and the end of 2015, Germany accumulated a balance of payments surplus of 2.7 trillion dollars and China 3.0 trillion. Relatively small countries such as Singapore achieved $563bn, Switzerland $785bn and the Netherlands $1,086bn. Oil producing countries such as Saudi Arabia with $1.089bn added to the surplus total. On the other side were the UK, with an accumulated deficit of $1,074bn, and the USA with a staggering $8.43 trillion gap between its foreign income and expenditure during the first decade and a half of the current century.[11]

Since these numbers are so large, it may well be asked how this situation could ever have been allowed to arise. At first sight it seems obvious that there would be great difficulties about repaying such large sums of money or even servicing the interest charges involved. There are, however, a number of reasons why it was not so obvious that the problems were as serious as they turned out to be and why there were such strong pressures for these huge debts to grow to their current size.

First, both the US dollar and the euro and, to a much lesser extent now, sterling are all reserve currencies. The US dollar, in particular, is used on a huge scale to finance globalised trade and to facilitate payments throughout the world. Being a reserve currency necessarily involves very large sums being required to be held as working balances both within the banking system and elsewhere, on which little interest is paid. As the world's economy expands, more and bigger balances are required, requiring larger and larger volumes of funding. This therefore provides a rational reason for the creation of debt which trade imbalances facilitate.

Second, although in theory all debts are due at some stage to be repaid, most lenders seldom expect this to happen in the reasonably near future. Nor do they need to be particularly worried as to whether repayment should be possible at any time, at least in individual cases, provided what appears to be a strong covenant and a solvent debtor is involved. This is because creditors do not need to be concerned about the debts owed to them provided that they can always rely on finding someone else to take over the debts owing to them if asked to do so. As long as markets are deep, liquid and confident in the capacity of debtors generally to meet their obligations, which for a long time had been the case in the West, the risks for each individual creditor, even large ones, appeared low enough for confidence to be maintained.

It is only when the realisation dawns that a significant number of major debtors at the same time are getting past the point where their liabilities are manageable that the systemic danger of so much debt being accumulated becomes apparent. This situation starts to be reached once it dawns on the markets that the rate at which debt is accumulating and the total interest payments due on it, are becoming beyond the capacity of debtors to pay. A big part of the reason why this realisation has been slow to materialise is that, as long as economies are growing, their capacity to service increasing amounts of debt keeps rising. It is when economies stop growing while their debts are still increasing – which is what has been happening to an increasing extent in recent years – that the line between solvency and insolvency suddenly hoves much more sharply into view.

Third, at least until very recently, it always looked as though at least western sovereign debt – debt owed by governments – was so nearly solidly reliable that virtually no risk was involved in holding it. There was always some danger that currencies would depreciate – providing an exchange rate risk that the value of debt denominated in a devaluing currency would be worth less than it was previously in other currencies – but no apparent risk that any developed western sovereign nation would default. As long as each currency had a central bank which, if need be, could create unlimited amounts of money, every sovereign nation could meet its obligations. Furthermore, if the policy of most governments was to avoid depreciation of their currencies if they could possibly avoid doing so, the exchange rate risk appeared also to be kept in bounds. Within the Eurozone, however, the situation is different. Because the Single Currency is managed by the European Central Bank and not by individual countries, the ability of the weaker economies to create whatever funds may be required to meet their obligations no longer exists and this is one of the major reasons why the Eurozone is currently in such difficulties. A major risk of sovereign defaults has been allowed to accumulate.

Fourth, if all balance of payments surpluses necessarily involve capital transfers of one sort or another to deficit countries, the huge sums of money involved as the surpluses are generated have to go somewhere and it was not obvious where else much of it could go unless it went into buying deficit countries' debt. Furthermore, if the result, for example, of the Chinese buying US Treasuries is also to provide a way of keeping China's currency and hence its exports highly competitive, by soaking up the funds from its export surplus, this policy clearly has a certain rationale to it. Although there might be a risk that the funds used to buy US Treasuries might never be repaid except in eventually heavily depreciated dollars, the gain to the Chinese economy in the short term from the huge boost to its economy from its success as an exporter, based on maintaining its undervalued currency to keep its manufactured output competitive in world markets, is evidently a major offsetting factor.

There have thus been a significant number of factors to persuade the herd instincts of the markets that the accumulation of debt on the scale which has materialised is sustainable. The danger is that, as market sentiment turns and becomes increasingly pessimistic, it precipitates precisely the recessionary conditions which make the world's major debt problems less and less manageable, resulting in just the sort of major financial crisis which it is in everyone's interest to avoid. The way a major crisis may envelop us all will be different in the USA and the UK than in the Eurozone countries, mainly because the EU's Single Currency makes the adjustments required even more difficult to accomplish than would be the case if it did not exist. The danger which is building up fast at the moment, however, on both sides of the Atlantic – and elsewhere, for example in China and the Ukraine – is broadly similar. Debt is building up more rapidly than the capacity of many governments and countries as well as some individuals and companies to service and repay it. This trend is unsustainable. It cannot and will not last indefinitely. This is why a fundamental review of economic policy objectives in the West – and elsewhere – is becoming so pressingly urgent.

The 2008 financial crisis and austerity

It is now time to turn to what happened in the UK, leading up to the 2008 crisis and the government's response. How much of what went wrong could have been avoided by better policies?

By the end of 1980s, it was apparent to everyone that the certainties promised by monetarism were not there in practice. Indeed, despite all the pain inflicted on the UK economy by the 1979 Conservative government, inflation was actually slightly higher when the Prime Minister, Margaret Thatcher (1925-2013) left office in 1990 than it was when she came to power in 1979.[12] During the late 1980s, Nigel Lawson (b. 1932), the then chancellor of the exchequer, therefore switched from controlling the money supply to contain inflation to shadowing the Deutsche Mark to achieve this objective. This was on the grounds that the relatively high exchange rate that this would entail would bear down on inflation – a doctrine favoured by both The Treasury and the Bank of England[13]. M1 and M3, having only recently been the lodestones by which UK economic policy was guided, were abandoned as policy determinants, and fell from view. The logical next step was for the UK to join the Exchange Rate mechanism (ERM) and this was achieved in October 1990 by John Major (b. 1943) who by then had become chancellor.[14] The exchange rate at which we joined, however, with a central rate of DM2.90 = £1.00 proved to be far too high, tipping the UK into a sharp recession. Unemployment rose to almost 13%[15] and the housing market nosedived.[16]

Eventually the dam broke and despite dire warnings of what the consequences might be, on 16th September 1992, following a final interest rise to 15%, it became apparent that maintaining an exchange rate of anything like DM2.90 was impossible. Sterling then fell out of the ERM and lost 14% of its value on a trade weighted basis before stabilising.[17] Far from the economy then suffering the promised downturn, however, it rapidly recovered from its ERM induced recession. Inflation fell from 5.9% in 1991 to 1.6% in 1993,[18] unemployment, having peaked at nearly 14% fell to 5.8% by 1999[19] and economic growth, which had been negative from 1990 to 1992, was positive for every year thereafter until 2009.[20]

Having abandoned the ERM, however, the authorities now needed a new central aim for economic policy to guide the economy. This turned out to be aiming to control the consumer price index (CPI) directly rather than through any intermediary and the era of inflation targeting began. In the UK's case this was to set the target inflation rate at 2% per annum, with policy initially in the hands of the chancellor but subsequently the Bank of England's Monetary Policy Committee when the Bank was made independent of government by the incoming Labour government in 1997.[21] Although inflation targeting was generally welcomed, and it stood the test of time better than those policies adopted previously, it had serious faults. Its most obvious flaw was that inflation was targeted strictly on the CPI[22] and not on what was happening to asset prices. The CPI remained reasonably close to its average of 2.5%[23] throughout the 1990s and 2000s while asset prices gyrated much more erratically. More fundamentally, however, inflation targeting did nothing to make the economy more competitive and thus to get it to grow faster and in a more sustainable way. Instead it turned out to mask all the underlying imbalances which steadily became more severe, mainly because inflation targeting at 2% tended to involve relatively high interest rates. For this and other reasons, the exchange rate got stronger and stronger, peaking at over $2.00 to the pound in 2007[24] as the City thrived and manufacturing declined between 1990 and the early 2010s from 20% to 10% of GDP.[25]

Nevertheless, despite the major fluctuations in asset prices round the dot.com boom period at the turn of the century and underlying concern about the increasingly unbalanced state of the economy, informed opinion became more and more convinced that the Great Moderation was here to stay. Major booms and slumps were a thing of the past. Neo-liberal ideas became more and more dominant as faith in the market system became increasingly entrenched. Buttressed by complex mathematical theorising round such concepts as Rational Expectations and the Efficient Market Hypothesis, most of the academic and financial worlds convinced themselves that the markets knew best, and that liberalisation and deregulation would lead to greater stability as risks were spread more widely. The financial system was essentially self-regulating and disturbances – with only limited help needed from government – would be self-correcting as equilibrium was automatically restored by market pressures.

This complacency was, of course, very rudely shaken by the crisis which built up in 2007 and which reached its climax in on 15th September 2008 with the collapse of Lehman Brothers, a major US investment bank.[26] Far from being stable, assets prices tumbled. The UK FTSE 100 index fell from 6,732 in May 2008 to 3,530 in March 2009, since when it had slowly recovered to just over 7,000 by the end of 2016.[27] The proximate cause of the 2008 crisis was the highly uncertain value of derivatives, such as sub-prime collateralised debt obligations, triggered by the US housing boom coming off the boil in 2006.[28] The total sums involved in this sector of the market – at around $200bn[29] – were, however, comparatively small and manageable in relation to the total amount of debt which was outstanding. The real problem was that identifying which mortgages were liable to default proved impossible and, as a result, no-one knew what all the huge bundles of collateralised mortgages – and the mountain of debt which had accumulated round increasingly exotic financial instruments – were really worth. Suddenly all the banks and other financial institutions, including many in the loosely regulated secondary banking market, did not know which organisations were solvent and which were not, including some of the biggest banks in the world.

The underlying case for the 2008 crisis, however, was the huge increase in debt which had built up over the period since the turn of the century. By 2008, the monetary base in the UK was over three times the size it had been in 2000 although the economy over this period grew by no more than 20%.[30] The capital base on which this huge expansion in debt – highly profitable though it was in a rising market – had been built had expanded much more slowly than the debt which it was supporting. During the peak running up to 2008 some financial institutions, including Lehman Brothers, had debt to equity ratios of in excess of 30. This meant that only a 3% to 4% default rate would wipe out their capital base – essentially what happened to Lehman[31] and which was at risk of happening to many other banks and financial institutions too.

This was why the solution adopted to counteract the 2008 crash was to flood the financial markets with still more debt, to ensure that financial institutions which were in danger of insolvency were not tipped on a widespread basis into bankruptcy because they became so illiquid that they could not meet their day to day obligations. In the UK both the Royal Bank of Scotland and Lloyds Bank were only saved by becoming partially nationalised – the latter after a disastrous take-over of HBOS.[32] The Quantitative Easing programme initially undertaken both in the USA and the UK but subsequently also by the European Central Bank allowed major financial institutions to improve their balance sheet ratios but did only a little to assist the rest of the economy, particularly industry and commerce to which lending had become much more constrained. The total amount of debt created, however, as a result of these programmes, continued to grow. By 2015 the monetary base in the UK was a staggering 12.4 times what it had been in 2000 against growth in GDP over the same period of no more than 29%.[33]

The immediate result of the 2008 crisis was the sharpest and deepest downturn in economic performance across the West since the Great Recession in the 1930s. GDP fell by 2.8% in the USA but by 4.2% in the UK.[34] Both households and the corporate sector pulled in their horns sharply, swinging between them from net lending of £9bn in 2007 to £143bn in 2009. The inevitable result was that government borrowing shot up from £38bn in 2007 to £159bn in 2009.[35] The main preoccupation of economic policy since then has been to get the government deficit reduced. Table 5.2 shows what has happened, providing – for context – the figures for borrowing and lending by the main sectors of the economy since 2000.

Table 5.2: UK net lending (+) and net borrowing (-) by sector in £bn

	Public sector	Corporations	Households	Rest of the world	Net totals
2000	11.8	−57.4	22.7	22.8	0
2001	4.1	−57.6	31.8	21.7	0
2002	−23.4	−20.8	20.1	24.1	0
2003	−40.6	13.6	6.4	20.6	0
2004	−45.1	29.1	−6.9	23.0	0
2005	−47.0	39.9	−10.4	17.6	0
2006	−41.0	24.0	−16.9	33.9	0
2007	−44.2	18.6	−12.1	37.7	0
2008	−76.8	35.0	−12.9	54.8	0
2009	−160.5	65.5	50.6	44.4	0
2010	−150.4	36.3	71.1	43.1	0
2011	−124.6	53.4	41.7	29.5	0
2012	−139.4	41.7	36.2	61.6	0
2013	−99.5	19.0	3.6	76.9	0
2014	−101.7	16.0	0.3	85.4	0
2015	−80.2	−6.5	−2.8	81.3	−4.8
2016 Q1	−16.3	0.2	−2.6	23.1	4.5
2016 Q2	−16.3	1.1	−2.1	22.4	5.1
2016 Q3	−19.5	4.0	−4.9	25.7	5.3
2016 Annualised	−69.4	7.1	−12.7	94.9	19.9

Source: Table I. Net Lending by Sector in ONS Statistical Bulletin – *Quarterly National Accounts 2016 Q3*. London: ONS, December 2016. Figures for 2015 and 2016 are still being reconciled by ONS and the net totals will also be very close to zero when this process is complete.

The really crucial conclusion to be drawn from these figures is how misguided the UK government's policy was from 2010 onwards if it really thought that getting the government deficit down was its main priority and that the policies it pursued would actually achieve this objective. The reality was – and still is – that the only way to get the government deficit down is to reduce substantially the balance of payments deficit. This is because all deficits and surpluses among the main four sectors of the economy – government, households, the corporate sector and the foreign payment balance – have, as an accounting identity, to sum to zero. All borrowing has to be exactly matched by all lending. Given a balance of payments deficit of £100bn a year, there is no way that the government deficit could be brought down to zero unless a combination of the corporate and household sectors borrowed £100bn – a prospect for which there was never the slightest possibility.

Of course, it may still appear that, if the government has a deficit, the most sensible way to reduce or eliminate it is to reduce expenditure and to increase taxation, which the government repeatedly said was its aim. This approach, however, entails a fallacy of composition, which is that what might be true for an individual or a company, each of which on its own has an impact on the economy as a whole which is much too small to make any material difference, is the same as for the government through whose hands goes about 40% of GDP. The reality is that the net borrowing or lending by the corporate and household sectors and by everyone involved in foreign payments, which is the outcome of millions of individual decisions, therefore leaves the government surplus or deficit as necessarily the equal and opposite residual. In these conditions, if the government tries to reduce its deficit by cutting expenditure or increasing taxation, the result will be that welfare claims on the state will go up and the actual tax yield will fall and the deficit will stay at about the same size as it was before.

Suppose, however, that there was a really determined government which was prepared to do whatever it took to get its deficit down to zero ignoring the fact that it had a large foreign payments balance at the starting point. It would cut spending and increase taxation but the borrowing and lending between the four main sectors would still have to sum to zero. The only way to achieve no government borrowing would then be to plunge the economy into such a recession that the foreign payments deficit was brought down to equal the net borrowing/lending balance achieved by the corporate and household sectors. As a major recession – on all the evidence from Table 5.2 – would drive these sectors into saving rather than borrowing the recession would have to be deep enough to get the foreign payments into surplus as imports were cut back sufficiently to make this happen. To achieve such an outcome, the economy would have to shrink massively. Greece, which was forced into this position, exemplifies what would have to happen. Greek money GDP fell 45% from \$354bn in 2008 to \$195bn in 2015[36] while real GDP, allowing for falling wages and prices, fell by 26% over the same period.[37] No government in the UK, which is not constrained by something like euro membership, as is Greece, is going to contemplate such an outcome.

This is why austerity policies based on cutting expenditure and raising taxation to reduce government deficits make no sense. They are based on a fundamental misconception about how borrowing and lending, and surpluses and deficits within the economy, have to balance. The reality is that only way to reduce government deficits is to rebalance the economy so as to avoid the balance of payments being in the red, or at least to reduce the foreign payment deficit to a point where government borrowing is reduced to a sustainable level. This might well be to have borrowing as a percentage of GDP no more than the growth rate – taking into account whatever borrowing or lending may be done by the household and corporate sectors. To bring the foreign payment deficit down to the level then required, the economy would have to be competitive enough to make this possible. As with so much to do with the weaknesses and imbalances of the UK economy, this comes back once more to the exchange rate.

Table 5.3: Government and consumer debt trends in the USA and UK. All at current prices

		2006	2007	2008	2009	2010
US Individuals US$bn	Consumer credit	2,385	2,522	2,561	2,449	2,403
	Mortgages	13,462	14,524	14,619	14,326	13,947
	Total	15,847	17,046	17,180	16,775	16,350
US Government		8,860	9,229	10,700	12,311	14,025
UK Individuals £bn	Consumer credit	198	201	208	205	197
	Mortgages	1,082	1,190	1,227	1,224	1,228
	Total	1,280	1,391	1,435	1,429	1,425
UK Government		648	696	862	1,050	1,238
Debt as a percentage of Gross Domestic Product:						
US GDP US$bn		13,399	14,062	14,369	14,119	14,660
US Individuals as a percentage of GDP		118	121	120	119	115
US Government as a percentage of GDP		66	66	74	87	96
Total as percentage of GDP		184	187	194	206	211
UK GDP £bn		1,328	1,405	1,446	1,395	1,454
UK Individuals as a percentage of GDP		98	99	99	102	98
UK Government as a percentage of GDP		49	50	60	75	85
Total as percentage of GDP		147	149	159	177	183

Sources: USA: Tables B-1, B-76, B77 and B-87 in *Economic Report to the President*. Washington DC: US government Printing Office, 2011. UK: Bank of England and *Credit Action* Internet Tables and pages 744 and 745 in *International Financial Statistics Yearbook* .Washington DC: IMF, 2011

Europe's Single Currency

The EU's Single Currency – the euro – which most EU political leads want to see operating across preferably all EU member states, has, as has already been described, roots going back to at least the 1970s. It was always a political rather than an economic project. The hope was that the establishment of the Single Currency would cause the performance of all the countries concerned to converge, although it was never clear why this should happen. The reality, on the contrary, as many people warned at the time, was that the countries which were to make up the Eurozone were too diverse for them to come together, all using the same currency, while retaining a large measure of sovereignty. Experience with the Snake and the Exchange Rate Mechanism had shown that some countries, particularly Germany, had highly entrenched capacities for holding down costs and increasing export competitiveness in relation to most others in the European Union, especially those in southern Europe.

In the USA, there is a relatively highly mobile labour force, speaking a common language and capable of moving to another part of the country to take advantage of changes in economic opportunities. In the EU, with many different languages and other ties to home countries, mobility has been much less easy to achieve. Furthermore, in the USA, even though a considerably lower proportion of GDP passes through government hands than the average in Europe, federal disbursements still account for about 20% of GDP.[38] This makes it possible for very substantial transfers to be made from the more to the less prosperous areas of the country. In the EU, no such mechanism exists. The EU's total budget is capped at no more than 1.23%[39] of EU GDP, and much of this, involved as it is with the Common Agricultural Policy, does little if anything to redistribute income from richer to poorer countries.

Locking the currencies of all the disparate countries making up the Eurozone in 1998 – supposedly irrevocably – and replacing all these currencies with the euro from the beginning of 2001 was always therefore a high risk strategy. As has happened with most currency unions in history, however, initially the project got off to quite a good start. The introduction of the euro from a technical standpoint was accomplished with commendable smoothness. In the relatively benign conditions which prevailed during the early years of the twenty-first century, the Eurozone did reasonably well. Again, however, as has been the case with all currency unions in the past which did not morph into being unitary states, as time went by, problems of disparate performance and compatibility gradually, and then later rapidly increased. When the Single Currency had been established, the Germans, having foreseen some of the problems which might ensue, had insisted in 1997 on a Growth and Stability Pact being implemented, which was designed to limit Eurozone country budget deficits to 3% of GDP and total borrowing to 60% of GDP.[40] The situation was not helped by the fact that both Germany and France ignored these restrictions early on when it suited them to do so, making it more difficult to establish any serious commitment to fiscal discipline later on among the more vulnerable Single Currency members.

Some of the problems stemmed from long established features of the constituent economies. Countries such as Greece, Italy and Spain had long histories of higher levels of inflation than Germany and other Nordic economies. Greece clearly joined the Single Currency on the basis of statistics which were wildly optimistic and unrealistic – and, by all accounts, known to be so by many people at the time. Others, such as Portugal, were uncompetitive from the beginning. These mismatches were then exacerbated by features intrinsic to the Single Currency concept. If there was only one currency, there could only be one interest rate. This tended to be too high in countries with low inflation rates but much too low in countries where prices were rising strongly. The result was unsustainable property booms particularly in Spain and Ireland, financed on low interest rates, with the 'feel good' impact of rising property values helping to push up the price level generally.

As always happens, the relatively rapidly rising price levels in the less disciplined countries began increasingly to bite into their capacity to pay their way in the world. All of them began to experience deteriorating balance of payments conditions. Initially, the increased indebtedness which was entailed was relatively easily absorbed by the markets, which felt confident that the Single Currency was such a solid project that Greek debt, for example, was as good – or almost as good – as German debt. As late as early in 2008 there was almost no interest premium to be paid on non-German euro bonds.[41] By early in 2011, however, the situation had completely changed. Greece was having to pay 12% and Ireland 10% per annum to service new sovereign bond issues. Later in the year, Italy was paying close to 7% while even France was starting to have to pay significantly more than Germany,[42] these spreads being a harsh but realistic indicator of market sentiment as to the decline of the relative creditworthiness of these different countries over the period concerned.

Initially with Greece, but then subsequently with Ireland and Portugal, it became apparent that all these countries were not going to be able to meet their debt obligations without much more assistance from other Single Currency members – and others – than had been envisaged. Contagion then began to spread to the much larger economies of Spain and Italy, with Belgium and even France being viewed as economies which might not be able to continue within the Single Currency without very substantial assistance from other Single Currency members. The first bail-out was for Greece in May 2010, followed by another one for Ireland in November 2010 and a third one for Portugal in April 2011.[43]

The dilemma faced by EU political leaders, particularly Chancellor Angela Merkel (b. 1954) the German Chancellor, became acute. It was increasingly clear that the Eurozone could not survive without massive transfers being made from the stronger economies to the weaker ones. As Germany was much the largest and most robust potential donor, it was obvious that there was no alternative but for the Germans to be the major paymasters. There was, however, huge reluctance in Germany for undertaking this open-ended commitment. It was also clear that, if major subventions from Germany were to be forthcoming, then there would have to be much tighter oversight of the budgets and economic management of the economies to whom the assistance was to be provided. This was evidently going to involve the imposition of drastic retrenchment on their economies, combined with insistence on wholesale reforms of labour markets, pension entitlement and institutional arrangements, for which there was no democratic mandate and to which there was certain to be strong resistance from entrenched interests. Furthermore, these changes were to be implemented in heavily deflationary employment and economic conditions, which were bound to increase hostility to any such programmes.

Since the crisis period earlier this decade, the situation in the Eurozone has been more quiescent but at the cost of very little growth and very high levels of unemployment, particularly in the southern countries which have been most-hard hit. Between the beginning of 2009 and the end of 2015, the Eurozone as a whole grew by 1.7% but the Spanish economy contacted by 4.6%, Italy by 7.3% and Greece by a heartrending 25%.[44] Over this period, unemployment in the Eurozone averaged 9.8% but 11.9% in Italy, 19.2% in Spain and 23.1% in Greece.[45] Youth unemployment was much higher. The Eurozone has recently been kept afloat largely as a result of huge Quantitative Easing lines of credit being created by the European Central Bank (ECB) doing, as its President, Mario Draghi (b. 1947) said it would at a conference held in London in July 2012: 'Within our mandate, the ECB is ready to do whatever it takes to preserve the euro. And believe me it will be enough.'[46]

It is still far from certain how this situation will get resolved. It seems very probable that there will be sufficient resolve among a majority of EU leaders to keep the Eurozone in being in substantially its present form for as long as they can. Even if, as seems likely, there are further attacks on the weaker members by nervous markets, they may be willing to do sufficient on the financial front to avoid defaults taking place and the Single Currency breaking up, at least for the time being. Whether they will be able to achieve this objective indefinitely, however, remains to be seen. Another threat is that leaders are elected to governing positions among Eurozone member states on platforms which entail abandoning Single Currency membership. This appears to be a scenario which might materialise in any one of several countries currently doing poorly from their presence in the Eurozone.

A major component of the Single Currency's current problems is that, when the Eurozone was established, cross border bank lending was positively encouraged by the EU Commission, as a way of promoting growth in those economies with relatively low GDP per head. This lending did increase living standards in the short term in countries such as Spain and Ireland, but only by creating unsustainable property booms. The legacy of encouraging banks in one country to lend in other is very large cross-country bank indebtedness, compounded by existing bad debts caused by large scale unwise property loans and speculation in sub-prime obligations, which put a major strain on EU banks' balance sheets. The danger is that if the EU breaks up, it will leave many European banks insolvent. Since having major banks going into liquidation would certainly plunge the EU economy – and the rest of the world – into a major crisis, the EU states would almost certainly want to avoid bank bankruptcies by refinancing all those in danger of collapse. The problem then, however, is whether even the sovereign states making up the EU would have the borrowing power to be able to do this, on top of all the other debt commitments they already have.

While it is therefore easy to understand the extreme reluctance of most EU leaders, to allow the Single Currency to break up there are two very major dangers in them pursuing the policy which they seem most likely to favour, as long as they have any hope of achieving it, which is to keep the Single Currency in being substantially as it is. The first is that this policy does nothing to overcome the root problem among the Eurozone's weaker members. This is not just one of solvency or liquidity. It is fundamentally one of competitiveness. It is therefore an exchange rate and cost base issue. If these economies were able to devalue substantially, there would no doubt be very serious short-term problems to overcome, but the longer-term outlook would be much more favourable – as happened in the case of Argentina, for example, which may provide some guidance to what could happen in the EU.

While Argentina always retained its own currency, the peso, this was tied supposedly irrevocably to the dollar in 1991 with the deliberate intention of stabilising and disciplining the Argentine economy. Because costs in Argentina still rose much more quickly than in the USA, economic conditions gradually worsened to a point where they became intolerable, leading to Argentina defaulting on its debts in 2002. The peso then fell in value against the dollar by 70% in four months, causing great hardship temporarily as GDP fell by 11%. The Argentine economy then rapidly recovered, however, growing cumulatively by 9% per annum between 2003 and 2007. By 2010, manufacturing output had doubled from its level in 2002,[47] providing a portent for what might happen in Europe if the Single Currency does break up.

The second fundamental problem faced by the EU leaders is that, far from the tensions within the Single Currency remaining bad but getting no worse, they are deteriorating all the time. This is happening partly because every month which goes by the total amount of debt which one way or another has to be financed goes up as both balance of payments and government deficits continue to accumulate. At the same time, if economic performance within the Eurozone shows no sign of sustained improvement, producing little or no economic growth, the capacity of all the deficit economies to meet their debt obligations will get steadily worse, making defaults eventually almost inevitable.

It is these developments which lead to proposals – although there is no sign at the moment of any of them being accepted – for coming to grips with the Eurozone's fundamental problems now rather than later, when the total amount of debt to be managed may be too great for the Eurozone countries to handle. Allowing the Single Currency to break up in an as orderly way as possible, while there is hopefully still time to do this in a controlled manner, might be a better option than having uncontrollable disorder as the markets completely lose confidence in Eurozone member states and a significant number of EU governments are no longer able to borrow while staying within the Eurozone. This could happen once it becomes more and more certain that the eventual outcome could only be defaults. Once this became clear, money is likely to be withdrawn from potentially defaulting countries faster and faster. This would put an intolerable strain on the solvency of the banks in these countries, potentially involving bail-out costs which would be so high as to be very difficult to finance. Problems of competitiveness within Single Currency areas eventually materialise as banking crises whereas with countries with their own currencies, once parities get too far out of line, they take the form of currency crises. The basic problems and solutions, however, are the same.[48]

Of course, the problem of dealing with Single Currency defaults is made hugely much more complicated and difficult by the fact that the same currency exists in all Eurozone countries. While most euro denominated debt and contracts could be dealt with by a defaulting country passing a law making all euros within its jurisdiction worth a fraction of those in Germany, but leaving the depreciated euro as legal tender until a new currency could be introduced, there would inevitably be many cases where it was not clear which euro value applied. Sooner or later, however, these problems are likely to have to be confronted and solutions to them found. Many currency unions have broken up in the past, with the problems involved in breaking up what had previously thought to be permanent arrangements being somehow or other overcome generally at the expense of a relatively short term period of turmoil. History has no examples of currency unions with less than about 15% of their GDPs being under the control of a central authority surviving, which is a far higher percentage than is the case with the Single Currency. It seems almost certain, therefore, that the Eurozone countries will either have to morph into becoming a unified state or that the euro will not survive indefinitely, although it is impossible to predict what timescales might be involved.

US and UK travails

The situations in the USA and the UK ought to be more manageable in a number of key respects than they are for countries which are in the Single Currency. Both the USA and the UK economies have their own currencies and central banks, and do not, therefore, suffer from the constraints faced by the Eurozone members. Although what happens in the Eurozone is bound to have a major impact on them, neither the USA nor the UK has very large commitments, through the IMF and in other ways, towards underwriting the continuation of the Single Currency, compared to those of Eurozone member states. If major changes in exchange rate policies are required, both are in a much better position to implement them than the economies which are in the Single Currency. There are, however, unfortunately different reasons why the sort of policies which are required fundamentally to stabilise and improve the position of both the USA and the UK in the world economy may be difficult to implement.

Perhaps the most important reason of all why this should be the case appears to stem from the fact that both the USA and the UK have been relatively unsuccessful in achieving reasonable rates of growth for longer than other major economies. This has allowed attitudes both to harden and to permeate public opinion more broadly than elsewhere in favour of the hard money, high exchange rate policies which have been the fundamental reason for their undoing.

First, both the US and the UK economies have very strong finance sectors and exceptionally successful and powerful importing companies combined with relatively weak and discredited manufacturing sectors. This leaves large sections of the apparently more successful business communities in both countries in a much stronger position to influence the policies which most immediately suit them well.

Second, no doubt significantly influenced by who in the commercial world calls the shots, the academic climate in both the USA and the UK has been much more orientated towards the hard money, neo-liberal school than is the case in most other countries. Although enthusiasm for the more extreme versions of monetarist theorising is much less common than it was a few decades ago, there is still a significant legacy left from those days which colours much of the way in which economics is taught, current affairs are discussed and policies are formulated. As long as fighting inflation is regarded as the major role which economic policy should fulfil, other objectives get side-lined because they are regarded as incompatible with financial stability or unachievable in the face of market forces.

Third, decades of relatively poor growth performance compared to many other places in the world seem to have inured many people to regarding slow growth as being inevitable. With widening dispersion of incomes leaving most influential commentators in a relatively favoured position, there is not as much pressure as there might be to embrace radical change designed to improve economic performance and correspondingly less willingness to search for solutions which go against the grain of conventional thinking. There is little doubt that the markedly widening distributions of income, wealth and life chances generally has had a major impact in this respect. Both sides of the Atlantic, a small elite section of the population, which enjoys a very high standard of living, has become more and more powerful in both controlling events and manipulating public opinion to its advantage.[49] These people have no great interest in altering the status quo thinking on economic policy and show little inclination to do so.

This situation may change, however, as both economic and

political pressures mount. In particular, the deficit problems faced by both the USA and the UK are becoming more acute. As of November 2016 the USA had net government debt which amounted to almost \$14.3trn, about 76% of GDP,[50] while the comparable figures for the UK in were £1.68trn and 83% of GDP.[51] These figures, however, exclude large potential liabilities. For example the British net government debt, if all financial sector intervention is included, is estimated to be about £2.6bn, which is almost 150% of GDP.[52] Both countries also had relatively high fiscal deficits, running in 2016 at \$587bn or 3.2% of GDP in the USA[53] and £80bn or 4.3% in the UK.[54] These figures are clearly much too high to be sustainable but it is far from clear that there are workable and achievable policies in either country to get them down to a manageable level, at least without severe deflationary implications. On the political front, in both the UK and the USA, mounting discontent with the adverse effects on large sections of the population from globalisation and trade liberalisation have recently had major impacts recently both sides of the Atlantic.

The reason for these developments not hard to find. They both stem from the same source, which is that both the USA and the UK have chronically underperforming export sectors, which have driven both economies into the imbalances which have undermined their performance. Table 5.1a showed how substantial the trade and payments deficits are for both countries. The same all too familiar consequences then emerge. It is impossible to run the economy at full throttle because of balance of payments constraints. As unemployment increases, so the many claims on public expenditure resulting from dependency on state support increase. Without the productivity increases which are so much easier to achieve in manufacturing than they are elsewhere in the economy, the growth rate falters and government revenues lack buoyancy. As public sector borrowing increases, so does the proportion of government revenues that have to be used to service debt. Slowly and then increasingly quickly both the US and the UK economies are teetering towards the point when both their sovereign and government debt positions will start to look increasingly unsustainable to the markets. Without major changes in policy, both the US and UK governments will then be faced with stark choices. With borrowing costs rising as their creditworthiness falters, they can fight off major exchange rate changes with higher interest rates, but these steps will depress their economies even further. On current form, nevertheless, this may well be what both will choose to do, at least as long as they can sustain this policy stance. Alternatively, even at this late stage, both could start taking steps before the markets turn against them to get their economies more competitive in international terms, to secure a stable long term future, to get their debts and borrowing back under control and to provide a much better future for all their citizens.

We turn now to seeing in more detail what the fundamental problems are and what we might be able to do about them.

6

Unmanageable Competition

This book argues that the root problem for the whole of the western world is that nearly all of it has for many years been deeply uncompetitive with the East, particularly China and other countries along the Pacific Rim, although there are also serious imbalances more locally, within the Eurozone. It is now time to look in detail at this overarching problem. The most compelling evidence is to be found in the increased shares of world trade secured by countries in the East, with corresponding reductions in the West. Table 6.1a shows the position.

Table 6.1a: Shares of world trade in percentages				
Country	1970	1985	2000	2015
China	0.5	1.3	3.9	14.1
South Korea	0.2	0.5	2.7	3.2
UK	6.9	5.4	4.4	2.9
USA	15.2	11.7	12.3	9.3
The Industrialised West	73.4	68.3	62.9	59.1
The Emerging East	4.9	11.0	19.9	21.0

Source: Successive editions of *International Financial Statistics Yearbook 1979, 2000, 2004 and 2016*. Washington DC: IMF Various Years.

Sluggish exports in the West have then taken their toll in the form of less stimulus for growth, deflationary problems caused by foreign payment deficits. The inevitable result has been much more slowly growing GDP. Table 6.1b shows the difference in growth rates which materialised, with the poor performance in the West very largely caused by their uncompetitive foreign sectors.

Table 6.1b: Ratio increase in real GDP in selected economic areas				
Country	**1970**	**1985**	**2000**	**2015**
China	100	290	915	3407
Singapore	100	320	1053	2135
South Korea	100	367	1109	1970
UK	100	134	200	253
USA	100	160	268	349
The Industrialised West	100	161	247	310
The Emerging East	100	176	397	1375

Source: Successive editions of *International Financial Statistics Yearbook*. Washington DC: IMF Various Years; and Table C from *The World Economy: A Millennial Perspective* by Angus Maddison. Paris: OECD, 2001.

We now return to the fact that the cause of these hugely discrepant outcomes is not hard to find. It was the enormous increases in western exchange rates during the monetarist era which were the fundamental reason why this happened. They were caused mainly by the very high interest rates which monetarist policies required, supplemented subsequently, in the UK's case – and that of the USA – by massive net asset sales which both pushed up the pound and the dollar on the foreign exchanges and sustained their high valuations. These developments were then combined with rapidly falling real exchange rates in the East. Figure 6.1 highlights what happened between the UK and China, which is a reasonable proxy for the changes which took place between almost the whole of the West and most of the Pacific Rim countries in the East.

The UK economy generally was none too competitive in the 1970s, but the impact of monetarist policies in raising interest rates and constricting – at least initially – the money supply across the period from the late 1970s to the early 1980s was dramatically to worsen the competitive position. Between 1977 and 1981 the UK's real effective exchange rate against all currencies rose by almost 60%.[1] It then stayed roughly constant for the next 15 years, falling about 12% after the UK left the Exchange Rate Mechanism (ERM) in 1992, before starting another steep rise in the late 1990s.[2] This was induced partly by UK interest being higher than those prevailing elsewhere,[3] but mainly because of changes in policy which enabled UK assets – particularly shares in existing businesses – to be purchased by foreign interests to a degree which prevailed

Figure 6.1: Chained real effective exchange rates

Sources: *International Financial Statistics Yearbooks 1989* (UK page 717), 2000 (UK page 981, China page 344-5), 2004 (UK page 651, China page 236) and 2015 (UK page 833, China page 246): IMF, Washington DC. Based in all cases on Relative Unit Labour Costs.

nowhere else in the world. Between 2000 and 2010, net sales of portfolio assets alone, excluding all direct investment in buildings and machinery which contributed directly to the health of the UK economy, came to £615bn[4] – equivalent to about half annual GDP at the time. The result was a further very large increase in the strength of sterling, peaking in 2008.

The rate fell between 2007 and 2009 by about 25% – from roughly $2.00 to the pound to $1.50 – but since then, at least up to the 2016 EU referendum, the rate had been slowly climbing back again. In 2009 the IMF real effective exchange rate index for the UK stood at 93.3. By 2015 it was 114.3, an increase of 22%.[5] As of the end of 2016, it was back to about where it had been in 2010[6] – still much too high for most low- and medium-tech manufacturing in the UK to be viable.

On the other side of the world, in China, the exchange rate regime has been completely different. When China joined the trading world around 1980 both wages and productivity were very low. China thus initially had a very weak exporting sector but with huge potential if it could be made competitive. This goal was very successfully realised as the yuan was devalued in stages from 1.50 to the US dollar in 1980 to 8.62 by 1994.[7] Inflation was higher in China than in the West over this period[8] but nevertheless the nominal devaluation of the yuan combined with the improvements in the way resources were used, particularly labour, as a result of market disciplines being introduced, led to a dramatic reduction in China's real effective exchange rate. The IMF index fell from 367 in 1980 to 147 in 1987 and then on down to 86 where it bottomed out in 1993.[9] As Figure 6.1 shows, the real effective exchange rate for China fell by about 70% between 1980 and the mid-1990s, leaving the Chinese in an extraordinarily competitive position. To a lesser extent, much of Asia followed the Chinese example, especially after the 1997 Asian crisis.[10]

The results were all too predictable. UK manufacturing – and particularly low- and medium-tech activity, which was especially sensitive to international competition – was hit correspondingly hard. It fell as a proportion of GDP from 32% in 1970 to 20% in 1990[11] as swathes of light industry went to the wall, and by 2016, it had fallen to just under 10%.[12] The trade surplus on manufactured goods, which the UK had managed to maintain every year after the end of World War II evaporated in 1983 and there has been a steadily mounting deficit every year since then.[13] The UK's total goods deficit in 2015 was £120bn.[14] The last time that the UK had an overall current balance of payments surplus was in 1985.[15]

In China by contrast, the position was reversed. Manufacturing as a percentage of GDP remained high. It was 32% in 2000 and was still as much as 30% in 2015.[16] Instead of balance of payments deficits, there were surpluses. There was no need for deflationary austerity policies to contain government deficits. The Chinese economy grew at about 10% per annum while productivity – and living standards – rose at an only slightly lower rate because the population was growing only slowly.[17]

By 2015, GDP per head in China was 10.6 times what it had been in 1985. In the UK it rose over this same 30-year period by 65% – reflecting roughly similar performance across the western world.[18] Chinese GDP per head is still well below what it is in Western Europe – estimated in 2015 to be $6,497 compared to $34,405 on

average in the EU[19] and $14,301 in China compared to $41,200 in
the UK on a Purchasing Power Parity basis[20] – but the Chinese
economy, although its rate of growth has slowed during the last
two or three years, is still growing much faster than ours, with
momentous consequences for our relative positions in the world.

Globalisation

Globalisation is by no means a new phenomenon. Measured by
the percentages of GDP involved in exports and imports added
together, taken as a ratio to GDP as a whole, the history of the UK's
exposure to foreign trade is exemplified in Table 6.2.

Table 6.2: Ratio of UK exports plus imports to GDP	
Year	Ratio
1885	66%
1913	63%
1933	31%
1950	24%
1970	44%
2000	68%
2015	58%

Sources: 1885 to 1970 Table UK.1 in *One Hundred Years of Economic Statistics*. New York: Facts on File,
1989. 2000 and 2015 Successive editions of *International Financial Statistics Yearbook*. Washington DC, IMF,
various years.

The UK economy was therefore in 2000 almost exactly as exposed
to foreign trade as it was at the end of the nineteenth century. There
was a very large drop during the inter-war period and then a slow
increase back to pre-World War I conditions up to the period before
the 2008 crash, followed by a significant fall. There are, however,
important trends within these overall figures, which have a heavy
bearing on the extent to which globalisation benefits a large majority
rather than perhaps only a substantial minority of the population
in the UK.

First, the make-up of our exports, as between manufactures,
commodities (particularly oil) and services, and whether we
have had a foreign payment surplus or deficit, has varied
substantially over the last 200 years. Some of these factors have

made a lot of difference to who has benefitted and who has lost out from globalisation. Certainly for all the period from the end of the nineteenth century to the 1980s, except for during the two world wars, the UK had a substantial export surplus on both manufactured goods and services. This was matched by a large deficit on imports of food, beverages, tobacco, raw materials and – later on – by oil, at least until the advent of sources of supply from the North Sea. Nevertheless, throughout this 100-year period, the UK, apart from during the World Wars, had a balance of payments surplus most years.[21]

North Sea oil began to have a significant impact on the UK balance of payments in the early 1980s and peaked contributing 5.2% of GDP to the balance of payments in 1984 before starting a slow decline.[22] Oil revenues, which were treated in the UK as a consumable resource, undoubtedly bore significant responsibility for sterling's strength particularly in the 1980s – in sharp contrast to what happened in Norway. There, oil revenues were used to buy foreign assets through a huge wealth fund, thus providing a strong offset to pushing up the exchange rate, a policy which has served the Norwegians much better than the corresponding stance taken in the UK.[23]

Second, in the nineteenth century the UK roughly broke even on imports and exports of goods and services but had a large net income from abroad UK. We therefore had a substantial current account surplus enabling us to sustain a constant flow of net investment abroad. Since the 1980s, this position has been reversed and the UK has run an increasingly large trade deficit, financed by selling assets and borrowing from overseas. This development, in turn, has been largely responsible for changing our net income from abroad from being a substantial positive figure to being one which is increasingly strongly negative. The overall balance of payments position has also been worsened recently by increasingly large net transfers abroad in the form of net payments to the European Union, remittances abroad mainly from migrants and the UK's aid programmes.[24]

Third, freedom of capital movements has made it much easier for serious imbalances to go on being accumulated without remedial action being taken to contain them. In the nineteenth century, the gold standard regime had at least some inbuilt tendency for foreign payment imbalances to be offset by higher inflation in countries accumulating gold, with the reverse happening in those that were losing it. Nowadays, with no similar countervailing forces in operation, the huge flows of money looking for a home mean that the pressures on deficit countries are much less than they were. The UK can currently go on borrowing at relatively low real rates of interest, supplemented by net sales of assets, to finance without difficulty an adverse foreign payment balance which at times has approached 6% of GDP. Very large imbalances can therefore be sustained for a long time.

Fourth, migration, which took place on a large scale in the nineteenth century, but which slowed down in the twentieth has recently increased again, made much easier by the falling cost of travel and by relatively liberal policies on free movement, at the same time as both economic and political pressures have tended to make more migration take place. Many of the impacts of migration have been positive but others have caused severe problems. In the nineteenth century, most migration was to relatively empty countries, such as the USA, Canada and Australia, whereas nowadays much more of it is to countries which are already densely populated.

Fifth, much more of the world is now involved on a major scale with trade and financial liberalisation than was the case 100 years ago when living standards in areas such as East and South Asia were a small fraction of what they are now.

The impact of globalisation on this scale has undoubtedly had a large number of very positive effects for some areas of the world and for some categories of people. Overall, as a result of the spread of industrialisation and the service economies which it then spawns, the world as a whole is much more prosperous, peaceful, well-fed, clean and healthy than it was 100 years ago. Millions of people, especially in Asia, have been lifted out of extreme poverty. Over almost all of the world, living standards are much higher than they were, although some have increased much more rapidly than others. International trade has brought opportunities for specialisation which have benefitted almost everyone. Diversification has made supplies of essentials such as food much more secure. On the whole, as Richard Cobden proclaimed nearly 200 years ago, trade has promoted peace.[25]

For all its benefits, however, globalisation has also brought substantial problems in train, especially for the countries and regions which have not responded as well as they might have done in the increasingly liberalised international markets which have materialised, because they have had problems competing. This is what has caused problems which have impacted countries in the West much more than those in the East, with huge global implications.

First, lack of competitiveness in the many countries which have suffered from it has led to relatively slow growth in exports, loss of share in world trade, a knock on effect on levels of investment, and a negative impact on the profitability and career attractions of light industry – the key to productivity increases. The balance of payments problems thus generated have then caused governments to rein in expenditure to try to avoid their economies running up still further deficits. As we have seen, the overall outcome has been far slower growth in the West than the East. Between 1970 and 2015, the average rate of growth in GDP in the industrialised West was 2.5% whereas in the Emerging and Developing Countries of Asia it was 6.0%.[26] This means that over this 45-year period the ratio increase in GDP in the West was 210% compared to 1,275% in Asia.[27] Of course, the East started from a much lower base than the West but the example of countries such as Singapore, with an average growth rate of 5.1% between 2000 and 2015[28] and a standard of living now about twice the mean in the UK, $87,100 compared to $42,500 according to CIA rankings,[29] shows that countries can go on growing fast as they get richer provided the right policies are pursued.

Second, the major balance of payments deficits which have been sustained by the countries which have had the largest problems competing with the East have led to a vast accumulation of debts which are unlikely ever to be repaid. Even just servicing them may generate increasingly severe problems, especially if interest rates increase from their current very low level. Despite all the efforts being made to stabilise banks, global debt is still increasing rapidly partly because financial liberalisation has made it all too easy for finance to be created in secondary markets which are much more difficult to control. The situation has been made much worse by the massive sums of money created by the central authorities – the Fed in the USA, the Bank of England in the UK and the European Central Bank in Frankfurt – in the form of Quantitative Easing. It has been used to try to stimulate their flagging economies into more activity, but unfortunately has been more successful at creating asset inflation than sustainable economic growth. The monetary base in the USA increased between 2000 and 2016 by 520% while in the UK it has been much higher still, at a staggering 1,140%.[30] Over this period the increase in money GDP in the USA was 80% and 91% in the UK.[31]

Third, the combination of trade liberalisation with deeply uncompetitive exchange rates for manufactured goods in much of the West, compared with the East, has led to the western world deindustrialising on a huge scale – to a greater extent in the UK than elsewhere but with a marked tendency for manufacturing as a percentage of GDP to fall right across the western world. To be fair, some of this apparent reduction to has been caused by price effects, as manufactured goods have fallen in price compared to services, and partly because the border line between producing goods and then providing services to look after them has blurred the distinction between the two. Nevertheless, after taking account of both these factors, the reduction in the UK from almost a third of GDP coming from manufacturing to just under 10% now is far too marked to be offset by them. Since it is manufacturing – and especially light industry – which more than any other area of the economy, produces increase in output per hour, rising productivity and higher real wages, as well as supplying enough goods to sell to the rest of the world to pay for our imports – the cost of deindustrialisation is very high.

And fourth, the impact of these changes has been very varied for different parts of the country and different people. They have been especially tough for those sections of the population who have lost out by seeing vast numbers of their erstwhile relatively high quality manufacturing jobs disappearing. Globalisation and liberalisation, by contrast, has undoubtedly brought huge benefits to those working in the right parts of the service sector, providing the well-educated metropolitan elites – so conspicuous in successful places such as parts of London and some other cities in the UK – with ideal working and living conditions. Because of their ability to function very successfully in this environment, they have managed to accrue to themselves much of what relatively little growth in GDP there has been. The losers, on the other hand, have been those outside these favoured areas, especially those in our former industrial heartlands. They have seen the good blue collar manufacturing jobs, which they and their forebears used to have, disappearing to the Pacific Rim – or to countries like Germany and Holland on the continent with much stronger manufacturing bases than the UK has – too often to be replaced by low productivity, low paid and relatively insecure service sector jobs. Nor is this a problem just confined to individuals. Whole cities and communities in some areas of the UK now simply do not have enough to sell to the rest of the world to support the living standards to which they are accustomed. They then become increasingly dependent on subsidies and grants from government as their environments and services – starved of funds – slowly deteriorate.

And there is a huge political dimension to what is now happening as a result of the gap which is now so obvious between those who have benefited the most from globalisation and those who have lost out from it. When the crisis hit everyone in 2008, most people turned to their established political leaders to find solutions. Nearly 10 years later, with perhaps half the population in the UK on lower real wages than they received a decade ago, while the rich have got richer and the bankers responsible for the 2008 crash almost all got away unscathed, the worm is turning. The result of the EU referendum in the UK, the election of Donald Trump to the US presidency, and the rise of parties such as the Front National in France, Alternative für Deutschland in Germany, Podemos in Spain, the Five Star Movement in Italy and Syriza in Greece, all have common roots. Although these movements are all different in style and political alignment, all of them are the result of large numbers of people feeling disenfranchised and economically marginalised. Hardly surprisingly, they resent what has happened and they no longer vote for the political leadership which – with some considerable justification – they think has let them down.

The tragedy is that it need not be like this. The reason why globalisation has worked so badly for so many people in the West is not inevitable. It has happened because misaligned exchange rates have allowed the East to become far too competitive compared to the West, thus depriving much too much of the West of industry, growth and hope. This has to change.

Borrowing and lending

To get to grips with the nub of the UK's economic dilemmas, we need to delve deeper into the sectoral imbalances already touched upon in Chapter 5. If the UK economy – or any other one for that matter – is going to be run on a stable and sustainable basis, borrowing and lending both need to be kept within manageable limits. The UK has not done well in this regard and any policy designed to get us on to a reasonably steady and sustainable growth path needs to achieve a much more balanced outcome than we have achieved for a long time.

Two tables are needed to set the scene. Table 6.3a shows the make-up of the balance of payments for the UK for the last decade. It demonstrates a reasonably stable position on the trade balance and on net transfers overseas, combined with an alarming deterioration in our net income from abroad culminating in a very substantial worsening in our overall balance of payments. As a percentage of GDP, this is trending towards an annualised figure for 2016 which, at not far short of £100bn, is about 5% of GDP and clearly far too high to be indefinitely sustainable.

Table 6.3b, which is a shorter version of Table 5.2 in the previous chapter, shows the borrowing and lending done by the four major sectors of the economy – the government, businesses, households and the foreign balance. As a matter of accounting logic, all the deficits and surpluses within these sectors have to sum to zero

	Trade balance	Net income from abroad	Net transfers from abroad	Net totals
Table 6.3a: UK balance of payments breakdown – net figures in £bn				
2006	−36.1	16.5	−12.7	−32.4
2007	−39.9	16.4	−14.0	−37.5
2008	−46.2	5.3	−14.1	−55.0
2009	−34.4	5.4	−15.8	−44.8
2010	−42.6	20.2	−20.7	−43.1
2011	−27.1	19.6	−21.7	−29.1
2012	−37.3	−2.2	−21.9	−61.4
2013	−39.2	−10.3	−26.9	−76.4
2014	−36.2	−23.8	−25.0	−85.0
2015	−29.8	−25.7	−24.7	−80.2
2016 Q1	−8.6	−9.5	−5.5	−23.6
2016 Q2	−7.3	−8.7	−6.0	−22.1
2016 Q3	−13.6	−5.0	−6.9	−23.5
2016 Annualised	−39.3	−36.4	−23.2	−91.4

Source: Time Series Dataset in *Balance of Payments Quarterly Report*. London: ONS, December 2016. ONAS codes are IKBJ, HBOJ, IKBP and HBOP.

because the total of all borrowing has to come to the exact total of all lending.

Total public sector borrowing, having peaked at a very high level immediately after the 2008 crash, is continuing to trend downwards but it is still a very long way from being eliminated. Consumers are becoming more significant borrowers, which partly explains why the government deficit is coming down despite the balance of payments deficit going up. Consumer borrowing, on these figures, is as high now in relation to GDP as it was during the run up to the 2008 crash and may not, therefore, be sustainable at this level. The corporate sector is hoarding cash rather than investing it, reflecting the current low levels of business investment, which badly need to be increased The public sector borrowing requirement is currently running at 3.8% of GDP, corporate lending at 0.4%, consumer borrowing at 0.7% and the balance of payments deficit at 5.2%.[32]

There are several key conclusions which need to be drawn from these figures in addition to those already covered in the previous chapter, showing that it is not possible to reduce the government

Table 6.3b: UK net lending (+) and net borrowing (-) by sector in £bn

Year	Public sector	Corpora- tions	House- holds	Rest of the world	Net Totals
2006	−41.0	24.0	−16.9	33.9	0
2007	−44.2	18.6	−12.1	37.7	0
2008	−76.8	35.0	−12.9	54.8	0
2009	−160.5	65.5	50.6	44.4	0
2010	−150.4	36.3	71.1	43.1	0
2011	−124.6	53.4	41.7	29.5	0
2012	−139.4	41.7	36.2	61.6	0
2013	−99.5	19.0	3.6	76.9	0
2014	−101.7	16.0	0.3	85.4	0
2015	−80.2	−6.5	−2.8	81.3	−4.8
2016 Q1	−16.3	0.2	−2.6	23.1	4.5
2016 Q2	−16.3	1.1	−2.1	22.4	5.1
2016 Q3	−19.5	4.0	−4.9	25.7	5.3
2016 Annualised	−69.4	7.1	−12.7	94.9	19.9

Source: Table I. Net Lending by Sector in ONS Statistical Bulletin – *Quarterly National Accounts 2016 Q3*. London: ONS, June 2016. Figures for 2015 and 2016 are still being reconciled by ONS and the net totals will also be very close to zero when this process is complete.

deficit substantially if there is a large balance of payments deficit, because to a large extent one is the mirror of the other. If this is the case, austerity policies to reduce the government borrowing do not make sense. The only realistic way to bring the government deficit down is to get the balance of payments deficit reduced, bringing us back to the range of policies which need to be implemented for many other reasons too.

There is, nevertheless, a counter-argument which needs to be considered. This is that it is not the UK's current account balance of payments which makes the government need to borrow so much, but that the causation goes the other way. In other words, it is the size of the government deficit which is responsible for the foreign payments position being so badly in the red. If this is the case, then the solution to the balance of payments problem would be to reduce the government deficit – and to do this somehow in a way which was not heavily deflationary.

The problem with this argument is that analysis of what causes the foreign payments deficit does not support it. At least two of the three major components of our balance of payments deficit – our negative net income from abroad and the UK's transfers overseas – would not be significantly changed by any general reduction in the government's deficit. Returns on investment are fixed by the markets and not by the government. Obviously, our overseas transfers – especially those to the EU and on our aid programmes – could be reduced if government policy changed on these specific topics, but this is an argument about the impact of particular policy alterations on government finances rather than a general argument for believing that reductions in the government's deficit per se will improve the foreign payments balance. Our trade deficit – the third major balance of payments co component – would be reduced if the economy was plunged into a sufficiently large recession to reduce our imports significantly – but this is not what the proponents of direct action on the scale of government borrowing have in mind. They do not want a recession. Their problem is that there is no discernible mechanism – while deflationary policies are avoided and while other policies remain broadly the same – to show why raising taxation or reducing expenditure would exercise any positive incidence on either the trade balance, net income from abroad or transfers to other countries.

At the same time, there are a number of other aspects of borrowing and lending which urgently need attention. If we are to get the economy to grow faster, we will need to invest a lot more of our GDP every year in physical assets than the barely 13% which we devote at the moment. The world average is about 25% and in China the ratio is nearly 50%, indicating that we need to get this ratio up to somewhere round at least 20%. At the moment, the savings ratio in the UK is very low – matching the low expenditure on investment – but if the proportion of GDP to be spent on investment is to rise to 20% or more, then about 8% of GDP is going to have to be shifted out of consumption and into investment. How is this to be done, especially if, at the same time, we are faced with doing something about the fact that a nearly 5% balance of payments deficit means that we are already living at a rate well above what we are earning? There are, in fact, three overlapping problems which then have to be confronted.

The first is that, at least as a proportion of GDP, consumption is going to have to fall. If, however, the economy can be made to grow much more rapidly than it has done recently, a relative fall does not have to be an absolute decrease as long as the economy is growing fast enough. As experience both from our own history and that of other countries shows, this is not an impossible condition to fulfil given the right mixture of policies and, in particular, high rates of return from light industry.

The second problem is that to shift an additional 8% or so of GDP out of consumption and into investment is going to entail a large increase in saving. This does not all have to be done by households. It can be spread over consumers, businesses, the government and from the foreign payment balance – probably about 2% each over a transition period. Again, for all the main sectors of the economy, revenues would rise but expenditure on consumption would have to increase more slowly.

The third issue is to ensure that finance is available for all the investment which would be needed. Quantitative Easing (QE) has fed increases in asset prices, leaving banks with a disproportionately large proportion of their total lending being for house purchase whereas where money needs crucially to be plentiful to get the economy to grow is on lending for industrial investment. This strongly suggests that we need to copy what was done in Japan after World War II when the whole of the banking sector was skewed towards lending on very soft terms to industry. On the back of an expanding economy it will then be possible – and important – to make sure that social investment in roads, rail, schools, hospitals and housing expands too.

It will then be possible to move away from QE and ultra-low interest rates. These policies have done something to stop the post 2008 recession being worse than it otherwise might have been but they are not sustainable. The accumulation of more and more debt combined with interest rates which do not provide a fair balance between savers and borrowers are not the way ahead. Sooner or later we will need less debt and higher interest rates, based on higher rates of real investment, more saving and debt ratios rising more slowly than GDP.

Economic imbalances

The UK is the fifth or sixth largest economy in the world.[33] Its population enjoys a living standard which is relatively high compared with much of the rest of the planet, although we have slipped a long way down from the top position which we held in the nineteenth century. According to the World Bank, in 2015 we ranked 13th with GDP per head of $43,902 compared to a world average $10,136.[34] On a Purchasing Power Parity basis, however, we did considerably worse, in 25th position, with GDP per head of $41,499 compared to $15,536 for the world as a whole.[35]

As we have seen, however, most of the rest of the world has growing much faster than us and, on present trends, this is likely to continue. There are therefore major causes for concern about our future prospects, if we continue as we are, while some of the trends in the economy are clearly unsustainable. Taking stock of where we are now and in the light of our economic history and all the trends which it exhibits, and drawing together comments made in previous chapters, what – has gone wrong and what needs to be corrected?

Investment

Ever since the beginning of the Industrial Revolution two and a half centuries ago, living standards in the UK – and elsewhere – have risen very largely as a result of investment in capital assets, particularly industrial plant and equipment. It is this investment more than any other that increases output per head and therefore living standards. The UK's problem is that this process of capital accumulation has now ground almost totally to a halt. Instead of investing in our future, we consume much too high a proportion of our national income – and that trend is getting worse. In 2008, the ratio of gross domestic investment to GDP in the UK, measured by the Office for National Statistics (ONS) in the way which was standard until it was recently changed to include intellectual property,[36] was just 16.7%, already far below the world average; but by 2016 it had fallen even further to a disastrous 12.7%.[37] That compares with an international average in 2014 of 25.7%, while the figure for China was 46.0%.[38]

Further international comparisons show how badly the UK performs measured by this crucial yardstick. A recent survey, based on 2012 data, ranked the UK at number 142 – equal with El Salvador – out of the 154 countries rated on how much each devoted to investment as a percentage of GDP.[39] Worse, however, is to come. To calculate how much we are really investing in our future it is necessary to deduct depreciation, otherwise known as capital consumption, from the gross domestic investment figure to produce a net rather than a gross figure. In 2015, this measure of depreciation of existing capital assets, including intellectual property, was running in the UK at 13.0% of GDP,[40] compared to a gross figure of 17.3%,[41] meaning that, on the widest and most generous interpretation, what we invest in our future is now on a net basis no more than 4.3% of GDP.

Even this figure, however, makes no allowance for the fact that the UK's population is growing by about 500,000 a year, taking into account both the indigenous birth rate and net immigration.[42] If the total fixed assets in the UK, estimated in 2015 by the Office for National Statistics to have a replacement value of £9.09trn,[43] is divided by the 65.1m mid-year population that year,[44] we arrive at a figure of about £140,000 of accumulated assets for each UK resident. Just to keep up with the UK's rising population, therefore, requires annual new investment of about 500,000 x £140,000, producing a total of £70bn. This is barely as high as the total new investment, net of depreciation, that was actually achieved, which in 2015 amounted to £80bn.[45] On this calculation, there is now almost no net new investment per head of the population taking place in the UK at all.

This failure to invest goes a long way towards explaining the fact that productivity increases in the UK, stalled after the 2008 crash and have only very slowly recovered since 2013. Over the whole period between 2007 and 2015, the UK economy grew by 7.4%[46] while the population has increased by 5.8%.[47] Over this eight-year period, therefore, output per head only went up by 1.5%. The increase in GDP which we are currently seeing is not therefore mostly the product of increased productivity. It is the result of slightly increased demand and our growing population pulling more people into the labour force – better than nothing in the short term, but no substitute for significantly growing output per head.

The bald fact is that our economy is clearly incapable of sustainable growth if there is almost no investment to support it. We therefore need urgently to lift the proportion of our GDP applied to investment from its current level to at least somewhere near the 26%[48] world average – an increase whose size demonstrates just how serious are the imbalances which currently handicap our economic performance.

Manufacturing

Manufacturing, as our economic history shows all too clearly, has a key role to play in the economy in three vitally important respects. One is that productivity increases are very much easier to achieve with the plant and equipment which typify manufacturing operations than it is almost anywhere else in the economy; no other form of economic activity does as much to stimulate incremental and continual innovation. Even in the UK economy, where the environment for manufacturing has been so adverse, as Table 1.2b shows, just under a quarter of the total increase in UK value added between 1990 and 2015 came from manufacturing, even as manufacturing gross value added fell over the same period from 15.3% of GDP to just 9.7%. A further 15% came from Information and Communications, whose contribution to GDP rose from 3.1 % to 6.3% as a result of investment in similarly productivity-enhancing assets. The contribution of the remaining 62% of value added over the period required all of the remaining 84% of economic activity.

A second key contribution made by manufacturing is the provision of higher-quality blue-collar jobs of the kind that services have never managed to generate in sufficient quantities. The collapse in the number of manufacturing jobs in the UK – down from 4.2m in 1997 to 2.6m in 2015[49] – has had a major impact on employment prospects and income per head throughout the regions where industry used to be strong. This is a major reason why the North East, one of the poorest regions in the UK, achieved gross value added per head in 2015 of only £18,927, compared to

£43,629 in London and a national average of £25,601.[50]

The hollowing out of high-quality manufacturing jobs has also contributed heavily to widening socio-economic inequality. In the mid-1970s, the Gini coefficient, which measures income inequality (with 0 representing complete equality and 100 where one person gets everything), was just over 23 for the UK, after allowing for taxes and transfers. At the beginning of 2015, it had risen to 34.[51] Comparable figures, recorded from the late 2000s, are 26 for Sweden, 38 for the USA and 48 for Mexico.[52]

Perhaps the greatest significance of manufacturing, however, is the vital part it plays in generating export earnings. Despite the decline in UK manufacturing, it remains the case that about 56% of all our exports are goods rather than services[53] and 80% of all our visible exports are manufactured goods of one sort or another.[54] The current weakness of manufacturing means that our exports are lower than they must be if we are to pay for all the imports we want or need to buy. Perennial balance of payments deficits are the consequence.

In 1972, 32% of the UK's GDP came from manufacturing.[55] By 1997, the percentage was down to 14.5% and by 2016 it had dropped to just under 10%, compared to about 21% in Germany and 19% in Japan.[56] This is why our record on exporting, which depends heavily on manufactures, has been correspondingly so poor, reflected in both our lower share of world trade and our balance of payments difficulties. In 1950, our share of world trade was 10.7%, but by 2014 it had shrunk by nearly three quarters to 2.9%.[57] Because manufacturing is so strong an element in increased productivity, the money value of its output – computers being a striking case in point – tends relatively to decline, even while the volume of manufactured products increases. But while manufacturing tends therefore – even in a successful manufacturing economy – to account for a lower percentage of GDP than it does in an emerging economy, international comparisons show that if it sinks below about 15% of GDP, foreign payments deficits are the virtually unavoidable consequence.

The balance of payments

Our overall balance of payments record tells a similar story. The last time we had a visible surplus was in 1982 and we have not had an overall surplus since 1985.[58] While the UK has done relatively very well on exports of services, on which we have a substantial and important competitive advantage, generating a surplus in 2015 of £90bn, this excellent result was overshadowed by a much larger deficit of £120bn on goods, producing an overall trade deficit that year of £30bn.[59] In 2015 we had a deficit of almost £84bn just on manufactures alone.[60]

The net trade deficit contributed to a total balance of payments deficit in 2015 of £80bn, accounted for by adding net transfers abroad of £25bn and net income paid abroad of £26bn.[61] The UK's trade deficit, although a negative drag on the economy every year, may not on its own be a large concern, but when the other two major components are taken into account, we arrive at an unmanageably large total, and one which is trending strongly in the wrong direction. In 2014 the total balance of payments deficit as a percentage of GDP was 4.7% and 4.4% in 2015[62] – one of the highest ratios in the whole of the developed world and on a potentially unsustainable rising trend. Extrapolating from the latest ONS figures, the total deficit for 2016 may well be close to £100bn.[63] Viewed against this background, what are the prospects looking further ahead for each of the components of that total deficit?

Of the three major elements in net transfers abroad, the largest is our net contribution to the European Union, which totalled £11.0bn in 2015.[64] The UK's payments to the EU are on a rising trend and the Office for Budget Responsibility (OBR) expects our net contribution to rise by another £10bn over the period 2013 to 2018,[65] a figure which Brexit is unlikely to reduce for some time. Other government transfers, mainly aid payments, amount to a net £8bn, with a further £7bn mostly made up of remittances sent abroad by immigrants to support their families abroad. Net transfers have steadily risen in recent years. They were £10bn in 2003, £14bn by 2008 and by 2015 they had reached £25bn.[66] It seems likely that this upward trend will continue.

The UK's net income from abroad in recent years has exhibited a rather more erratic pattern than the figures for net transfers but again – unfortunately – the figures are again moving strongly in the wrong direction. During the 2000s, the net income per year earned by the UK averaged about £17bn, but since 2011, when the figure was a positive £23bn, there has been a very sharp deterioration to a deficit of £24bn in 2014 and of £26bn in 2015.[67] Part of the reason for this huge swing must have been the loss of profit flows as a result of the enormous net sales of UK portfolio assets which have taken place over the past decade and a half. Over the period 2000 to 2010 alone, net sales of UK shares, bonds and property came to a total of £615bn[68] – equivalent to almost half our annual GDP at the time.[69] It may be that the fall in the value of sterling after the EU referendum will reduce the scale of our negative net income from abroad, however, and a further reduction in sterling's parity would clearly help in this regard.

The change from the UK having a substantial net income from abroad to the reverse has had a very material impact on UK living standards. GDP measures all the output produced in the UK but not who benefits from it. Gross national income (GNI), which is the aggregate of all UK incomes, does. If this GNI component goes from positive £20bn a year to negative £30bn, this means that UK total incomes have gone down, in relation to what they would otherwise have been, by £50bn per annum – or nearly 2.5% of GDP. Set against the slow increase in UK GDP we have seen in recent years, this is a very significant figure.

All of this means that our long-standing trade deficit on goods is only partially offset by the better figures on services, while the overall trade deficit position is heavily undermined by major further deficits on both transfers and net income from abroad, neither of which looks like diminishing and both of which may well increase further. To finance these deficits, we have either to borrow from abroad, adding to the interest charges we have to pay, or we have to sell UK assets to foreign interests, foregoing the returns on them and increasing our foreign income deficit. We have done both. There is, however, obviously a limit to how long we can go on running up deficits and debts, with little or no growth in prospect, before our creditors lose confidence and may demand higher interest rates and deflation to bring the position back under control. It is therefore essential that we take immediate and effective action to prevent the current balance of payments deficit from continuing to operate as a very serious constraint on the UK's economic prospects.

Debt

Ever since the dawn of economic history, borrowing and debt have been unavoidable features of economic activity, oiling the wheels of both commerce and government. Provided debtors are in a position to service their borrowings and to retain the confidence of their creditors, debt is not a problem. Difficulties start to materialise only when these conditions are no longer met and creditors start to doubt the creditworthiness of the borrowers. For both governments and countries, the danger point arises when debt is accumulating faster than the capacity to service and repay it – in other words when the rate at which debt is rising as a percentage of GDP is higher than the growth rate.

For the period between 1945 and 2008, UK governments succeeded in generating the occasional surplus, while for most years there were modest deficits. As a ratio to GDP, peak deficits were reached in 1975 at 1.7% of GDP, in 1983 at 2.5% but at 7.0% in 1993.[70] In 1945, as the UK emerged from World War II, total government debt was about 240% of GDP[71] but by the early 2000s it had fallen to a little under 40%[72] as a result of inflation eroding away the value of the capital sum and economic growth increasing the size of the economy. It then rose slowly to 43% by 2007 before climbing very steeply as the financial crisis broke in 2008. By 2014, gross government debt was 87.5% of GDP[73] and still increasing fast – by about 2% of GDP per annum, this being the difference between the government deficit as a percentage of GDP and a combination of the rate of inflation and the rate of growth.

The big differences between the earlier years and the recent period since 2008, therefore, are first, that inflation has recently been relatively low, averaging about 2.6%;[74] second, that government deficits have been very high – 11.4% in 2009, 10.0% in 2010, falling to 4.4% in 2015[75] – and third, and perhaps most importantly, that there has been relatively very little growth.

Asset inflation

Both of the two main indices of inflation – the CPI which measures prices in the market sector of the economy, and the ONS deflator, which takes account of price and cost movements in the public as well as the private sector – have recently been relatively subdued. Between 2008 and 2015, the CPI rose by an average of 2.0% per annum[76] and the deflator by 2.6%.[77]

Over this period, however, the prices of assets – especially housing, and shares as registered by the FTSE 100 index – have been far more volatile. After the long boom in asset prices during the early 2000s, average house prices in the UK rose by a further 15.6% between the end of 2005 and 2007, fell 16.2% in 2008, continued to fall slowly until 2012 but then started to rise sharply in 2013.[78] By the third quarter of 2016 they were 20% higher than they had been three years earlier while in Greater London, house prices followed the same pattern but with much sharper rises – by just over 40% over the same three years.[79]

These figures mean that house prices have been rising much faster than incomes, increasing 126% between 2001 and 2015 nationally and 180%[80] in London while average earnings rose only about 50% over the same period.[81] The banks' preference for lending on mortgages rather than for productive investment and the failure to restrain that lending with all its inflationary consequences have meant that there is now an unacceptably unbalanced relationship between average incomes and average houses prices. Home ownership has, in consequence, become the preserve only of those with well above average incomes or of people who already owned a house when the ratio was smaller. This is especially true in London where houses prices have soared at the fastest rate in 14 years to an average price at the end of 2016 of some £470,000.[82] We are seeing the emergence of an older generation that is asset-rich and a young generation that is asset-poor.

Share prices have been even more erratic. The FTSE 100 index peaked at 6,722 in October 2007. It then fell to 3,830 in February 2009 before recovering sharply to 5,909 by March 2010, since when it has climbed fairly steadily. It stood at just over 7,000 in December 2016. Bearing in mind the unsustainable increase in asset prices that preceded the crisis which broke in 2008, it is probably not unfair to suggest that the asset valuations in 2009 were a good deal more realistic than some of those seen since.

The recent sharp increases in the value of both houses and shares have much more to do with current very lax monetary policies and the banks' predilection for lending for essentially financial transactions than it has with any sustainable trend increase in their underlying value, although shortages are no doubt also a major factor in the case of housing. It is, however, the increase in these asset values which underpins a large proportion of the present 'feel good' factor, which in turn is responsible, through boosting consumer demand, for the increase in GDP. While housing and shares might hold their current value for a time, thus continuing to encourage consumer confidence, this does not provide by itself a secure basis for our economic future.

Overall, therefore, the prospects for the coming years look bleak. Without a radical change in policies, we could very easily follow the Japanese pattern from 1990 onwards with one decade of stagnation following another.[83] We have steadily lost ground economically vis-à-vis the rest of the world ever since the end of World War II. We badly need to do better.

The response from academia

Bearing in mind how crucial it is that economic policies are rational, well founded in terms of logical coherence, firmly grounded in history and fact and capable of guiding economic strategy successfully, the role which academic economics has played as history has unfolded needs some examination. The record has been very mixed. In particular, neither between the wars when the slump precipitated the events leading up to World War II, nor more recently as the West has stagnated – two really seminal economic events – has the academic world united round any persuasive prescriptions about how to make our economies perform better. Not only has there been no consensus but views among professional economists diverge now perhaps more than they have ever done, reflecting the long and chequered history of changing fashions in ideas about economic theory and practice.

The Wealth of Nations, written by Adam Smith and published in 1776, gave the world its first comprehensive overview on how the Industrial Revolution was shaping the economic future. Its really big achievement was to show the irrationality of mercantilist policies based on accumulating pecuniary assets and to point out that true wealth came from the production of goods and services and not the accumulation of bullion. Adam Smith was followed by three key political economists, Thomas Malthus, David Ricardo and Jean-Baptiste Say (1767-1832), each of whom produced seminal ideas which unfortunately turned out not be correct but which led economics in unhelpful directions. Malthus predicted that it would never be possible to increase working class living standards because rising populations would always expand at a rate which would press so hard on the supply of food and other necessities that subsistence living standards would never be alleviated. Ricardo expanded on the Labour Theory of Value developed by Adam Smith, reinforcing the pessimistic view of the future taken by almost all early economists, who completely failed to foresee the possibility of the exponential increases in productivity which actually materialised. Say propounded the law named after him which claimed that there could never be more serious economic downturns that those involving frictional unemployment and temporarily underused resources because the payments for all the goods and services which were being produced would always generate sufficient demand to keep resources essentially fully employed.

These ideas had a very powerful impact on the way in which economic policy developed in the nineteenth century. If there was no hope of raising living standards among most of the working population and the economy was as self-regulating as Say said it was, even relatively activist economists such as John Stuart Mill

(1806-1873) were unable to move policy away from the state taking a minimalist role, leaving economics to become a discipline which described what was happening rather than prescribing what should be done. There were exceptions, such as the drive for free trade, promulgated by Richard Cobden (1804-1865), and Karl Marx (1818-1883) whose aim was not to improve the performance of capitalism but to overthrow it, but the main impetus was towards building a corpus of ideas, turning economics into a quasi-scientific subject based on micro-economic analysis. Its capstone was the marginal revolution, propounded more or less contemporaneously by Auguste Walras (1801-1877), William Stanley Jevons (1835-1882) and Karl Menger (1840-1921), which replaced the Labour Theory of Value as the accepted way in which prices and value were determined by general equilibrium between supply and demand.

With this quietist approach underlying most economic thinking, it is not altogether surprising that, once the relative world economic stability was upturned by World War I, disastrous policy mistakes were made round the treatment of Germany at the Versailles Conference and subsequently more widely as the Great Depression set in. With the exception of John Maynard Keynes (1883-1946) and his associates, the economic profession had little of any value to say about what had gone wrong and what to do to get the world economy to function without the huge waste of resources generated by the slump. The really major change in approach spearheaded by Keynes was the realisation that Say's law was not correct, that it was entirely possible that economies could suffer prolonged periods of lack of demand if savings intentions exceeded investment plans, and that there was vital role for the state in ensuring that full employment and the maximum use of resources were maintained.

It was the Keynesian revolution which underpinned the enormous success achieved by the West during the quarter of a century after the conclusion of World War II, with its example spreading throughout the world. By the 1970s, however, the post-War settlement based essentially on free trade but limited capital movements, was being undermined by a combination of inflationary pressures, weaknesses caused by the US economy becoming overstretched and asymmetry between the treatment of surplus and deficit countries. Those with surpluses were under no pressure to take any remedial action while those – such as the UK – with perennial balance of payments weakness – were forced to deflate. In 1971 the USA removed the link between the dollar and gold.

The explosion in the money supply which followed, exacerbated by the Yom Kippur War, triggered a huge increase in inflation and over a short period Keynesianism was replaced by monetarism with Milton Friedman (1912-2006) as its leading proponent. The monetarists, harking back to traditions on hard money going back to the nineteenth century, believed that inflation was caused exclusively by increases in the money supply and that by constricting the money supply, inflation could be controlled within tight limits. Within a short period most countries, particularly in the West and most conspicuously the USA and the UK raised interest rates to previously unheard of rates with measurements of the money supply being the talisman by which policy was determined.

As explained in Chapter 4, in fact the link between the money supply and inflation proved to be much weaker and less reliable than monetarists claimed it would be, but the notion that controlling inflation was the target to which economic policy should give primacy was retained. Monetarism morphed into neo-liberalism which in turn spun off ever more complex mathematically driven theories about how markets worked, all justifying deregulation, liberalisation and the notion that markets should as far as possible be left alone. These were all approaches to economic policy which commended themselves strongly to the social and political elites who were becoming ever more powerful and influential. It was in this intellectual climate that theories such as the Efficient Market Hypothesis, which claimed that share prices always incorporated and reflected all relevant information, flourished and discouraged external interference and control. On the international front, the Washington Consensus, championed by the IMF, held that the policy solution for economies with financial crises was privatisation and deregulation.[84] When the 2008 crash materialised, however, the weakness of 'the market knows best' polices became all too apparent and economic strategy became increasingly pragmatic and less guided by any over-arching view, with guidance from economic theory from professional economists becoming conspicuously less influential.

In the meantime, those opposed to neo-liberalism produced a proliferation of varying critiques of what was still broadly the mainstream approach.[85] Pragmatists' major concern has been to make sense of the crisis as it unfolded and to take whatever practical actions seemed most appropriate in the short term to stabilise the situation, focusing on the need for regulatory reform to prevent future financial melt downs. Market fundamentalists believe that government intervention was the major cause of the crisis, including maintaining low interest rates for much too long, thus fuelling housing booms, followed by supposedly misguided policies to bail out banks. Institutionalists blame liberalisation, deregulation and poor regulation as being the major factors which caused insufficient action to be taken to curb the perennial tendency for booms to generate themselves in the housing and banking sectors, allowing financial innovation to run riot. Keynesian collectivists, by contrast, tend to argue that the problem is one of demand deficiency and falling consumption, as a result of loss of household wealth, leaving only the government to fill the demand gap. Structuralists see the fundamental cause of the West's present malaise in widening inequality, which prompted governments to augment stagnant incomes by tolerating excessive borrowing both by consumers and the state. While there may be elements of truth in all these points of view, it is striking that almost none of their adherents attach much significance to exchange rates, which are almost never mentioned in the literature they have produced. Hardly surprisingly, therefore, their proposals seldom – if ever – claim to provide coherent, comprehensive and realistic programmes for getting the West's economies to grow fast and sustainably enough to reduce unemployment and inequality and to generate a significant increase in living standards.

The reality is that economics is not a scientific subject like physics, with large numbers of reliable causes and consequences which can be validated by replicable experiments. It is much more like history – with one thing happening after another, often without any very clearly discernible patterns. All the efforts which have been made to turn economics into a system of axioms and precepts from which universal conclusions can safely be drawn have proved to fall well short of being really convincing and indeed the whole process has been attacked as being unsound even within its own parameters.[86]

Instead, it is much better to recognise the limitations from which economics suffers. It is not a study of objective facts and chains of causation. To a much greater extent it has become a systemised way of providing common-sense signposts for muddling through, taking account of the extent to which economics has become a battleground for doctrines which favour one interest group or another. Because economics has been able to masquerade as being scientific, it has provided cover for the fact that its precepts have been subject to a huge amount of pressure from the rich and powerful, who have been very good at bending economic conventional wisdom in directions which suits them best, not least by funding think tanks, newspapers and academic posts to advocate views which they find congenial.

Nowhere is this truer than in relation to exchange rate policy. Those who make and sell things have an interest in a low and competitive exchange rate while those who make their living in finance derive no such benefit – at least in the short term. The City – and the Bank of England – has always tended to want to see sterling as strong as possible because they believe that a high exchange rate bears down on inflation and that it gives them more international financial leverage. It is because the UK, and the USA, have such concentrations of political and social power in finance rather than industry that their views on economic policy and the supposed benefits of a strong currency are so widely accepted. This is in sharp contrast to the position in countries such as Germany and Japan, which have much stronger industrial bodies than we do in the UK to make the case for keeping manufacturing competitive.

The contribution by academic economics to economic progress has been patchy at best and sometimes counter-productive. It needs to do better than this.

7

Competitiveness

The central case which this book sets out is that, for any country, maintaining an exchange rate which enables it to compete successfully in our more and more globalised and liberalised world economy is much more important than is often realised both by economists, politicians, the commentariat and public opinion. Neglecting its importance as a critically significant variable – as has happened particularly strongly in the UK – has been both puzzling and extremely damaging. How and why has this come about, and why is it so important for us to have as much focus on exchange rate policy as we do to managing our fiscal and monetary affairs?

During the period of fixed exchange rates, up to the breakdown of the Bretton Woods system in 1971, the pressure which sterling might be under on the foreign exchanges was a matter of constant preoccupation. Once floating rates came into play, however, as essentially they have done for the last 45 years, interest in the exchange rate evaporated. It became a residual in the UK, blown hither and thither largely by market sentiment, with a general bias towards keeping it as strong as possible, both to bear down on inflation and because substantial sections of the population always favoured a strong pound. The City has always tended to like a high exchange rate because of the additional leverage it provides in dealing with foreign transactions. The sizable percentage of the population who holiday abroad strongly favour the currency strength which makes vacations overseas seem cheaper and better value for money. Savers have tended to benefit – at least in the short term – from the higher interest rates which are associated with an over-valued currency. Furthermore, policymakers and public opinion, supported by both the Bank of England and The Treasury, appear firmly to believe – despite the lack of evidence to support their view – that a strong pound bears down on inflation and that loss of output thus caused is a price worth paying for lower price increase.

These reasons have been buttressed both by concerns about whether the value of sterling on the foreign exchanges could really be changed substantially by government policy and by worries about whether a lower pound would actually do any good. The consequence has been that the UK has had no policy for one of the most powerful influences on the performance of the economy for almost all of the last four and a half decades, other than a general proclivity for favouring it being high rather than low. The impact of this insouciance – reflecting a lack of appreciation as to what the impact of the exchange rate is on economic performance going back to the beginning of the Industrial Revolution 250 years ago – has been enormous. It has not only been very damaging but unnecessarily so, had better knowledge and understanding as to what was involved been part of the conventional wisdom. In varying degrees this perception applies to the whole of the western world while many of the countries elsewhere, particularly along the Pacific Rim, have taken a contrary view and have prospered as a result well beyond the dreams of what was believed in the West to be feasible.

This is why the exchange rate so important. It is because it has an enormous influence not only on the economic performance of any country which gets it wrong but also because of the huge political implications which follow on. The immediately obvious impact that an over-valued currency has is that the trade balance suffers and that there is a chronic tendency for imports to exceed exports, reflected in a worsening of the government's fiscal position, both pointing towards the apparent need for deflationary policies. The consequent tendency for the economy to slow down reinforces the tendency for investment in manufacturing industries to fall away as the prospect of profitable investment in both home and export markets declines. As light industry, in particular suffers and goes down as a percentage of GDP, major opportunities for the type of investment – mechanisation and the application of technology which tradable manufacturing pre-eminently provides – evaporate, productivity fails to increase and real wages stagnate. Because, in these circumstances, this vital sector of the economy struggles to produce profitability it also fails to attract the most talented people to make a career in making and selling products rather than going into financial services, the media, academic life or any of the other occupations which enjoy nowadays a much higher social status than manufacturing industry. Hardly surprisingly, then the quality of management goes down making a bad situation worse.

These are the immediate economic implications but there are profound political consequences too both externally and internally. As the economy's performance, reflected in its growth rate, weakens in relation to others in the world, its country's status, influence and capacity to secure its future, all diminish. Both hard military power and softer capacity to influence by example decline – and national self-confidence wanes. Internally, slow growth tends to accentuate the tendency for income, wealth and life chances to become more and more unevenly distributed. In a country like the UK, with a long – if now diminished – industrial history, it has produced enormous regional imbalances. Combining trade liberalisation with too high an exchange rate tends to accentuate inequality strongly by favouring those who have done well out of the opportunities which globalisation has produced but at the expense of the large percentage of the population which has done badly out of globalisation as they have seen far too many good manufacturing jobs disappearing to the Far East and elsewhere. The result, as we have seen, is the widespread discontent among those who feel left out, exemplified in the Brexit vote in the UK in June 2016, the election of Donald Trump to the presidency of the USA in November of the same year, and the increasing voter appeal, power and influence of populist parties all over continental Europe.

So the exchange rate is not a matter of minor importance, to be left to the markets to determine, with a bit of help from the Bank of England to keep it as high as possible. On the contrary, as a policy instrument, it is as important as fiscal policy is in keeping the government's finances in reasonable order and the economy fully employed. It is as crucial as monetary policy is in determining interest rates and regulating the relationship between borrowers and lenders. The exchange rate is the key metric which has a very large influence on all our commercial and financial relationships with foreign countries and the more liberalisation there is, the more transactions there are and the more critically important it becomes. For a variety of reasons, most – although not all – of the western world seems to have lost the plot. The Eurozone has tied itself into inter-country relationships through the establishment of the Single Currency which have made exchange rate changes impossible within the system, with all the baleful effect described above clearly manifest especially in the weaker Eurozone countries. The USA controls the world's reserve currency, and this plus the sheer size of the US economy make it much more difficult than it would otherwise be to opt for an activist exchange rate policy. To a large extent, however, the UK suffers from none of these constraints. This may provide us with a unique opportunity.

History recapitulated

Looking back of the UK's economic history, it is obvious just how important the prevailing preconceptions about monetary policy have been in shaping the way in which events have unfolded, especially since the Industrial Revolution began and trade began to depend on manufactured goods rather than on commodities or raw materials. This switch made a huge difference. Whereas sellers for commodities and raw materials are up against world prices set by supply and demand, and are therefore price-takers, those selling manufactures are much more inclined to be price-makers. This is because they are dealing in more variegated products, usually with both close substitutes and significant economies of scale in their production, with all the scope this provides for battling for increased sales and using price competitiveness to gain market share

At the start of the nineteenth century, Britain was indeed the Workshop of the World. For many decades the UK led the world in industrialisation, with manufactured exports exceeding imports by a wide margin. The British economy never achieved a significant overall visible trade surpluses during the whole of the nineteenth century, however, because of the scale of its imports of food and raw materials. The statistics from the early part of the century are relatively sparse and incomplete but by about 1870, when more reliable figures become available, the UK clearly had a significant overall deficit in goods offset by a substantial surplus on both export of services, such as shipping and insurance, and on net income from investments overseas. The figures for 1885, for example, show visible exports of £272m against imports of £341m, a deficit of £69m, while services contributed £91m in exports compared to £29m in imports, a surplus of £62m. Within these totals, exports of manufactures were £188m against imports of £59m, providing a healthy overall surplus in manufactured goods of £129m.[1] With net income from abroad running at £70m, there was a £62m[2] net overall surplus which was invested abroad. The UK had an overall balance of payments surplus along these lines each year throughout almost all of the nineteenth century, enabling a continuous accumulation of net assets overseas.

While the performance of the UK economy during this period was, therefore, in many ways impressive, its weakness was the slowdown in its rate with compared to its competitors, becoming more apparent as decades went by. Having been the fastest growing major economy in Europe between 1820 and 1870, as the table below shows, Britain was the slowest – apart from France – between 1870 and 1913.

Table 7.1: Ratio increases in GDP 1820-1913 in selected western countries:		
	1820-1870	1870-1913
France	1.27	1.63
Germany	2.01	2.83
Italy	1.24	1.94
Netherlands	1.70	2.16
UK	2.05	1.90
West Europe Average	1.71	2.14
USA	4.20	3.94

Source: Table A1-e, page 187, in *The World Economy: A Millennial Perspective* by Angus Maddison: Paris, OECD, 2001

What went wrong was that British exports, although they started from a relatively high level, as a result of our Industrial Revolution first mover advantage, grew relatively slowly throughout the nineteenth century as other countries' share of world trade grew at our expense. The fundamental reason why this happened was the familiar process which occurs when any economy has a relatively high exchange rate compared with its competitors. Exporting was difficult and unprofitable, investment was discouraged, management talent went to other economic activities and the growth rate slowed up.

The reason why the UK was in this position is that, for the reasons described in Chapter 1, the UK did not begin the Industrial Revolution with a particularly competitive exchange rate. This position was then made substantially worse by the outcome of the High Price of Gold Bullion report, produced at the end of the Napoleonic Wars, which locked the UK into a still less competitive value for the pound. This in turn got subsumed into the gold standard regime as the nineteenth century wore on, making it in practice impossible to change to a more competitive level, even if the desire to do so had been present, which it was not. On the contrary, the abolition of duties by the UK at the same time as our competitors were raising tariffs against our exports effectively amounted to a revaluation of sterling – making UK sales abroad more difficult and importing easier. As a result of these policies, whereas in 1850 GDP per head was about half in the rest of western Europe what it was in the UK by the outbreak of World War this gap had narrowed to about a quarter.[3]

World War I was hugely disruptive to the pre-war roughly competitive equilibrium. Between 1913 and 1920, the price level in the UK grew to 250% of its former level[4] compared to 175% in the USA.[5] Notwithstanding this, the Cunliffe Committee recommended that the pre-war parity of $4.86 to the pound should be re-established. The consequent downward pressure on wages and prices lead to the wasted 1920s during which the British economy stagnated. UK real GDP was actually slightly lower in 1931 than it had been in 1919. The devaluation in 1931, however, made a massive difference. By 1938, the economy had grown by

21% compared to 1931,[6] although by 1938, all the competitive advantage which had been secured at the beginning of the decade had disappeared. This was the result of devaluations elsewhere with which the British authorities acquiesced without making any effort to main the competitive conditions which had made so much difference earlier in the decade.

Inflation in the UK was handled much better during World War II than during World War I, with a rise between 1938 and 1946 of no more than just over 50%,[7] although the USA did better with an increase of only 40%.[8] Nevertheless, once again the UK authorities tried to maintain the same exchange rate (£1.00 = $4.03) as had prevailed in 1940 at the start of the war when hostilities finished despite the huge extent to which the UK foreign investment position had been weakened during the war, on top of the UK's extra inflation compared to the USA.[9] This led to the 1949 devaluation to $2.80, which went a considerable way to resolving the UK's imbalance in its dollar trade but not nearly enough to combat the rising competitiveness of our continental competitors, most of whom also devalued in 1949 – unnecessarily in the light of their rapidly emerging competitiveness – at the same time as the UK.

The next 20 years, between 1950 and 1970 therefore saw the UK once more back in the same condition as had prevailed during the nineteenth century and in even more accentuated form in the 1920s. UK prices were uncompetitive on world markets. The UK's share of world trade gradually decreased – from 11.1% in 1950 to 9.3% in 1960 and 6.9% in 1970.[10] Balance of payments problems added deflation to the lack of stimulus to the economy from export led growth, leading to the economy growing more slowly than those of our competitors. Between 1950 and 1970 the German economy expanded to 3.4 times its 1950 size, France by a factor of 2.7 and Italy 3.2. The UK achieved a ratio of 1.7 while the USA chalked up 2.1 and Japan 6.3.[11]

The UK was not therefore in the best of shape to weather the problems inflicted on the world when the Bretton Woods system broke up in 1971 and the consequent monetary expansion, accentuated by oil price hikes, led to much higher levels of inflation in the 1970s. It was the monetarist policies adopted by most of the

West from the late 1970s onwards to deal with inflation – with almost no regard being paid to their competitiveness consequences – however, which did the real damage. The UK's exchange rate against all currencies rose between 1977 and 1981 by almost 60% as the UK interest base rate averaged over 15% for the whole of 1980.[12] Over the next two decades the proportion of UK GDP coming from manufacturing declined by over a third – from 32% in 1970 to 20% in 1990.[13] The decline slowed after we came out of the Exchange Rate Mechanism in 1992, triggering a weighted devaluation of about 14%,[14] but accelerated again as, towards the end of the 1990s, the exchange rate soared once more, rising from an average of about $1.50 during the first half of the decade to an average of almost $2.00 to the pound for the mid-2000s.[15] Price-sensitive tradable manufacturing reeled again as manufacturing as a percentage of GDP halved between 1990 and the early 2010s from 20% to 10%.

As the UK deindustrialised, the UK economy became more and more unbalanced. Physical investment as a percentage of GDP tumbled to less than 13%, compared to a world average of about 25% and almost 50% in China.[16] Almost half of UK exports were still manufactures in 2015 but, with a visible trade deficit of £120bn there were far too little of them to provide us with a positive trade balance despite a much better performance on services with an export surplus of £90bn, leaving an overall trade deficit of £30bn.[17] On its own, this might have been manageable but the overall balance of payments figure was much worse, partly as a result of net income from abroad, which had for a long time been in substantial surplus turning heavily negative at -£26bn. Net transfers were also on the rise, reaching £26bn in 2015, all contributing to an unsustainable overall balance of payments deficit of £80bn[18] that year – 4.4% of GDP.[19]

As government borrowing in the UK at the moment is largely a mirror image of the balance of payments deficit, unsurprisingly this failed to respond to government efforts to bring its deficit down to zero. In 2015 it was still £81bn,[20] buttressed by heavy borrowing by the household sector and, to a lesser extent, by businesses. Consumer price index inflation was very low but Quantitative Easing and the consequent ultra-low interest rates for those in a position to borrow pushed up asset inflation. Inequality soared as the prosperous London and South East became an increasingly different place from the North of England and the Midlands. In quite large areas of the north of England living standards were barely half what they were in the South. The UK median wage in 2015 was still barely higher than it had been in 2008.[21] Hardly surprisingly, the EU referendum vote in June 2016 was seized on by just over half the population as an opportunity to express their anger at policies – not least globalisation – which had been so much to their disadvantage.

These are the problems to which we have to find solutions if the UK economy is to provide enough well distributed growth to provide us with a sustainable future.

The cost base

Almost all output, whether manufactured goods, services or commodities has some sensitivity to the prices asked for it. Nobody wants to pay more than they have to for goods, services or commodities. Seeing whether buyers receive value for money from sellers, however, is much more difficult to determine in some sectors than others.

For commodities such as oil, foodstuffs or metallic ores, where quality standards are well established, there are world prices, which may well, fluctuate but where sellers have to match the market price or no sales take place. If, in any particular country, there are sources of supply which can be marketed at profitable prices, trading will take place and if not, not. The exchange rate will make a big difference as to whether this profitability condition is or is not met but, except for a small number of countries which have cornered large shares of the market for particular commodities – oil in Saudi Arabia for example – no country and the companies which operate within it can make much, if any, difference to the prevailing price levels. If the cost of extracting North Sea oil rises above the world price, production may continue for a while, as the marginal cost is lower than the full cost. The companies involved may persevere with production temporarily in the hope that prices will be higher in future, but if North Sea oil costs more than the world price for long, production will stop.

For services, the situation is different. Nearly all service outputs come in forms which are relatively small, differentiated and more difficult to compare with each other. How good is this lawyer compared to that one? How nice is this hotel bedroom compared to the one in another hotel? How does the teaching in this university compare with that one? Of course, everyone still wants to obtain value for money but measuring what is worth buying and what is not is much more difficult than it is with commodities. Services are therefore price sensitive to a less immediate extent and in a less obvious way than commodities.

Manufactured goods are in a different category again, partly because nearly all manufacturing involves falling costs as production volumes increase in a way which does not apply to most services, and partly because most manufactured products have obvious close substitutes, making price comparisons relatively easy. Most manufactured goods are, therefore, very price sensitive. Companies capable of capturing sufficient market share to benefit strongly from higher and higher volumes of production find themselves in a cumulatively stronger and stronger position to capture still more market share.

What impact do these differences in price sensitivity have on the way that trade develops? The answer is that this depends on the way in which the cost base in any particularly country is charged out to the rest of the world and it is then easy to see how crucial the exchange rate is in determining what happens. It is the relative difference in cost bases between different countries which shapes world trade.

The cost base consists of all the costs involved in producing anything – commodities, services or manufactured goods – which are incurred in the domestic currency. These include wages and salaries, nearly all overhead costs as well as provisions for profit and taxation. ONS figures show that for manufacturing in the UK, on average about 33% of total costs involve inputs which are bought in at world prices, particularly machinery, raw materials and components[22] leaving about 67% paid for in sterling. For commodities such as oil, the ratio for domestically incurred costs tends to be rather higher and in services higher still. Most services have only a small import content – typically less than 20%. For the UK economy as a whole, the ratio is about 22%.[23]

The ability of any economy to flourish – or otherwise – in world markets then depends crucially on how the cost base is charged out to the rest of the world – and this is entirely an exchange rate issue. Suppose two countries start both with an exchange rate which is sufficiently competitive to enable each of them to maintain their share of world trade, in which case both are very likely to grow at close to the same speed as the world average. Suppose then that one of them increases its exchange rate by 50% – which is less than what happened in the UK between 1977 and 1981. What happens to export prices? The country with the rising exchange rate, as a first approximation, will have to raise its export prices measured in world currency terms by 50% times the percentage of production costs which are paid in the domestic currency.

What happens then is that, subject to various caveats which would apply in the real world, the proportion of total costs incurred at world prices – machinery, raw materials and components in the case of manufacturing – will stay the same as they were before, measured in world currency terms, say in US dollars. The domestically incurred costs, however – about 67% on average in the case of manufactures and around 80% for services – will all go up by 50%. Suppose that before the currency got stronger, export prices in the revaluing country were 100, then, after the currency had strengthened, measured in world terms, manufactured goods will have to be charged out on average at 30 + (67 x 150%), which comes to about 130. Services would be even higher. 20 + (80 x 150%) comes to 140. In practice these increases might be rather less, as profit margins were squeezed, but the principle is clear. Furthermore, these higher charges will impact not only on export competitiveness but also on the tendency of the economy to import more than it otherwise would have done.

Unfortunately, the economic history of the UK over the 250 years since industrialisation began and GDP per head and living standards started to rise shows that for most of this period we have had an exchange rate which has been too high for the economy as a whole. The evidence is that over most of this time we have seen our share of world trade declining, dragging down our growth rate with it, compared to other countries. The reason for this is that the prices at which we have tried to sell our domestically incurred costs – our cost base – to the rest of the world has been, on average, much too high. The picture is not; however, the same on services as it is on manufacturers.

On services, we have done much better than on goods. Not only in the nineteenth century but right through to the present day, the UK has run an export surplus which in 2015 came to £90bn compared to the £120bn deficit on goods.[24] This is because the UK has a large number of important competitive advantages on services – the English language, our geographical location, our legal system our high quality universities and all the biases which have led to talent being concentrated in this part of the UK economy. Combining these advantages with the general lack of price sensitivity in the service sector means that the UK's export position on services has between positive and successful with the exchange rate as high as it has been recently.

In manufacturing, however, we unfortunately do not have the same natural competitive advantages. This is why, with the exchange rate where it has been over the last 40 years; nearly all of the internationally tradable manufacturing capacity which the UK had in the 1970s has been run out of business. Apart from industries essentially serving the local market as a result of having to be close to it, such as food production, jobbing printing and repairs and maintenance of existing equipment, the UK has little manufacturing capacity left other than high tech operations such as aerospace, vehicles, arms and pharmaceuticals, which are not very price sensitive for other reasons. These types of industries require substantial accumulations of experience and skills, and large amounts of historical research and development. They are heavily protected by branding and intellectual property rights. They therefore have monopolistic characteristics which have enabled them to survive – although even these industries may be under threat before long, as the Chinese get more proficient at aerospace production, the Indians at pharmaceuticals and the South Koreans at car manufacturing.

The dilemma faced by UK policymakers, therefore, is that the exchange rate requirements of the service and manufacturing sector of the economy diverge sharply. $1.50 to the pound may work for the service sector but it is lethal for manufacturing, which needs an exchange rate of the order of anything up to one third lower to have any realistic chance of reversing deindustrialisation. Hardly surprisingly, because the service sector is so much more successful in the UK than manufacturing, the prevailing conventional wisdom tends strongly to favour the current conditions, which suit the service sector well enough – and this is one of the major reasons why there is little pressure for a lower exchange rate.

The problem is that our foreign sales still depend very heavily on goods rather than services. Despite the huge difficulties under which manufacturing in the UK has laboured over past decades, 55% of our exports are goods rather than services,[25] despite the fact that about 80% of the UK's GDP comes from the service sector.[26] To avoid us slipping further and further down the world-exporting league, therefore, we cannot rely on our services export. We have to do better on manufacturing – and this can only happen if we have an exchange rate which works for our highly price sensitive manufacturing sector.

Elasticities

If the UK economy has for many years suffered from an overvalued currency – as judged by its falling share of world trade, low growth rate and other imbalances – and still does, despite the fall post the June 2016 EU referendum, it seems that there should be an obvious remedy. This would be to bring down the value of the pound to the level required to enable the UK to compete successfully in the world economy. There are a number of reasons – dealt with in the next section – about the practical difficulties of implementing such a policy, which are generally relatively easy to refute. There is, however, a more substantial objection. This is that the price sensitivity of the UK economy is just too low to make a more competitive exchange rate strategy work.

Reasons for thinking that this might be the case rest partly on some elements of our recent experience, particularly the relatively anaemic response of the UK economy to the fall in the exchange rate from about $2.00 in 2007 to $1.50 in 2009 and partly on academic work which has shown that the price sensitivity – the price elasticity – of demand for British exports and imports is too low to make a devaluation strategy work.

Price elasticity is defined as the ratio between the increase in quantity of sales of goods to the change in prices at they which are offered. Thus, if a fall in price of 1% produces an increase in sales volumes of 2%, the elasticity would be two. Similarly, with imports. In other words, to achieve, for example, an elasticity of more than one, the loss of money value of exports due to their fall in price must be more than offset by their increase in volume, while on the import side the increase in cost of imports must be more than offset by their reduction in volume. The condition which has to be fulfilled to make a devaluation produce a better *ex post* trade balance than the one *ex ante* is called the Marshall Lerner condition and it is that the sum of the elasticities for exports and imports (ignoring any negative signs) is more than unity. Thus the elasticities for exports and imports, viewed separately, may each be less than one but their combined total can still be above unity. Studies of these elasticities are normally broken down into short-term effects – within one year – and those which are longer term – over two to three years – once the economy has had time fully to adjust. Since it takes less time for increased import cost to work their way through the system than it does for additional export capacity to become available, the longer-term elasticities, especially for exports, tend to be considerably greater over two to three years than they are immediately.

A substantial amount of work has been done both by academics and by organisations such as the IMF over the years to try to determine what these price elasticities are in practice. Table 7.2a summarises work done by academics covering the last quarter of the twentieth century. Table 7.2b shows estimates produced by the

Table 7.2a: The elasticity of demand for exports and imports of 16 industrial and eight developing countries. Summary of numerous late 20th century academic studies

Industrial countries	Elasticity of demand for exports	Elasticity of demand for imports	Sum
Austria	1.02	1.23	2.25
Belgium	1.12	1.27	2.39
Canada	0.68	1.28	1.96
Denmark	1.04	0.91	1.95
France	1.28	0.93	2.21
Germany	1.02	0.79	1.81
Iceland	0.83	0.87	1.70
Italy	1.26	0.78	2.04
Japan	1.40	0.95	2.35
Korea	2.50	0.80	3.30
Netherlands	1.46	0.74	2.20
Norway	0.92	1.19	2.11
Sweden	1.58	0.88	2.46
Switzerland	1.03	1.13	2.16
United Kingdom	0.86	0.65	1.51
United States	1.19	1.24	2.43
Average	1.11	0.99	2.10

Developing countries	Elasticity of demand for exports	Elasticity of demand for imports	Sum
Argentina	0.60	0.90	1.50
Brazil	0.40	1.70	2.10
India	0.50	2.20	2.70
Kenya	1.00	0.80	1.80
Morocco	0.70	1.00	1.70
Pakistan	1.80	0.80	2.60
Philippines	0.90	2.70	3.60
Turkey	1.40	2.70	4.10
Average	1.10	1.50	2.60

Notes: The estimates above refer to elasticities over a two to three-year period. The figures are based upon the result of a number of different studies. Individual studies give differing estimates depending on the time periods involved, the econometric methodology employed and the particular data sets used. Source: Does Exchange Rate Policy Matter? European Economic Review vol 30 (1987), p 377, reproduced on page 63 of International Finance by Keith Pilbeam, Basingstoke, UK: Macmillan, 1994.

IMF covering the early part of the twenty-first century. These tables show relatively high elasticities both for the UK and other countries. More recent work, however, has indicated that the elasticities, at least for the UK, are considerably lower than those in these tables – indeed with the sum of the elasticities being barely above unity.[27] These figures are consistent with the relatively poor response of the UK economy to the 2007/09 devaluation.

There is, however, a clear explanation as to why these elasticities have altered, which relates back to the comments on price sensitivity in the previous section. We know that services, which comprise about 45%[28] of our export revenues, are not very price sensitive. We also know that the export industries which are left – high tech ones such as aerospace, arms, vehicles and pharmaceuticals are equally price insensitive. What would be much more price sensitive – the output of tradable light industrial products – is no longer there as nearly all this industry has been put of business as the proportion of GDP coming from manufacturing has fallen from almost a third to barely 10%. In sum, the current elasticities for UK exports and imports are as low as they are now because the high exchange rates over the last few years have eliminated nearly all the sectors of the economy – essentially medium- and low-tech light industry – where they would be higher if they still existed.

Now there are two essentially separate variables which price elasticities measure. One is the responsiveness of whatever is being exported and imported now to changes in price. To what extent would production from existing operations increase if the exchange rate was lower? The other concerns decisions about where new manufacturing production might be located if the exchange rate was different. At what point would the UK cost base become low enough for it to be more profitable to site a new factory in the UK rather than in, say, the Far East? The crucial insight is that price elasticities relating to location are much higher than those stemming from responses in sales volumes for existing products. This is why two or three year elasticities are much greater than those in year one and why the UK responded so relatively sluggishly to the 2007/09 devaluation. The drop from $2.00 to $1.50 to the pound, made almost no difference to where it was worth locating new light

Table 7.2b: Elasticity of demand for exports and imports 2001-2004. Estimates produced by the IMF and published in 2010

	Export long run	Import long run	Total
Australia	0.70	1.61	2.31
Austria	1.20	0.88	2.08
Belgium	2.10	0.56	2.66
Canada	1.32	0.83	2.15
Czech Republic	0.82	1.20	2.02
Denmark	1.27	0.78	2.05
Finland	1.23	0.01	1.24
France	1.14	1.03	2.17
Germany	2.51	0.10	2.61
Greece	1.13	1.11	2.24
Hungary	0.88	0.83	1.71
Iceland	0.91	1.46	2.37
Ireland	0.84	0.34	1.18
Italy	0.99	0.97	1.96
Japan	1.72	0.75	2.47
Korea	1.02	0.21	1.23
Luxembourg	2.65	2.63	5.28
Netherlands	1.04	0.73	1.77
New Zealand	1.01	0.94	1.95
Norway	0.33	1.61	1.94
Portugal	1.65	1.46	3.11
Slovakia	0.84	0.83	1.67
Spain	1.08	1.33	2.41
Sweden	1.84	0.04	1.88
Switzerland	1.27	0.78	2.05
United States	1.77	1.52	3.29
United Kingdom	1.37	1.68	3.05
Mean	1.28	0.97	2.25
Median	1.14	0.88	2.02

Sources: Export Supply Elasticities Table 2, page 21, and Import Demand Elasticities Table 1, page 15 in A Method for Calculating Export Supply and Import Demand Elasticities by Stephen Tokarick. Washington DC: IMF Working Paper WP/10/180, published 2010. NB Signs have been reversed for Imports in the table above for the sake of clarity.

industrial capacity. It was completely uneconomical in nearly all cases at both $2.00 and $1.50 to the pound. The parity needed to be much lower than this to make reshoring on any major sale feasible. Instead, deindustrialisation continued its relentless progress, falling as a percentage of GDP from 15% in 2000 to 10% in 2015.[29]

The crucial issue, then, is what exchange rate would be needed to make the establishment of UK light industrial manufacturing capacity viable again, which means that it would need to be clearly expected to be profitable, otherwise the necessary investment would never take place. Figure 6.1, in the previous chapter, gives some indication, as does the history of the UK's real exchange rate over the past few decades. So does the difference in the costs of producing a swathe of light industrial goods in the UK rather than in the Far East or in Germany. This evidence, plus more detailed calculations based on all the evidence from elasticities,[30] indicate that sterling would need to fall to somewhere between $1.00 and $1.10. As, post the EU referendum, the dollar sterling exchange rate has already fallen from about $1.45 to $1.25, the additional amount of depreciation required is much lower than it was previously and therefore correspondingly easier to achieve. Furthermore, for a number of reasons, sterling should not need to fall further than this, again making a potential transition more manageable.

One is that it costs about 10% to ship goods from the Far East to the UK, so that we would not have to compete directly with Chinese production costs. Another is that our strong service sector sales mean that, to rebalance our economy, so that we could pay our way in the world, we would not have to reindustrialise to the same extent as countries such as Germany where manufacturing in 2015 accounted for 22% of GDP, Japan 19% and Switzerland 18%. We would, however, need to get this ratio up to some 15% to enable us to close our foreign payments balance to a sustainable level.

Two other key aspects of any successful policy to reindustrialise the country need highlighting. The first is that the government would need to have an exchange rate target in the public domain and to be determined to take whatever steps were necessary to keep it within the target range. No-one is going to invest heavily in manufacturing capacity if there is a serious risk that, as soon as the economy shows signs of doing better, the exchange rate is encouraged to rise again as, unfortunately, has for many years been the pattern.

The second is that, both to provide the necessary new industrial capacity and to move the overall level of investment in the economy as a percentage of GDP up to a level capable of supporting sustainable growth, while at the same time shifting the economy away from running its current very large current account deficit, there would have to be a major shift towards a higher level of saving. Some of this could be done by consumers, some by business, some by the government and some by temporarily running a large balance of payments deficit. To make this happen, however, there would need to be radical changes to the ease of financing industrial investment. To do this we need to borrow from the financial policies developed largely at the instigation of Dr Osamu Shimomura (1910-1989) to support the enormous increase in industrial output achieved by Japan during its huge economic expansion after World War II. This was achieved by using the state, through its banking system, to make almost unlimited credit available to light industry. Either existing UK banks – or new ones which may well be required if the old ones won't change – are going to have to adopt radically different lending strategies to those currently in place to help to finance the much larger scale industrial investment which is going to be needed.

Changing the exchange rate

It is one thing to say that the exchange rate for sterling ought to be lower than it is. It is another to say how this could be done. Suppose that the government was convinced that a more competitive exchange rate strategy was to be adopted to rebalance the economy. What steps would the government then need to take to make sure that this happened?

The first requirement would need to be for the government to state what its new policy on exchange rate targeting was and to explain to all concerned the rationale behind it. It would be to make it profitable for a sufficient amount of light industry to get re-sited in the UK rather than for the country to rely on imports so as to bring the proportion of GDP contributed by manufacturing up to about 15%. In parallel with this change, there would have to be major switch in physical investment in the UK from under 13% to rather more than 20%. Especially initially, it would be vital to ensure that a substantial proportion of this extra investment went into the sectors of the economy – principally mechanisation and technology – which would produce the largest and quickest returns, but it would also be important to increase social investment – in schools, roads, hospitals, rail and housing – as soon as possible.

Although the balance of payments might well have to become increasingly negative for a period while these transitions were taking place – which would help to get the exchange rate down – the objective should be to get the balance of payments reduced within the short to medium term future to a much more manageable level than we have seen recently. At the very least, the foreign payments deficit should be below the growth rate, so that the capacity of the country to service its debts should no longer be allowed to deteriorate year by year. The way this would be done would be by achieving a much better balance on our goods export/import balance, instead of seeing our net trade position deteriorating every year. A much lower foreign deficit would automatically reduce the government deficit to an annual rate below the grow rate, thus at least stabilising it and making it possible for total government debt as a percentage of GDP to be slowly reduced.

In these conditions, the government could have a target increase in the growth rate to 4% or 5% per annum, which would allow there to be an increase in real wages as the economy was rebalanced strongly towards the regions of the country outside London and the South East. The stimulus for growth would no longer come primarily from consumer demand but from exports and investment.

To make all this happen, the government would not only have to announce the exchange rate it wanted to see – probably in the range of between $1.00 and $1.10 to the pound – but it would need to make clear its determination to keep it within the bounds it had set. The investment required will never take place if it is not clear that the conditions to make it profitable are here to stay, and not allowed to be dissipated as soon as the economy shows strong signs of recovery.

What would the government have to do to make sure that the exchange rate it wanted to see materialised? The size of our current foreign payments deficit and the impossibility of this continuing at its present level indefinitely should enable the government to mobilise a reasonable amount of market sentiment to support its new strategy but in addition, there are a number of key steps which it could take and it would need to choose some combination of all the following policy options:

Capital receipts

The large deficit which we have currently can only exist because it is matched by sale of capital assets and borrowing to finance it. Few people would like to see a rigid system of capital controls reintroduced along the lines which used to exist under the Bretton Woods system but there is a considerable amount which the government could do to discourage the acquisition by foreign interests along the lines used by almost all other countries. We could have a public interest test on foreign takeovers. We could have a tax regime which discouraged the acquisition of UK assets much more strongly than it does at the moment. We could introduce a withholding tax which made it much less attractive for foreign interests to own UK assets.

Bank of England

The role of the Bank of England has generally been to keep sterling as strong as possible, partly reflecting the preference of the City and other sections of the economy, including importers, foreign travellers and pensioners, for a high pound and partly because the Bank has always thought that a strong pound would bear down on inflation. It would need to have its objectives changed to giving priority to keeping sterling within the new agreed bands and supporting a growth strategy based on net trade and investment rather than consumer demand and asset inflation. This would involve no longer supporting sterling but, as required, selling it to bring the exchange rate down.

Fiscal and monetary policy

Other policy instruments would need to be aligned with the new strategy for the economy. As well as having fiscal and monetary policies in place which were generally compatible with the new approach, it would be essential for financing facilities to be readily available on easy terms for manufacturing industry, to make sure that the required investment was not held up by lack of finance. The pressure on resources generally which these conditions would produce would help to achieve a lower exchange rate. It is possible also that the outcome of the current Brexit negotiations may put further downward pressure on sterling, as has already happened since the EU referendum in June 2016. An important aim should be no longer to use Quantitative Easing as a way of underpinning the economy. Eventually interest rates would need to rise to somewhere closer to where they have been historically, with a small premium over the rate of inflation.

Inflation

Historical evidence shows that devaluations do not generally produce much more inflation than would have occurred in their absence but it also shows that it is difficult to have a sustained rate of real growth of 4% or 5% per annum with year on year price increase averaging less than 3% or perhaps even 4% per annum. During the period when European economies were growing at 4.9% per annum after World War II, the average inflation rate was 2.8% per annum. In Japan, during the same period, the economy grew at 9.9% a year while inflation averaged 4.3%.[31] The fear of increased inflation, even if driven by much faster growth, may help to get the exchange rate down.

The key requirement is for the government to have an economic strategy geared to rebalancing the UK economy so that it can be launched on to a sustainable growth trajectory, using the same stimuli as have worked so well in the past in many parts of the world, including our own in all too isolated periods, such as the mid-1930s.

Objections

Many people, even if they were persuaded by the logic of the case for a more competitive exchange rate for sterling which has been presented in this book, might still be inclined to shy away from trying to implement it because of deeply held suspicions that such a policy would neither be achievable nor would it work even if it could be put into practice. What are these contentions and how can they be countered?

There are six main arguments which are regularly advanced to support these concerns. They are, first, that devaluation always produces extra inflation which negates any gains in competitiveness; second, that devaluation is impossible to combine with an open economy; third, that if we did devalue, we would be bound to be met by retaliation which would undermine its benefit; fourth, that reducing sterling's parity would make us all poorer; fifth, that we have tried devaluation in the past and it does not work; and sixth, that the UK is no good at manufacturing and that our economy would not therefore respond positively to a lower exchange rate. None of these allegations stands up to close scrutiny and a central part of the case put forward in this book is to understand why this is so.

Devaluation and inflation

The contention that devaluation always produces a rise in inflation is true in so far as it applies to goods and services which are imported. Price rises here are inevitable and a necessary part of switching demand from foreign to domestic suppliers. It does not, however, follow that the price level generally will rise more quickly than it would have done without a devaluation, and a wealth of evidence from the dozens of devaluations which have occurred among relatively rich and diversified economies such as ours in recent decades shows that in fact lower parities sometimes produce a little more inflation, sometimes a bit less, but most of the time little if any change. This may seem a very surprising result to many people but this is unequivocally what the statistics show. Looking at recent examples, when the UK left the Exchange Rate Mechanism in 1992, sterling fell by trade-weighted 12%,[32] but inflation fell from 5.9% in 1991 to 1.6% in 1993.[33] When sterling dropped from about $2.00 to the pound in 2007 to $1.50 in 2009, a drop of 25%, the rate of inflation barely flickered,[34] and what increase there was in 2011 was very largely driven by an increase in commodity prices, which fell away as soon as they dropped back again.[35]

The reason why these are common outcomes is that, while higher import prices push up the price level, many factors to do with a lower parity tend to bring it down. Market interest rates tend to be lower after a devaluation, and so do tax rates. Production runs become longer, bringing down average costs. Investment, especially in the most productive parts of the economy, tends to rise significantly, increasing output per head, reducing costs and producing a wage climate more conducive to keeping income increases in line with productivity growth. Furthermore, as domestic supplies of goods and services become more competitive with those from abroad, demand switches to local sources, negating the need to pay higher import prices even if foreign suppliers reduce their prices to try to retain market share.

For all these reasons, the plain fact is that neither theory nor historical experience, based on a wide range of individual cases, show evidence of devaluations having any systematic effect on increasing inflation above what it would have been anyway. Still less does either theory or practice show that competitive gains from a devaluation tend rapidly to be eroded away by higher inflation, although this is a central tenet of monetarist thinking, which perhaps explains why so many people believe it to be the case even though it isn't. On the contrary, the longer term evidence very firmly indicates that economies which have strongly competitive international pricing tend to perform better and better as talent and highly productive investment is attracted to those sectors of the economy most likely to produce rising productivity and increasing competitiveness. This is the environment into which a considerably lower parity needs to draw the UK economy.

Changing the exchange rate in an open economy

Next, it is frequently contended that the parity of sterling is determined by market forces over which the authorities have little control, so that any policy to change the exchange rate in any direction is bound to fail. Again, historical experience indicates that this proposition cannot be correct. The Japanese, to provide a recent example, brought the parity of the yen down against the dollar by a third between the beginning of 2013 and the start of 2015[36] as a result of deliberate policy. Further back, the Plaza Accord, negotiated in 1985, produced a massive change in parities among the major trading nations of the world at the time, causing the dollar, for example, to fall against the yen by just over 50% between 1985 and 1987.[37]

It is of course true is that market forces have a major influence on exchange rate parities but it does not follow from this that the authorities cannot influence the factors which determine what market outcomes are. If the UK pursues policies which makes it very easy for foreign interests to buy British assets, for example, this will exert a strong upward pressure on sterling's parity. If the markets think that the Bank of England is going to raise interest rates, this will also push sterling higher. If the Bank evidently wants to help to keep the parity of the pound up by buying sterling and selling dollars, this will have a correspondingly strengthening impact on sterling.

Sooner or later, the parlous state of our balance of payments is also likely to be a major factor. Up to now, the ability of the UK to finance its increasing deficit by selling assets has kept the markets confident that the rate at which sterling is trading on the foreign exchanges is sustainable. It is far from clear that this confidence will continue indefinitely for two main reasons. One is that the UK may soon have sold so many assets that it may become increasingly difficult to find enough to sell in future, especially if more safeguards relating to the sale of UK assets are put in place, thus making it more difficult to keep the exchange rate as high as it is at the moment. The second is that every £100bn annual deficit, financed by selling assets with an average gross return of the order of 3%, adds another £3bn to the underlying deficit every year, as we forfeit the returns we would have had from the assets had we not sold them. The laws of economic gravity can be ignored for a long time but as Herbert Stein had it – incidentally with balance of payments deficits as a prime example – 'Trends that can't continue, won't.'[38] It may, therefore, very well be the case that in the foreseeable future there will be a change in market sentiment which will bring sterling down to a lower parity with or without the assistance of the authorities. The fall in the value of sterling following the EU referendum in June 2016 has already shown this happening, although the fall from $1.45 to $1.25 is unfortunately still not enough to precipitate a large scale industrial revival.

Retaliation

If the UK were to devalue by a sufficient amount – probably about 20% from its current $1.25 level – to enable the economy to reindustrialise to a point where we could pay our way in the world, is it likely that there would be retaliation from other countries which would negate any benefits in the form of increased competitiveness which the devaluation had secured? The answer to this question needs to come in several parts.

In the first place, it depends on the position from which the devaluing country starts. The curse of foreign payment imbalances starts not with countries like the UK, with massive deficits, but with countries such as Germany, Switzerland and the Netherlands with huge surpluses – in 2015 almost 8% of GDP in Germany's and the Netherlands' cases, and 15% for Switzerland.[39] These surpluses have to be matched by deficits somewhere else in the world economy. Unfortunately, surplus countries are never under any immediate pressure to reduce the beggar-thy-neighbour impact of their surpluses by revaluing their currencies and this leaves economies such as ours, carrying big deficits, with no alternative but devaluation to get the situation under control. There is thus a very strong principled case for countries such as the UK to make for getting sterling to a more competitive level.

In terms of practicalities, the UK has a number of advantages which other countries do not share. We are not in the EU's Single Currency, membership of which would clearly preclude the UK from doing anything about our exchange rate. We still have our own central bank and control over our own interest rate and monetary policy. Sterling is not a world reserve currency like the dollar, making it much easier for us to alter our exchange rate without there being major international consequences. The fact that our share of world trade is now so low – at 2.9% in 2015[40] – means that what happens to sterling has relatively little impact on the rest of the world.

As to recent evidence, the quite major changes in the parity of sterling when the UK left the ERM in 1992 – a trade weighted drop of 12%[41] – and the fall in the rate for sterling against the dollar between 2007 and 2009 – about 25%[42] – as well as the post-EU referendum drop in sterling's parity, all engendered no retaliation. All were evidently seen by other countries – the markets and the authorities – as being exchange rate adjustments which were clearly warranted by the state of the UK economy. Against the background of our currently ballooning foreign exchange deficit, there is no reason why the same could not be made to happen again. If the manifest imbalances in the UK economy are clearly associated with an unsustainably high exchange rate this should also enable us to overcome any objections from our G7 partners, with whom we have jointly agreed not to indulge in unwarranted competitive devaluations.

Sterling and living standards

It is frequently argued that a devaluation must make us all poorer and this argument tends to take two forms, one of which is manifestly incorrect while the other can relatively easily be counteracted.

The first is that if we reduced the value of the pound by, say, 20%, in world currency terms, we would make ourselves 20% worse off and we would therefore genuinely be poorer by this amount. The fallacy with this argument is that, while it might be well founded if we did all our shopping in international currencies such as dollars, this is not what UK residents do except perhaps when they go on holiday. UK citizens pay for almost everything they buy in sterling and it is therefore GDP measured in sterling, not in dollars, which counts. This is the way in which international accounting is done and this explains why IMF figures do not generally show falls in GDP when countries devalue. On the contrary, they almost invariably show the growth rate rising and GDP increasing in consequence. Since living standards closely approximate to GDP per head, especially over time, if the economy is increasing in size and the population does not change from what it would have been anyway, GDP per head and thus living standards must, as a matter of logic, go up rather than down.

The second potentially more substantial argument is that if we are going to increase our net trade balance to a point where we are not enjoying a standard of living far beyond what we are earning – as we are at the moment – living standards will have to suffer. Relatively speaking, this has to be correct. If we produce more for export, too, there will be less for the home market. Furthermore, if, to get the economy to grow faster, we have to spend a considerably higher proportion of our GDP than we do at the moment on investment, there will again have to be a corresponding reduction in consumption as a percentage of GDP. The crucial question then is whether the economy can be made to grow fast enough to enable both the shift towards exports and investment to be accommodated without living standards falling – and indeed preferably rising. Careful calculations show that this would be possible – provided that a high enough proportion of increased investment goes to the most productive parts of the economy, mostly manufacturing. It can be done.[43]

Past devaluations

Sterling may be too strong now for the good of our manufacturing base, but there is a powerful case to be made that this is no new phenomenon. Controversies over banking prudence and the link between sterling and gold, combined with the dominance of financial interests over those of industry, all stretching back to the beginning of the nineteenth century when industrialisation in the UK really got under way, have always hobbled British industry. Although we initially showed the way, other countries have overtaken us as their industrial bases have got stronger and their more competitive currencies have allowed them to secure better net trade advantages.

As these other countries have invested more heavily in the future than we have, their output per head has grown more rapidly than ours, their wage climates have been better and their inflation rates have been lower. As an extreme example, in Switzerland, between 1970 and 2010, the price level rose by 88%. In the UK it increased by 780%. The average annual Swiss inflation rate over these 40 years was 1.6% while in the UK it was

5.6%.[44] It was against this kind of background that from time to time the over-valuation of sterling became so obvious that either the markets or the authorities or both tolerated, engineered or encouraged the parity for sterling to fall. Perhaps it is worth reiterating the oft-forgotten fact that sterling's fall by about 30% in 1931, after near stagnation during the 1920s,enabled the UK economy to have its fastest spurt of growth ever during the middle of the 1930s – over 4% per annum cumulatively for the four years between 1933 and 1937.[45]

When World War II ended and the continent began to recover from wartime devastation, it soon became apparent that the UK had no chance of maintaining the pre-War dollar parity of $4.03 to the pound, and sterling was devalued in 1949 to $2.80.[46] Higher than average inflation in the UK than elsewhere and underinvestment in export industries resulted in a steady trade deterioration in the 1950s and 1960s, culminating in the pound being devalued in 1967 from $2.80 to $2.40.[47] Once currencies started to fluctuate against each other in the 1970s, following the break-up of the Bretton Woods fixed parity system in 1971,[48] rapidly rising prices combined with high interest rates kept sterling much too strong. This was especially so early in the 1980s and later in that decade as the UK entered the Exchange Rate Mechanism, which we left in 1992 with a devaluation of about 12% against all currencies,[49] to escape from a sharp economic downturn. After showing some signs of recovery, the UK economy then became more and more unbalanced as asset sales, starting in the late 1990s on a scale unparalleled anywhere else, pushed sterling up to absurdly high levels in the 2000s. Its value fell between 2007 and 2009 – still by not nearly enough – since when it has climbed back a bit and then fallen to roughly where we were in 2009 post the EU referendum. Meanwhile, in the East, over past decades, exactly the opposite policies were followed as they massively devalued.

The reality is that the UK's exchange rate has been much too strong to allow our industrial base to flourish for most of the last two centuries. The devaluations that have taken place have made the situation rather better than it otherwise would have been but they have almost always been too little and too late.

Devaluation and the UK response

Finally, it is argued that the UK has no bent for manufacturing and that, even if industry was presented with a much more favourable competitive environment, it would not respond. While it is true that a wide swathe particularly of low- and medium-tech manufacturing is uneconomic in the UK at present, because the exchange rate and the cost base for it is much too high, there is no evidence whatever that, if more favourable conditions prevailed, UK entrepreneurs would not be just as good as those anywhere else in the world at taking advantage of the new opportunities which would then open up.

Evidence for this proposition comes from a wide variety of sources. Perhaps the most obvious is to consider how implausible it is that the nation which was the very birthplace of the Industrial Revolution should be incapable of running manufacturing operations successfully, given a reasonably favourable environment. Nor is there the slightest evidence that the UK lacks entrepreneurial people who would be willing to try their hands at making money out of making and selling, if the right opportunities were there. The problem with the UK, as a manufacturing environment, is that these conditions simply do not exist at the moment, because the cost base is too high, and entrepreneurs rightly shun investing in ventures which they can see from the beginning have poor prospects of being profitable and successful.

The reason why the UK has allowed manufacturing as a percentage of its GDP to fall from almost one third in 1970 to barely 10% now is obvious. Nearly all our internationally traded low- and medium-tech manufacturing has been driven out of business and there is insufficient high-tech activity – also subject to long term threat – to fill the gap. We cannot allow this condition to continue if our economy is to grow at a reasonable rate in future. There is, however, a significant school of thought which is sceptical about whether this is what we should be aiming to achieve, even if such objectives were attainable. Are there wider arguments, covered in the next chapter, which need to be considered which potentially throw in doubt whether faster growth in GDP and higher living standards are what we ought to be aiming for at all?

8

Sustainability

It is impossible to deny that changes in policy which were successful in increasing the rate of economic growth among western economies would inevitably increase the pressure on the world's ecology. Extra output would entail the consumption of more raw materials and the production of additional waste. Raising living standards could, unless carefully handled, increase rather than reduce the risk of destabilising the world's climate – especially if the world's population goes on rising strongly. Meanwhile more migration, encouraged by rising living standards, could enhance other pressures. Is there, therefore, a convincing case to make that any policy orientated to producing better economic performance, as conventionally measured, is likely to be self-defeating? While this line of attack has always had a vocal constituency, there is a strong case to argue that this is much too pessimistic a view to take. On the contrary, from all major perspectives, this chapter argues that the prospects for producing a sustainable future – and increasing human happiness – are likely to be much better if the developed countries of the world are stable and prosperous than if they are stagnant, and financially and politically stressed, with all the social and economic problems that such a scenario brings in train.

There are many global risks which are going to have to be managed over the coming decades. Some of them, such as major outbreaks of disease or volcanic activity or widespread terrorist activity, are difficult to forecast and most, on past performance, are also not very likely to occur on a world scale, even if they cause serious local disruption. Trying to anticipate them is not likely to be fruitful. If they do materialise, again on past performance, it seems likely that humanity will find a way of dealing with them. Other large scale potential problems for the future are much easier to foresee and to quantify, and it is to these that we turn in the following sections. Those which it is generally agreed are likely to be much the most pressing are the availability of sufficient resources of all kinds to support ever rising economic output, the impact on the future of the world of its still rapidly rising human population and the migration pressures rising from it, and the changes in climate which are forecast to result from mankind's rising living standards.

Before reviewing resource, population, migration and climate issues, however, there is still the question as to whether trying to improve economic performance is a worthy objective at all, even supposing that the problems involved in making this possible could be overcome. Is it the case that more output – at least beyond a minimum level, which is well below what prevails in most of the western world – does not improve happiness and therefore is a goal which it is pointless to pursue? There is now a significant literature which shows that, on the vast majority of measures which can be used, most people do not seem to be much, if any, happier now than they were decades ago when their living standards were substantially lower.[1] There are complex reasons for this state of affairs, with incomes relative to other people playing a substantially larger role than the absolute levels involved. It may well be the case that if living standards go on rising, if other things remain equal, limited increases in happiness will generally go on being found. Even if this turns out to be true – which seems likely – there are nevertheless very important exceptions to the happiness thesis which suggest strongly that better performance by the developed world would still improve rather than have little influence on the human happiness condition.

First, being unemployed involuntarily is one of the major causes of unhappiness and so is job insecurity.[2] If this is the case, running the economy with much lower levels of unemployment and more secure jobs must improve the happiness quotient. Indeed, this may be perhaps the most important way in which economic performance can increase happiness because so many of the other factors which affect people's attitude to life – such as family relationship, community and friends, health, personal freedom and personal values – are not really related closely to levels of income at all.[3]

Second, if the major contribution which the economic world can make to human happiness is to provide satisfying work, there is great danger in allowing conditions of little or no growth to materialise, especially over a long period. This is because there is no reason to believe that these conditions would stop productivity continuing to rise by something of the order of 2% per annum – as it has done ever since the Industrial Revolution started – among those still working even if there is no overall growth. If this happens, and the same amount of output can be produced by fewer and fewer people, unemployment – or more probably underemployment in low productivity jobs on low and insecure wages – is bound to go up, exactly as has happened now across the western world. This is why there are good reasons for believing that poor economic performance is very likely to reduce happiness however measured.

Third, while happiness may not increase with living standards once a reasonable minimum level has been achieved, there are large numbers of people in the world whose income per head is far below this point. It is one thing not to feel more content with life when your income goes up but when you nevertheless always enough to eat, when you or the state provide you with remedies for any illness from which you may suffer, and when you have somewhere tolerable to live. It is quite another to eke out life in severe poverty. Both within western societies and among the Third World, which depends heavily on the West for economic support, there are very large numbers of people whose condition very obviously would be improved by higher living standards.

Fourth, while it may well be true that having more and more material goods does not make people happier, there can be little doubt that most people still have an urge to buy more goods and services than they did before, given the opportunity to do so. Frustrating their capacity to do so may not have the dire effects on their individual personal wellbeing that which might be anticipated, but it may well have collective disadvantages if a sense of overall failure and degeneration overcomes the whole of the society in which they live.

Those who claim that increasing living standards beyond a certain point do not generally increase human happiness may well be right, but this is not an argument against making sure that economic policy contributes to contentment where it can.

Population

Arguably, the greatest threat of all to the sustainability of human existence on earth must be the number of people alive increasing to a point which puts completely intolerable strains on the earth's resources. This situation is certainly likely to be made worse if it is accompanied – as it almost certainly would be – by widespread determination everywhere to increase living standards in parallel to the rise in the total number of people to be accommodated. There are therefore very pressing arguments for creating conditions which ensure that the total number of human beings plateaus at a manageable number. What sort of policies are most likely to achieve this objective?

At the turn of the twenty-first century, the world's population was 6.1bn, up from 2.5bn in 1950. At the end of 2016 it was 7.5bn.[4] The number of people alive more than doubled during the last 50 years of the last century. The peak rise in percentage terms was in 1964 – at 2.2%. Since then, the rate of increase has steadily declined, standing at 1.1% in 2000[5] and expected to go on slowly dropping. The absolute number of people added to the world's population – 87m – reached its peak in 1990, falling to 76m in 2000 with a continuing downwards trend.[6] Nevertheless, the number of people on earth is still increasing at the rate of a little over 200,000 per day,[7] although there are wide variations in different parts of the world.

There are two major reasons why the population has grown so fast over the last 100 years, compared to previous experience. One is the fall in mortality among young age groups, particularly children up to about five years old. The other is that the average age to which those who survive are living is much higher than used to be the case. Average life expectancy in the developed countries is now about 80 years – and 67 years on average for the world as a whole.[8] Before the industrial revolution, average life expectancy at birth was seldom higher than 30 years anywhere in the world, and generally closer to an average of about 24.[9] During the Black Death in Europe, which, during the fourteenth century, killed off about a third of the population,[10] it fell as low as 18.[11] As late as 1930, life expectancy in China was only 24 years. It is now 70.[12] Significant widespread improvements in the probability of survival date back anywhere only to the nineteenth century and have been especially impressive since the end of World War II.[13]

While mortality has thus fallen dramatically across all age groups, the reduction in fertility needed to bring the rate of increase in population down to manageable proportions has taken considerably longer to materialise. In the early 1950s, women in developing countries gave birth to an average of more than six children – compared to an average of 3.1 today.[14] The reason why the rate of increase in the population in developing countries – compared with those in the developed world – is still so high is that the steps taken to reduce mortality have turned out to be much easier to introduce than the changes in attitude and perception needed to reduce the number of children which parents decide that they want to have. It has been relatively easy and cheap to eradicate disease-carrying insects and rodents, to chlorinate drinking water, to carry out vaccination programmes and to introduce drugs and dietary supplements, combined with better personal hygiene and rehydration therapy, to reduce infant mortality.[15] Changes in gender roles, attitudes towards authority, sexual norms and perceptions of advantage, leading to lower planned births, have been found to be much more difficult to influence.[16]

High fertility and low mortality produce a young population which, as it moves into child-bearing age, generates a further increase in children being born. The momentum thus generated means that, even if replacement level fertility was achieved today in fast growing population areas, there would still be big increases in the number of people to be accommodated because of the age structure.[17] Nor are these the only major consequence of changes to fertility and mortality. In many countries, the dependency ratio – which is the ratio between those outside the normal working ages and those within them – is much higher than it used to be, generating major new redistributive problems. In countries with very high birth rates, such as much of sub-Saharan Africa, almost 45% of the entire population is under 15 years old.[18] In the developed world, by contrast, there are now far more people aged over 65 than there have ever been before as a proportion of the population. It was about 18% in 2011[19] with this percentage expected to be on a steadily rising trend to 24% in 2050.[20]

With all these caveats in place, what can now be said about future population trends? The starting point is the work done by the United Nations whose Population Division produces a biennial report with updated projections for the world as a whole and for each individual country. The current projections run to 2100 with varying population estimates, depending on different assumptions, for each country produced at five year intervals between now and then. The projections are summarised into three main categories. The central estimate is called the Medium Variant. There are then Low and High Variants, which are essentially the product of varying assumptions about the lower and upper probable bands of fertility.[21]

The Medium Variant estimate in the 2015 Revision for the world's population in 2050 is 9.7bn. The rate at which the world's population is increasing – currently at about 84m a year – is slowly falling, but variations in the rate at which this happens make a big difference to the total population projections in the future. The Low Variant world total figure for 2050 is 8.7bn and the High Variant 10.8bn, compared to the 7.4bn people alive on earth in 2016.[22] The Medium Variant thus implies an increase in population between 2016 and 2050 of 31%, the Low Variant 12% and the High Variant 46%.

Clearly, since these very large differences are mostly the product of different fertility rate projections, what actually happens to fertility trends over the decades to 2050 is going to be of crucial importance to the world's future. Not all of the increase in population, however, is due to increased births. A significant proportion of it is the result of people being expected to live longer. By 2045-2050, the less developed regions are expected to attain a life expectancy of 75 years, whereas in the more developed regions the projected level is 82 years, implying that the gap between the two groups will narrow significantly.[23] Globally, on using the Medium Variant projections, the number of people over 60 years old is expected to rise from 231m in 2000 to just over 2.1bn by 2050, while those over 80 increase from 37m to 435m. In the developed world in 2050, for every child, there are likely to be two people over 60 – comprising about one third of the total population.[24]

This age transition, which is caused by the interaction of changes in fertility, mortality and migration, represents a shift from a very young population in which there are slightly more males than females, to an older population in which there are more females than males. This shift represents a powerful force for social, economic and political change.[25] At ages 75 and over, two-thirds of the people alive in the USA are women in comparison to Pakistan where the reverse is true, largely due to the low status of women there and their correspondingly poor life expectancy, though the trend is moving in the other direction.[26]

Obviously, there is not an unlimited number of people which the earth can support. A view therefore has to be taken about the extent to which the world's population can expand before one or other aspect of the world's carrying capacity is exhausted. Opinions on exact numbers may differ but it is clear that even the lower end of the UN projections for 2050 must be pushing towards a tolerable limit. Beyond that, to have the population as much as 50% larger than it is at the moment – which would happen if current fertility rates continued largely unchecked, reflecting the High Variant projections – and still rising by the middle of the current century, would be to put the future manifestly at risk. Generally speaking, it must be the case that the smaller the population that the world has to sustain as the number of human beings plateaus or peaks, the more likely it is that humanity as a whole will have a sustainable future. What then can be done to keep the population increase down as low as is feasibly possible? Not surprisingly, the mixture of policies which looks most likely to be successful is complex, not least because fertility – the key variable factor – is fundamentally the aggregate of millions of individual decisions which are private and which can therefore only indirectly be addressed by public policy.

Unquestionably, however, the greatest single cause of high levels of fertility is poverty. All the statistical data shows a high correlation between low living standards and high numbers of children per woman in the population. Table 8.1 shows how strong the relationship is between living standards and fertility. Births per woman start to fall sharply once annual GDP per head reaches about $2,500 (measured in 2009 US dollars) and then continue to fall as it climbs to $5,000[27] in almost all countries, whatever the religion or culture of their peoples. The table also shows how resistant poor countries have generally been to all the many well-meaning initiatives which have been undertaken in the least developed parts of the world to reduce birth rates in the absence of rising living standards.

Figure 8.1: Total fertility rate (children per woman) plotted against GDP per capita (US$ 2009). Only countries with over five million population are included, to reduce outliers.

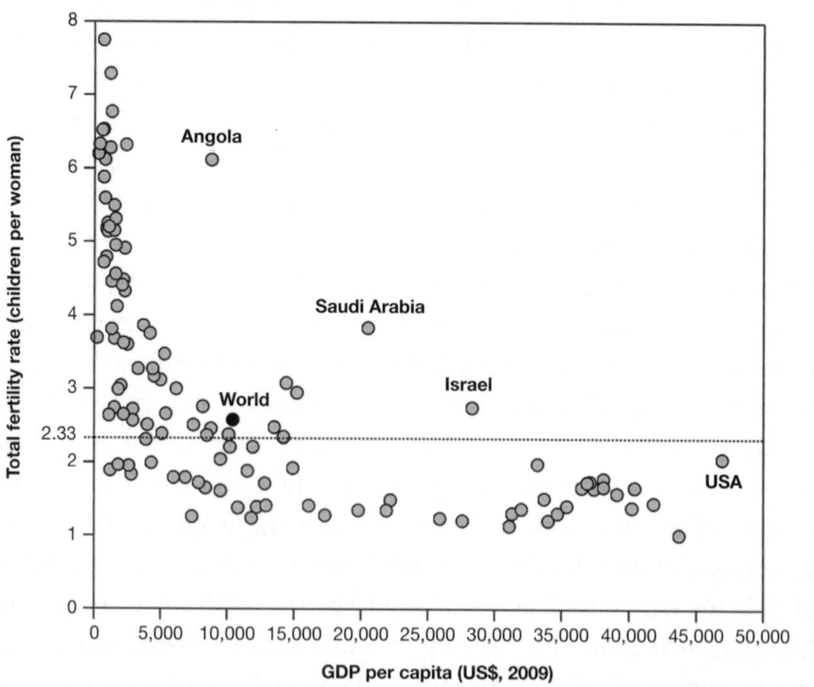

Source: Wikipedia Commons

The figures for the last 25 years of the twentieth century are particularly striking. Whereas the numbers of children per woman declined from an average of 5.27 in 1970-1975 to 2.78 in 1995-2000 in the less developed regions it only went down from 6.60 to 5.47 in the least developed and thus poorest countries. It is equally noticeable that during the same 25 years, annual GDP per head for the world's population as a whole rose from just under $2,600 (measured in 2000 US dollars) to almost $5,400, whereas in the least developed countries it remained almost completely static, moving only from $1,613 to $1,661.[28] In many countries in the poorest category, income per head actually fell over this period, sometimes precipitately. In Somalia and Zambia, it fell by nearly one third and in Sierra Leone it almost halved although both countries are doing much better now as a result of rapidly rising commodity exports.[29] The whole world has a huge interest in ensuring that the poverty in these very poor countries is alleviated.

The key to ensuring that the world's population eventually plateaus at a manageable figure is thus inextricably connected with the rate at which those part of the world with the lowest living standards can be brought up to a level where the demographic transition to lower family sizes occurs. Even then, it will take decades before the world's population stabilises. Crucial to living standards being raised in poor countries is going to be the attitude not so much to aid as to trade in the rest of the world. The only way for poor countries to become richer is for their output per head to rise, and by far the most likely way for this to happens is for them to be able to develop trade relationships with the rest of the world which will enable them to follow the same export led paths to prosperity as were shown to be so viable by many of the Pacific Rim countries.

For this to happen, however, the rest of the world has to provide trade opportunities which at the moment far too many countries are unwilling make available. Protectionism – particularly in agriculture but also in ways which adversely impact on industrial development – is much too widely prevalent. Reducing tariffs is never easy, as successive WTO rounds have shown, but the worse that economic conditions generally are, the harder it becomes to get them removed. One of the most overwhelming arguments therefore for improving the economic performance of the western world is that this is the only way there is likely to be to provide the world with the opportunity it needs to contain the expansion of the world's population to a level which will be viable for the long-term future.

Resources

If far the best solution to the world's population problem is to raise living standards as widely as possible to bring down the birth rate towards the one in the Lower rather than the Higher UN Variant, will this mean that we simply bring forward the time when sufficient resources cease to be available to support the growth in economic output which would otherwise materialise? This has been a constant pre-occupation at least since the publication of *The Limits to Growth* by the Club of Rome in 1972.[30] Warnings of resource depletion have been taken up by many others, leading to a widely held view that increasing the growth rate, especially in the already relatively well-off western world, even if desirable, may not be feasible. A systematic review of the available evidence, however, suggests that such a view is very likely to be misplaced. There are two main reasons why predictions of critical resource scarcity in the future are likely to be wrong. One is that a careful view of the resources on which the world depends shows that few, if any, of them are likely to run short to an extent that will prevent living standards from continuing to rise. The other is the capacity of human ingenuity to solve problems once the urgency of doing so, and the resources required to get this done, generally driven by market forces, both materialise.

Turning first to resources, these clearly come in a variety of different categories and a brief synopsis[31] of their availability indicates that there are actually remarkably few key raw materials on which our industrialised existence depends. 80% of by value of all them consist of seven raw materials, cement (of which limestone is the main component),[32] aluminium, iron ore, copper, gold, nitrogen and zinc, all of which are in ample supply.[33] Of the remaining 20%, three quarters are made up of 16 more raw materials,[34] supplies of none of which look anywhere near running out in the foreseeable future. This leaves a quarter – 5% of the total – still to be considered. Of these a study carried out in 1988, followed by further investigations, showed that, of the 47 raw material known to have significant applications, supplies of only one – tantalum, which is used for high-tech alloys and for some electronic applications – might be likely to run short. Particularly when account is taken both of the scope for recycling, the likelihood that more reserves will be found as potential shortages appear, and improvements materialise in the efficiency with which all raw materials can be used, it does not appear at all likely that there will be significant constraints on growth for the foreseeable future because of lack of sources of supply of any of them.

This view is reinforced by the fact that there is overwhelming evidence that, as GDP per head rises beyond fairly low levels, the resource intensity of further increases in living standards rapidly reduces proportionately the raw material resources required to sustain them. This happens partly because of a shift towards a substantially higher proportion of increasing incomes being spent on services rather than goods. It is also worth noting that the total value of all raw material production only represents 1.1% of world GDP.[35] Even if the costs of producing them were to rise significantly, it would not therefore be likely to put a serious strain on the world's growth prospects.

Second, will the world be able to produce enough food to be able to feed a population of perhaps 10bn people, especially as the demand for better nutrition rises with higher living standards? The main reason for optimism is the astonishing rate at which food production has risen both in quantity and quality over the past century. As a result, even though calorie counts have at the same time risen strongly, food prices have tended to fall dramatically, although with inevitable fluctuations. The main reason for the increase in food production has been the Green Revolution, involving higher crop yields; improved irrigation and water supply; more and more widespread and intensive use of fertilisers and pesticides; and a significant increase in farmer's management skills.

Can these trends continue? They almost certainly will. Technical advance is still taking place, not least in genetically modified foodstuffs, which are likely to become more and more widely used despite the objections to them in some quarters. There is a huge gap between best and worst agricultural practice, allowing large increases in output still to be achieved. Improved communication and cheaper transport have enabled world food production to be more and more heavily concentrated in those areas best suited for growing each individual crop. There is also scope for bringing more land into agricultural use, particularly in Africa. The problem with providing everyone with enough to eat does not, at least in principle, lie in getting enough food produced. The reason why far too many people are still hungry is that they do not have enough money to pay for the nourishment they need and the best solution to this problem is to raise their incomes.

Third, will there be enough water? There is certainly no shortage of it in aggregate. Total rainfall capable of being captured is equivalent to about 5,700 litres for water for everyone on earth per day.[36] The problem is with its distribution. Just to survive on a day to day basis, a human being only requires about two litres of water per 24 hours. This figure rises to 100 litres, however, if household needs and personal hygiene are included, and by anything from 500 to 2,000 litres a day if account taken of the requirements for agriculture and industry. Globally, of all the water available, agriculture uses about 69%, industry 23% and households 8%. Especially taking seasonal variations into account, this leaves potentially almost 20% of humanity short of water. There are, however, solutions. Desalination, although expensive, may be one. Avoiding growing highly water consuming crops in water-short areas is another. Much the most hopeful, however, is to stop massive waste of water by pricing it more appropriately, particularly in agriculture, where most of the waste takes place. It is interesting to note that 'water wars' have turned out largely to be a figment of copy writers' imaginations. The lack of warfare over water needs to be recorded alongside the no less than 3,600 treaties concerning international water resources which history shows as having been negotiated over the centuries.[37]

Fourth, what about energy? The average person in Europe now enjoys from non-human energy sources the equivalent of 150 times the power that the average human being could produce. In America the ratio is about 300 and even in India it is 15.[38] Of total energy consumption, oil represents about 41% of the total, gas 24% and coal 23%. Clearly, at some stage in the future reserves or oil and gas are going to become scarcer and more difficult to exploit and thus more expensive, although this seems unlikely to be the case for a long time in the case of coal and may not be that soon either in the case of oil and gas, as surveying for new deposits intensifies, technology develops and new ways of extracting oil and gas are developed. There are also other obvious pressures for reducing the consumption of carbon-based energy supplies arising from fears of global warming. The issue is therefore whether it is possible to bring other sources of energy on to the market as the world's economy grows, in sufficient quantities and at manageable prices, to fill the gap which will be left as, sooner or later, carbon based fuels provide a declining proportion of total energy.

Part of the solution will undoubtedly come from dramatic improvements in the efficiency with which fuels of all sorts can be used, especially if energy prices rise. Energy consumption per unit of output halved between 1971 and 1992.[39] It also falls as a proportion of GDP as incomes rise to western standards, relieving some of the pressure on resources. Nevertheless, it is clear that alternatives to fossil fuels are going to be needed in major quantities. Renewable energy from wind and waves will no doubt fill some of the gap, although it tends to be expensive and not always reliable when most needed. Nuclear energy is another possibility, although this also has high costs and other well-known drawbacks. Capturing the heat delivered to earth by the sun may turn out to be a better medium-term bet. The heat received by the earth from the sun presents about 7,000 times our current energy use.[40] The problem up to now has been the cost of photovoltaic cells, but these are steadily falling. Just over 3.0% of the area of the Sahara Desert could supply the entire world's energy needs at present levels of consumption,[41] although clearly there would be major distribution problems.

Finally, however, it is worth noting that, for all the importance attached to them energy costs only make up about 2% of world GDP.[42] Even if there were significant increases in energy costs above their present level, therefore, the impact on the world's economy would not be as substantial as is often supposed. If energy was, say, 50% more expensive than it is now, at an extra cost of 1% of GDP, a wide range of energy technologies would become economically viable. Energy therefore may well become more expensive relative to everything else in future but we are not likely to run short of it in aggregate.

Finally, there is another potential constraint on economic growth which is the accumulation of unmanageable amounts of waste and pollution. Waste production tends to rise at least as fast as living standards and, if anything, slightly faster. Recycling provides a limited solution, but at fairly heavy cost both environmentally and in financial terms, leaving some form of land fill as the only alternative. This problem is clearly more acute in densely populated countries than those with low densities, suggesting that moving waste round the world to under-populated areas may turn out to be the best way to solve a problem which looks difficult but not insurmountable.

Pollution problems, essentially break down into two main categories, these being those to do with air quality on the one hand and water contamination on the other. In terms of risks to human health, far the biggest problems relate to air pollution, especially in under-developed countries. Traffic fumes, open fires in poorly ventilated buildings, and industrial emissions are all major contributors. All these problems can be largely solved, however, by spending enough money on them and, as a recent World Bank survey showed, once living standards rise through $5,000 to $10,000 per head per annum, the pressure to clean up the environment rises exponentially, ensuring that resources are made available to do it.[43]

The single biggest cause of water pollution has been ocean oil tanker operations, which are now much more tightly controlled that they used to be, as are sewage discharges into the sea. Of more concern, however, is oxygen depletion in coastal areas, caused by agricultural run-off containing nitrates and phosphates, though these problems are on a limited scale in world terms. On balance the UN recently declared: 'The open sea is still relatively clean'.[44] Rivers are a more serious problem, especially during the early stages of industrialisation. The urge to improve the environment as living standards rise, however, tends to ensure – as has happened all over the West – that sufficient resources are deployed to overcome these problems too. There is little doubt that the same pressures will result in similar outcomes in developing countries.

This brief survey of the constraints on growth strongly suggests that with reasonably good management, there are no insuperable problems to be encountered in resource terms which will constrain humanity from increasing its living standards into the foreseeable future, whether or not the West takes steps to make its economies grow much faster. Looking just at resources is not, however, enough. It is also very important to factor in the capacity of humanity to adapt to new circumstances via the power or market pressures and the use of technology. No-one 50 years ago, for example, would have been able confidently to predict the results achieved by the Green Revolution in agriculture or the improvement in fuel efficiency of motor cars and aircraft. Something of a leap of faith may be required to assume that the improvements in technology and resource management which humanity has achieved over past decades will be accomplished again in the years to come. To plan ahead on the assumption that this will not happen, however, is surely to take much too pessimistic a view. It must be an error of monumental proportions to assume that the ingenuity which has achieved so much since the Industrial Revolution began is no longer going to be available to help us to find solutions to resource and production problems as well in the future as we have done in the past.

Climate change

There is, however, another type of constraint which needs to be considered in the light of any proposals to increase the world's growth rate which entails improving the performance of the western economies. Should the impact of increased output on climate change and global warming preclude increasing growth, especially in the West, being a reasonable objective?

While there are some differing views about the extent to which climate change is a threat to the world environment, there is no doubt that there is a widely held consensus on a number of aspects of the impact of increased industrialisation on the world's atmosphere. There is no serious dispute that a number of gases, of which carbon dioxide is the most important, representing about 60% of the total, trap heat in the atmosphere, although they can also cause it to be reflected back into space.[45] When observations started in 1960, the CO^2 concentration in the atmosphere was 315 parts per million. By 2016 the reading was 407.[46] There is therefore no doubt that the concentration like CO^2 has increased and is still rising as a result of emissions caused by industrialisation. There is also no dispute that there has been an increase in average world temperatures over the last century and a half of about 0.8°, although the rise took place almost entirely over two relatively short periods, one between 1910 and 1945 and the other from 1975 until the end of the twentieth century, with a plateau between 1945 and 1975, and much slower growth in temperature than almost all the climate models predicted since then.[47]

There is less agreement on the mechanism by which the concentrations of carbon dioxide and other greenhouse gases have caused the temperature rise, although all the climate change models based on empirical data indicate that there is a strong connection. The main problem has been providing sufficiently detailed and accurate descriptions as to how the world's climate works, particularly the cooling effect of particles and the effect of water vapour on temperature and weather. The impact of different sorts of clouds on the earth's temperature have been especially difficult to model comprehensively.[48] There is also a good deal of disagreement about the extent to which other factors, especially sun spot activity, may influence the earth's temperature fluctuations in addition to those to do with increasing gas concentrations, especially over relatively short timescales. Evidence suggest that the brightness of the sun has increased sufficiently over the last 200 to 300 years to raise the earth's temperature on its own by about 0.4°.[49] If it is true that as much as 40% of the increase in surface temperatures which has been recorded may be due to this effect rather than that of greenhouse gases, the significance of the contribution of carbon dioxide and other gases to global warming may have to be correspondingly scaled down.[50]

Despite these differences of opinion, however, there is a very broad scientific consensus that emissions of carbon dioxide and other gases resulting from economic growth have caused the earth's temperature to rise and will continue to do so in future. Taking it, therefore, as a given that increased economic activity accentuates climate change along the lines predicted by the UN, involving an increases in temperature on present trends through to 2100 which cluster round estimates of between 1.3° and 3.2°, accompanied by and a rise is sea level of between 31cm and 49cm,[51] what impact should this have on proposals to increase the growth rate of western economies?

A major difference between climate change and other considerations which bear on the pros and cons of increasing economic growth is the long timescales involved. Although cumulatively very substantial, the impact of increases in the average temperature of the earth, is inevitably spread over a long period, generating difficult concerns about how much to discount benefits due to materialise a long time into the future compared to others more immediately available. Even if the Kyoto proposals, flowing from the 1992 Rio de Janeiro Climate Change Conference, were implemented in full, they would only put off by about six years, at very high cost in terms of output foregone, the increase in average earth temperature which would happen anyway.[52]

This has raised questions as to whether curbing emissions as drastically as this is a rational approach, if the alternative is a reasonable expectation that economic growth will continue over the coming decades at roughly the same rate as over the last century, thus providing a huge flow of resources to deal with whatever costs climate change may bring. There also appear to be considerably less expensive ways of achieving most of the Kyoto targets by using policies such as carbon taxes, which would use market forces to encourage the use of energy sources which produce less greenhouse gases.[53] If the earth nevertheless does warm up as predicted, estimates produced by the UN indicate that the cost of offsetting the impact of climate change will be of the order of $5,000bn, with roughly half this sum falling on the developed world and the other half on other countries. This is a very large sum of money but not one which is necessarily unmanageable, representing 1.5% to 2.0% per annum[54] of world GDP, a ratio which should fall in the future as the world's economic output increases.

Even if global warming on the scale which the UN predicts – unless very vigorous action is taken to retard it – is regarded as too risky, however, it is not at all clear that the result of holding down economic growth to stop this happening, particularly in the West, would have the longer term effects on global warming that its proponents hope would be achieved. If the economic condition of many western countries is as poor and fragile as it appears to be, with resumption of at least some reasonable rate of economic growth being the only route out of their current financial difficulties, blocking off this escape route may plunge the world into a major financial crisis. In the short term, this may reduce carbon emissions, but in the medium to long term it is very unlikely to do so. This is because a financial crisis in the West will almost certainly have a major negative impact on economic conditions in countries where the birth rate is still very high, thus putting off the time when the demographic transition towards smaller families there takes place. The result of a prolonged period of slow or negative growth among the world's developed countries is therefore all too likely to be that the total number of human beings which the world has eventually to accommodate will be significantly larger than would otherwise be the case. As all these extra people will, sooner or later, almost certainly want to have western standards of living, the impact on the world's ecology and global warming will be correspondingly greater.

There are, moreover, other ways of combating climate change than letting it happen and paying the costs. There may be ways of offsetting the factors which drive global warming by technological developments – so called geo-engineering. Possible suggestions include fertilising the oceans with algae capable of absorbing carbon, putting sulphur particles into the atmosphere to help to cool it, and capturing carbon dioxide from fossil fuel combustion and returning it to permanent storage in appropriate geological formations.[55] A number of proposals such as these – and others – are already under consideration, whose cost, while high, should be manageable in relation to the adaptation costs which might otherwise be incurred.

There is also a possibility that the cost of renewable fuels will fall to below that of fossil fuels, in which case there is likely to be a major switch towards their use without any taxation or subsidies being involved. There may be additional help from even greater improvements in fuel use efficiency than are currently anticipated, thus reducing the amount of greenhouse gases emitted. The ratio between GDP per head and fuel consumption has doubled about every 50 years in the developed world,[56] and hopefully this trend will continue. With assumptions of this sort in place, the central projections for temperature increases from global warming come in at considerably lower figures, suggesting a rise in temperature of 0.7° by 2100, followed by a decline as renewable energy sources become more widely used. Even a somewhat more pessimistic scenario indicates a total temperature rise over the twenty-first century of no more than 1.5°, followed by a slow decline.[57] Furthermore, not all the impacts of climate change are negative. UN reports conclude, for example, that, while there will be winners and losers, the overall effect on agricultural output should be positive rather than negative.[58]

Overall, therefore, the policy mix on climate change which seems most likely to achieve the best results at minimum outlay is to constrain greenhouse emissions everywhere where this can be done at bearable cost, not least to reduce as much as possible the risk of the world reaching some kind of climatic or environmental tipping point. At the same time, however, we need to avoid the calamities which could befall us both in connection with global warming and in other ways if we fail to keep up the world's growth rate, among either developed countries or the Third World. This seems to be the most sensible way to minimise the risks from global warming, while putting everyone in the best position both to afford to make the contributions which will need to be made to counteract the costs of climate change and to do so without doing so prejudicing other important but much more immediately pressing objectives.

Migration

Migration has always been part of the human experience and, as the world's population has grown, so, with ups and downs, has the number of people migrating increased. From the eighteenth century onwards, 55m Europeans migrated overseas, many of them to the USA, peaking with nearly 9m arrivals in the first decade of the twentieth century. By the end of the first decade of the twenty-first century, including legal international migrants, refugees and illegal migrants, the total number of people worldwide who were living in a country other than were they were born was estimated to be about 215m,[59] and this number is growing at a faster rate than total population growth.[60] The influx of migrants to western countries has now approached in absolute numbers the scale of nineteenth century western emigration, prompted partly by crises like the one currently in Syria. When Europeans migrated, they were generally filling up territory that contained very few people. Now migration tends to increase already relatively high population densities.[61]

There is no doubt that migration has positive aspects to it. Diasporas spread information and facilitate trade and the spread of ideas. They can and often do generate flows of remittances to poor countries. A recent study by Duke University showed that, while immigrants make up an eighth of America's population, they founded a quarter of the country's technology and engineering firms.[62] Generally, however, migration between countries with roughly the same standard of living works more smoothly than where there is a very steep economic gradient to be traversed.

By far the largest category of migrants move from one country to another for economic reasons. Migrants move because they believe that they can better their life chances somewhere else, although the data consistently show that when families move, the employment opportunities for women are apt to be less favourable than they were prior to the move.[63] The process of taking such decisions therefore frequently includes family members who are left behind, especially in poorer countries where remittances from those who have migrated to more developed economies represent a major economic benefit.[64] Hardly surprisingly, the flow of migrants is largely from poorer countries to those that are richer. Sometimes a large degree of integration is relatively easily achieved. At the other extreme immigrants may find themselves almost wholly excluded from the host society. Those who have moved, however, often maintain substantial elements of their culture, including religious affiliations and language, at least for one generation.[65] The flow of migrants from Mexico to the USA is now the greatest in the world, although low Mexican educational levels have made assimilation difficult,[66] and there is large scale migration both into the EU and within it, sometimes presenting similar problems to Mexican migrants to the USA.

Who benefits from economically driven migration? Undoubtedly, it is migrants themselves who generally gain most from moving from one country to another. Clearly, too, the bigger the gap there is between migrants' earning power in their countries of origin and those to which they make the transition, the greater their economic gains will be. With travel as cheap as it now is, movement from poorer to richer areas of the world is now much easier than it was, and the larger the gap there is in living standards between the developed and developing countries, the greater the migration pressure are likely to be. The key issue here, then, is whether, on balance, the overall gains from large scale international migration, especially from poor countries to rich ones, outweigh the disbenefits. Much depends on the scale on which migration takes place and thus on the capacity of both host and donor countries to cope with its impacts. On balance, therefore, whether overall the gainers exceed the losers tends to depend largely on both how easy it is for migrants to be assimilated and the scale on which migration takes place. What are the pros and cons of migration generally?

First, it is argued that there are large numbers of jobs in high living standard countries which the indigenous work force in the developed world does not want to do but which migrants are willing to take on. This may be true, but in many cases there are other ways of getting the necessary work done other than by employing large numbers of unskilled people at low wages to get it carried out. There is therefore, not surprisingly, evidence that large scale immigration of people prepared to work for relatively poor remuneration discourages investment in labour-saving machinery and the improvements in productivity which go with it. Furthermore, the losers, when there is large influx of people who are prepared to work for low wages, tend to be those competing with them, although the evidence on this point is not wholly conclusive with some studies showing much more pronounced effects than others.[67]

Second, it is maintained that immigrants are required to redress imbalances in the age structure of developed countries with low fertility rates and thus aging populations, particular cases in point being potentially much of continental Europe and Japan. There are, however, two main problems with this approach. One is that immigrants themselves get older and will, therefore, sooner or later themselves become part of the dependency problem, even if – as is usually the case – they have larger families than the indigenous population in the meantime. The second is that the scale of immigration required to fill the gaps in the population left by low fertility rates is on a scale which would be completely impractical because the number of immigrants required to allow this to happen would be far greater than any estimates of the host countries' capacity to absorb them.

Third, it is maintained that immigration provides cultural diversity which would not otherwise be there and that this is a positive good in itself. There is surely something in this argument but it is one which needs to be balanced against the resentment which large cultural and life style differences can easily bring in train, especially if those involved are forced to live in close proximity to each other. Again, there may well be significant differences in perception among those who are well off who, for example, enjoy dining out at a variety of ethnic restaurants, from those living on high density housing estates with neighbours who cannot speak the host country language and who live their lives in different ways from the indigenous population.

Finally, it is argued that immigrants have a lot to offer because they tend to be exceptionally hard working, positively motivated and entrepreneurial. There is no doubt that there is considerable force in this contention. In the British context, for example, although not all immigrant groups have done so well, Huguenots, Jews and Ugandan Asians are all groups who have made conspicuously successful contributions particularly to the business world but often more broadly too. The obverse of this benefit, however, is the loss sustained by the countries from which exceptionally talented and motivated groups come. All too often, they tend to be the best educated and worldly wise migrating from poor countries which can ill afford to lose their skills.

In summary, therefore, while large scale migration for economic reasons has some merits, especially, in most cases, for the migrants themselves, the positive implications for everyone else are less obvious. Those who are on lower incomes in the developed world tend to find their earning capacity reduced while the pressure generated on social resources such as housing and the infrastructure generally increases, especially in countries or urban environments where the population density is already high. At the same time the poorer countries from which migrants tend to come can ill afford to lose the skills and abilities of the sort of people who want to migrate.

What is also clear is that, as the scale of migration increases, the strains in all directions get greater and the tolerance of those in host countries, particularly its poorer members, gets stretched beyond a point where it can be contained. If migration is to be kept within reasonable bounds, therefore, there are two major requirements. One is that, as far as possible, the gap in living standards between poor and rich countries is kept as small as possible, and reduced rather than increased. The other is that the living standards of the poorest countries are raised as quickly as possible to the point where the transition to smaller families take place, thus reducing the number of potential migrants and the pressure on them to move to more manageable levels.

The major problem facing the world in migration terms, therefore, if the numbers of migrants is to be kept to manageable proportions, is the low GDP per head in the poorest countries, with the highest birth rates and the poorest economic prospects. No doubt, the wider the gap becomes, the greater the pressure for large scale migration for economic reasons will become. If the poorest countries are to become better off, however, it is even more important that the rich world is doing well enough to provide the trading opportunities and aid which poor countries need to raise their living standards. If the West falters, the result therefore, over coming decades is likely to be more and not less migration. There are already signs that there is limited capacity among host developed countries to absorb immigrants from poor countries on a larger and larger scale without tensions rising to an intolerable level. At the least, it has to be in the developed world's interest to adopt policies which will raise the living standards in the least developed economies in the world to a point where the birth rate starts to fall steeply, as has happened everywhere else once the GDP per head tipping point has been reached. Both the developed and the developing world therefore have a huge interest in ensuring that the pressures for economic migration are kept within bounds with which both donor and host countries can cope.

Conclusion

2016 was the year when the UK voted for Brexit and when Donald Trump was elected president of the USA. Both were events which the political elites either side of the Atlantic neither expected nor wanted to see happening. They both occurred because of heavily discontented electorates. Across the whole of the western world there is an increasing divide between those who are doing well and who are confident and contented and those who feel left behind, undervalued and alienated, with these discontents manifesting themselves in increasingly strident populist nationalism. In 2017, Europe faces the prospects of elections in major countries such as Holland, Germany and France, where the outcomes may mirror the upsets in the UK and the USA.

There is a clear reason why this is happening. The big divide in western societies nowadays is between those who have done well out of globalisation and those who have not benefited from the changes which increasingly liberalised trade and financial flows have brought in train – or at least by nothing like as much as those who have. This divide is now showing serious signs of destabilising the reasonably stable political environment which the West has enjoyed for many years. Indeed, at worst, it may pose a potentially existential threat to liberal democracy itself, if nothing is done to stop our politics sliding further and further towards irrationalism, protectionism and xenophobia as a result of electorates losing more and more faith in the capacity of those governing them to do so reasonably competently and fairly. All societies are unequal and history shows that free electorates are willing to tolerate this state of affairs, recognising its inevitability, but only provided that it is not to excess. Current developments, however, suggest that we are pushing against the limits of what an increasingly large percentage of voters are prepared to accept as part of what they think is a reasonable social compact.

This might not matter so much if those protesting about the unfairness of the way they feel treated had leaders with policy platforms which were reasonably likely to improve the conditions of their supporters. Unfortunately, this does not generally appear to be the case. Lashing out against austerity is not a policy if there is no understanding about how to get the economy to grow and to become less unbalanced, so that austerity becomes unnecessary. Declaiming about the downsides of globalisation and trade liberalisation – which may well have not have benefited many people very much – is not a policy for making the situation less unfair. Protectionism may help some sectors of society but always at the expense of making others worse off. Retreating from international obligations generally gets reciprocated, making everyone's future less secure. Instead, we need rational policies which will deal with the underlying problems of dashed hopes, resentment at static living standards and mounting inequality by making the beneficial impact of global trends more widely felt; by getting the economy to grow so that everyone is better off; and by restoring sufficient faith in the competence and good intentions of our political governing class to make our democratic future more assured and appreciated.

The message in this book is that the reason why we suffer from the increasingly dystopian predicament felt by many people to be overtaking them is that the UK as a country – mirroring conditions across most of the West – is too heavily divided between those who are doing well and those who are having a much rougher time economically, with the former too ready to blame the latter for their lack of good fortune. The South of England is now a different place from the Midlands and the North. Those who voted Leave in the June 2016 EU referendum generally have a very different view of life than those who chose Remain. If we want to restore the cohesion which is vital to make liberal democracy work, we need to bind our communities back together again. Sharing out the fruits of prosperity more evenly must be the best way of doing this. Most of the reason why this has not been happening to anything like a sufficient extent is that for a long time, we have run our economy so relatively poorly as a result of policy deficiencies which chapter after chapter in this book have highlighted. At the risk of over-gilding the lily, perhaps it is worth reiterating once more what the major imbalances and deficiencies in our economy are and what we need to do to put them right.

We have allowed the proportion of our GDP which we invest to drop to a point where productivity growth has almost completely stalled and where, as a result, median wages, allowing for inflation, are barely higher than they were before the 2008 crash. We have deindustrialised to such an extent that literally millions of people have lost their good blue-collar jobs, leaving them in far too many cases with low productivity, unfulfilling, low paid and insecure service sector employment. Because we have lost nearly all our light industry, we have foregone the increases in output per hour which this sector of our economy is uniquely good at generating. We have also allowed disparities in income, wealth and life chances generally in different parts of our country to proliferate to a completely unacceptable extent. In addition – crucially – we have lost our capacity to pay our way in the world, leaving us with a vast balance of payments gap every year, which we have only been able to fill by selling off national assets on a scale unmatched anywhere else in the world and by getting deeper and deeper in debt to foreign countries.

Because we are not earning the standard of living which, as a nation, we enjoy, we have had to borrow vast sums of money to fill the gap both as a nation, as consumers and through our government. To try to stimulate the economy, base rates are lower than they have ever been but the result has been to make it much easier for the rich than the poor to benefit from the asset inflation which ultra-low interest rates have generated, exacerbating the tendency for inequality to become both greater and increasingly obvious to everyone. Our society has become more and more divided on both a socio-economic and a regional basis. Those who have done well out of liberalisation and globalisation enjoy wonderfully secure, well paid and interesting lifestyles, while those who have lost out struggle with tight budgets, static or declining life chances and dwindling hope.

The fundamental reason why we suffer from all these problems is that we have allowed our country to become so deeply uncompetitive with those along the Pacific Rim – and with others, such as Germany and Holland, which have wage rates just as high as ours but who enjoy much higher productivity as a result of greater capital equipment per worker and much better trained workforces than we have. The reason why we have allowed ourselves to drift into this condition is that for many decades our exchange rate has been far too high for manufacturing to thrive. It is true that we have a vibrant and very successful service sector with a large export surplus, but this does not make up for the much larger deficit we have on goods, about 80% of which are manufactures.

Because most services are not very price sensitive, the exchange rate does not make a huge difference to those who sell them abroad, buttressed by the fact that we have strong competitive advantages in our language, geography, legal system, etc which make our services attractive to foreign buyers. For manufacturing, however, where we lack comparable natural advantages, and especially for light manufacturing which is very price sensitive, the exchange rate – essentially what we charge the rest of the world for our labour costs – is absolutely crucial. If we charge too much – as manifestly, for a long time, we have done in relation to the level of productivity we have actually achieved – all the usual adverse consequences described in this book are bound to follow. Our share of world trade has gone down because we have not had enough to sell to the rest of world at prices foreign buyers are prepared to pay; investment has faltered because most manufacturing has been unprofitable and large amounts of it have been closed down; because of poor prospects competent people have been put off a career making and selling, so our industrial management in too many cases has got worse and worse; balance of payments problems have become increasingly acute; and deflation, low growth, static incomes and increasing inequality have all followed.

If we are going to break out of this vicious downward spiral, we need to recognise what the fundamental cause of it is and to take action to counteract it. We need to get our economy rebalanced. We do not need to have as large an industrial base as countries such as Germany and Singapore because we have such a strong exporting service sector, but we do need a bigger manufacturing base than 10% of GDP. Something like 15% of GDP looks like being a reasonable target, if we are going to be able to pay our way in the world at least to a point where we are not accumulating debt on an exponential basis in relation to our capacity to service and eventually to repay it.

To retrieve the degree of industrial strength we need, we will have to have a much larger percentage of our GDP than at present spent on physical investment – perhaps 20% or more rather than the current barely 13%. This will only happen if light industry is profitable. No industrial strategy is going to work without this condition being fulfilled. Public sector investment – in roads, schools, hospitals, rail and housing – requires resources but not profitability to make it happen. In the private sector, without positive returns on investment being clearly achievable, there is no prospect of expenditure on the required scale materialising.

If we ran policies to get sufficient industry back to get our economy rebalanced, it would obviously make sense for most of the new manufacturing to be located in our erstwhile industrial areas rather than in London and the South East, and this will go a long way towards evening up prospects between different regions of the country. It will also produce a fund of new well paid jobs where they are most needed. The already well-favoured areas of the country – London in particular – need to continue to be encouraged to flourish while other parts of the country, which have no done so well, are given maximum opportunity to catch up.

The key to getting all this done is for the authorities – and politicians, the commentariat, the academic world and public opinion – to realise just how crucial competitiveness is in regulating our relationships with everywhere else in the world. We need an exchange rate policy just as badly as we need to make sure that we have fiscal and monetary policies which make sense. We cannot afford any longer the neo-liberal insouciance as to the value of the pound on the foreign exchanges – leaving it to market forces on their own to fix the going rate, with no official guidance or involvement. Very few other countries in the world with the capacity for controlling their own destinies do so, and nor should we. This does not mean that we would need to operate on a beggar-thy-neighbour basis, running a surplus which has to be someone else's deficit. Instead the most sensible policy would be to run a manageably small deficit while making sure that we maintain a fair and sustainable share of world trade and the manufacturing capacity to underpin it, so that we are not falling behind everyone else all the time.

For the UK electorate does not look likely to tolerate in future the static wages and lost opportunities from which far too many of its members have suffered. Those who have done well need to pay more attention to the lot of those who have not been so lucky. Using an activist but benign exchange rate policy as the lever for doing so has a much better chance of success than any other policy option on the horizon.

Notes

Preface

1   Wikipedia entry on the Bank of England.
2   Wikipedia entry on The Club of Rome.
3   Wikipedia entry on Climate Change.

Introduction

1   Table C5-b in the *World Economy – A Millennial Perspective* by Angus Maddison. Paris: OECD, 2001; and Tables on page113 in International Statistics Yearbook 2004 and op cit page 78 in the 2015 edition.
2   Wikipedia entry on World Population, using figures supplied by the US Census Bureau.
3   Estimates by the World Bank.
4   Page 84 in *International Financial Statistics Yearbook 2016*. Washington DC: IMF, 2016.
5   Table 10-6 in *China Statistical Yearbook 201*. Beijing: National Bureau of Statistics of China. 2016.
6   Ibid.
7   Tables A2 and F in *Quarterly National Accounts 2016 Q3*. London: ONS, 2016.

1. Economic Evolution

1   Table 1-2, page 28, in *The World Economy – A Millennial Perspective* by Angus Maddison. Paris: OECD, 2001.
2   Op cit, Table 1-9b, page 46.
3   Op cit, Table 19c, page 46.
4   The description of the development of credit and money in this section draw heavily on an as yet unpublished work by Christopher Meakin and Geoffrey Gardiner.
5   Wikipedia entry on money.
6   Pages 242 and 276 in *Hutchinson's Encyclopaedia*. Oxford: Helicon, 1998.
7   Wikipedia entry on the Industrial Revolution.
8   Page 50, in *The World Economy – A Millennial Perspective* by Angus Maddison. Paris: OECD, 2001.
9   Wikipedia.

10 Page 1009 in *Hutchinson's Encyclopaedia*. Oxford: Helicon, 1998.

11 Ibid, page 390.

12 Page 29 in *Frozen Desire* by James Buchan. London: Picador, 1997.

13 Wikipedia entry on banking.

14 Wikipedia entry on banknotes.

15 Page 96 in *Hutchinson's Encyclopaedia*. Oxford: Helicon, 1998.

16 Correspondence with Professor John Black.

17 Page 96 in *The Wealth and Poverty of Nations* by David Landes. London: Little Brown, 1998.

18 Table US.1 and US.4 in *Economic Statistics* 1900-1983 by Helma Leisner. London: *The Economist*, 1985. The measurement in this case is against private and not total investment.

19 Ibid Tables UK.1.

20 Ibid, tables J.1 and J.2.

21 Ibid, Table J.1.

22 Ibid Table UK.1.

23 Pages 283-5 in *Economic History of Europe* by Herbert Heaton. New York and London: Harper Bros, 1935.

24 Wikipedia entry on the British Empire.

25 Wikipedia entry on the Atlantic Slave Trade.

26 Table B-21, page 264, in *The World Economy: A Millennial Perspective* by Angus Maddison. Paris: OECD, 2001.

27 Page 310 in *A History of Europe* by J.M. Roberts. Oxford: helicon, 1996.

28 Page 168 in *The Death of Inflation* by Roger Bootle. London: Nicholas Brealey, 1996.

29 Calculation from Shaun Stewart.

30 Wikipedia entry on the Six Acts.

31 Table B-10a in *Monitoring the World Economy 1820-1992* by Angus Maddison. Paris: OECD, 1995.

32 Page 673 in *Economic History of Europe* by Herbert Heaton. New York and London: Harper Bros, 1935.

33 Page 390 in *Economic Development in Europe* by Clive Day. New York: Macmillan, 1946.

34 Wikipedia entry on Prussia.

35 Statistics provided by Shaun Stewart.

36 Figures calculated from Table B-10a in *Monitoring the World Economy 1820-1992* by Angus Maddison. Paris: OECD, 1995.

37 Ibid, Table D-1a.

38 Tables UK.3 and G.2 in *Economic Statistics 1900-1983* by Thelma Liesner. London; The Economist, 1985.

39 Ibid, Tables UK.3 and G.2.

40 Table A-2 in *Monitoring the World Economy 1820-1992* by Angus Maddison. Paris: OECD, 1995.

41 Pages 12 and 13 in *American Economic History* by John O'Sullivan and Edward K. Keuchel. Princeton and New York: Markus Wiener Publishing, 1989.

42 Ibid, page 49.

43 Table C88-114 in *Historical Statistics of the United States*. Washington DC: US Department of Commerce, 1960.

44 Table B-16a in *Monitoring the World Economy 1820-1992* by Angus Maddison. Paris: OECD, 1995.

45 Ibid, Table B-10a and D-1a.

46 Ibid, Table A-3a.

47 Ibid, Table C-16a.

48 Figure 3.2 page 76 in *Monitoring the World Economy 1820-1992* by Angus Maddison. Paris: OECD, 1995.

49 Ibid, Table D-1a.

50 Ibid, Table C-16a.

51 Various Tables in *Historical Statistics of the United States*. Washington DC: US Department of Commerce, 1960.

52 Table K-1 in *Monitoring the World Economy 1820-1992* by Angus Maddison. Paris: OECD, 1995.

53 Ibid, pages 40-42.

54 World Bank website.

55 Table B-12 in *Economic Report of the President*. Washington DC: US Government Printing Office, 2011.

56 Pages 67 and 68 in *American Economic History* by John O'Sullivan and Edward K. Keuchel. Princeton and New York: Markus Wiener Publishing, 1989.

57 Ibid, pages 59 and 70.

58 Page 320 in *A History of the American People* by Paul Johnson. London: Weidenfeld and Nicolson, 1997.

59 Tables E1-12 and E13-24 in *Historical Statistics of the United States*. Washington DC: US Department of Commerce, 1960.

60 Page 57 in *American Economic History* by John O'Sullivan and Edward K. Keuchel. Princeton and New York: Markus Wiener Publishing, 1989.

61 Ibid, page 345.

62 Table U1-14 in *Historical Statistics of the United States*. Washington DC: US Department of Commerce, 1960.

63 World Bank figures.

64 Page 464 in *A History of the American People* by Paul Johnson. London: Weidenfeld and Nicolson, 1997.

65 Table 1-2 in *Monitoring the World Economy 1820-1992* by Angus Maddison. Paris: OECD, 1995.

66 Ibid, Table K-1.

67 A series of tables in Part 1 of *The Productivity Race* by S.N. Broadberry. Cambridge: Cambridge University Press, 1997.

68 Table E-2 in *Monitoring the World Economy 1820-1992* by Angus Maddison. Paris: OECD, 1995.

69 Internet Archive on *The Final Report of the Royal Commission on the Depression of Trade and Industry*

70 Wikipedia entry on Thomas Malthus.

2. International Turmoil: 1914 to 1945

1   Page 1156 in *Hutchinson's Encyclopedia*. Oxford: Helicon, 1998.

2   Page 331 in *the End of History and the Last Man* by Francis Fukuyama. London: Penguin, 1992.

3   Calculated for figures in Table UK.1 in *Economic Statistics 1900-1982* by Thelma Liesner. London: the Economist 1985.

4   Ibid, Table US.1.

5   Ibid, Table US.7, UK.7, F.3 and G.7.

6   Page 1155 in *Hutchinson's Encyclopedia*. Oxford: Helicon, 1998.

7   Table F.2 in *Economic Statistics 1900-1983* by Thelma Leisner. London: *The Economist*, 1985.

8   Ibid, Table G.2

9   Ibid, Table UK.2.

10 For a full account see *the Great Inflation* by william Guttmann and Patricia Meehan. Farnborough. Saxon House, 1975.

11 Table G.3 in *Economic Statistics 1900-1983* by Thelma Leisner. London: *The Economist*, 1985.

12 Ibid, Table F.2.

13 Ibid, Tables G.1 and G.2.

14 Ibid, Tables G.1 and G.2.

15 Ibid, Table G.6.

16 Ibid, Tables UK.1, UK.2 and UK.10.

17 Page 73 in *the European Economy 1914-1990* by Derek H. Aldcroft. London: Croom Helm, 1993.

18 Table G.6 in *Economic Statistics 1900-1983* by Thelma Leisner. London: *The Economist*, 1985.

19 Ibid, Table G.1.

20 Page 85 in *the European Economy 1914-1990* by Derek H. Aldcroft. London: Croom Helm, 1993.

21 Table G.1 in *Economic Statistics 1900-1983* by Thelma Leisner. London: The Economist, 1985.

22 Ibid, Table G.3.

23 Ibid, Table G.1.

24 Ibid, Table UK.15.

25 Calculations by Shaun Stewart.

26 Table UK.15 in *Economic Statistics 1900-1983* by Thelma Leisner. London: *The Economist*, 1985.

27 Correspondence with Geoffrey Gardiner.

28 Study by the Manchester Statistical Society. Correspondence with Geoffrey Gardiner.

29 Table UK.2 in *Economic Statistics 1900-1983* by Thelma Leisner. London: *The Economist*, 1985.

30 Ibid, Table UK.9.

31 Ibid, Table UK.7.

32 Ibid, Table UK.2.

33 Ibid, Table UK.15.

34 Note from Shaun Stewart.

35 Tables F.1, F.2 and F.6 in *Economic Statistics 1900-1983* by Thelma Leisner. London: *The Economist*, 1985.

36 Ibid, Tables F.2, G.2 and UK.3

37 Table US.1 in *Economic Statistics 1900-1983* by Thelma Liesner. London The Economist,1985.

38 Ibid, Table US.1.

39 Ibid, Tables US.1, US.2 and US.9.

40 Page 163 in *American Economic History* by John O'Sullivan and Edward F. Keuchel. Princeton and New York: Markus Wiener Publishing, 1989.

41 Tables US.1, US.6 and US.7 in *Economic Statistics 1900-1983* by Thelma Liesner. London *The Economist*,1985.

42 Page 165 in *American Economic History* by John O'Sullivan and Edward F. Keuchel. Princeton and New York: Markus Wiener Publishing, 1989.

43 Ibid, page 167.

44 Tables US.1, US.2 and US.10 in *Economic Statistics 1900-1983* by Thelma Liesner. London The Economist,1985.

45 Chapter 10 in *American Economic History by* John O'Sullivan and Edward F. Keuchel. Princeton and New York: Markus Wiener Publishing, 1989.

46 Table US.15 in E*conomic Statistics 1900-1983* by Thelma Liesner. London T*he Economist*,1985.

47 Ibid, Tables US.1, US.2 and US.10.

48 Page 187 in *American Economic History* by John O'Sullivan and Edward F. Keuchel. Princeton and New York: Markus Wiener Publishing, 1989.

49 Table US.7 in *Economic Statistics 1900-1983* by Thelma Liesner. London *The Economist*,1985.

50 Page 187 in *American Economic History* by John O'Sullivan and Edward F. Keuchel. Princeton and New York: Markus Wiener Publishing, 1989.

51 Tables US.1 and US.2 in *Economic Statistics 1900-1983* by Thelma Liesner. London *The Economist*,1985.

52 Ibid, Tables US.1, US.2, US.7 and US.9.

53 Table B-10a in *Monitoring the World Economy 1820-1992* by Angus Madison. Paris: OECD, 1995.

54 Page 169 in *Towards True Monetarism* by Geoffrey Gardiner. London: The Dulwich Press, 1993.

55 Pages 233-235 in *A History of Economics* by John Kenneth Galbraith. London: Penguin , 1987.

56 *The Economic Consequences of Mr Churchill* by John Maynard Keynes. London: Published by Leonard and Virginia Woolf at the Hogarth Press, 1925.

57 Wikipedia entry on John Maynard Keynes.

58 House of Lords Record of Debates.

59 Page 239 in *A History of the World Economy* by James Foreman-Peck. Hemel Hempstead: Harvester Wheatsheaf, 1995.

60 Ibid, page 239 *et seq.*

61 Table G-2 in *Monitoring the World Economy 1820-1992* by Angus Maddison. Paris: OECD, 1995.

62 Ibid, Table C-16a.

63 GDP Volume Measure Tables in *International Monetary Statistics*. Washington DC: IMF, 2000.

64 GDP Volume Measure Tables in *International Monetary Statistics*. Washington DC: IMF 2000 and 2011.

3. Post-World War II

1 Table G.2 in E*conomic Statistics 1900-1983I by Thelma Liesner*. London: The Economist, 1985.

2 Ibid, Tables UK.2 and F.2.

3 Ibid, Tables G.1, G.2 and G.7.

4 Ibid, Tables F.1, F.2 and F.7.

5 Ibid, Table UK.1.

6 Ibid, Table UK.15.

7 Ibid, Tables UK.1, F.1. F2, G.1, G.2. It.1 and It.2.

8 Page 173 in *Treaties establishing the European Communities*. Luxembourg: Office for Official Publications of the European Communities, 1973.

9 Page 23 in *The New European Economy* by Loukas Tsoulakis. Oxford: Oxford University Press, 1993.

10 Table UK.1 in *Economic Statistics 1900-1983* by Thelma Liesner. London The Economist, 1985.

11 EC and UK Tables in *National Accounts 1960-1992*. Paris: OECD, 1994.

12 Page 450 in *National Accounts of OECD Countries 1953-1969*. Paris: OECD, 1970.

13 Table US.1 in *Economic Statistics 1900-1983* by Thelma Leisner. London: *The Economist*, 1985.

14 Table I-2 in *Monitoring the World Economy 1820-1992* by Angus Maddison. Paris: OECD, 1995.

15 Tables B-79 and B-80 in *Economic Report of the President* Washington DC: US Government Printing Office, 1999.

16 Ibid, Tables B-1 and B-29.

17 Ibid, Table B-79.

18 Ibid, Table B-2.

19 Page 345 in *American Economic History* by John O'Sullivan and Edward F. Keuchel. Princeton and New York: Markus Weiner Publishing, 1989.

20 Table B-63 in *Economic Report of the President* Washington DC: US Government Printing Office, 1999.

21 Ibid, Table B-103.

22 Table US.11 in *Economic Statistics 1900-1983* by Thelma Leisner. London: *The Economist*, 1985.

23 Table B-63 in *Economic Report of the President* Washington DC: US Government Printing Office, 1999.

24 Ibid, Table B-35.

25 Ibid, Table B-103.

26 Page 154 in *National Accounts 1960-1992*. Paris: OECD, 1994.

27 Table G-2 in *Monitoring the World Economy 1820-1992* by Angus Maddison. Paris: OECD, 1995.

28 Page 172 in *International Financial Statistics Yearbook*. Washington DC: IMF, 1998.

29 Table B-4 in *Economic Report of the President* Washington DC: US Government Printing Office, 1999.

30 Ibid, Table B-63.

31 Page 52 *et seq* in *Monitoring the World Economy 1820-1992* by Angus Maddison, Paris: OECD 1995.

32 Ibid, Tables D-1a and D-1e.

33 Page 569, *Hutchinson's Encyclopaedia*. Oxford: Helicon, 1998.

34 Chapter 23 in *The Wealth and Poverty of Nations* by David Landes. London: Little Brown, 1998.

35 Wikipedia entry on Emperor Meiji.

36 Page 53 in *Monitoring the World Economy 1820-1992* by Angus Maddison, Paris: OECD 1995.

37 Ibid, Table B-16a.

38 Ibid, Table D-1a.

39 Table J.5 in *Economic Statistics 1900-1983* by Thelma Liesner. London: *The Economist*,1985.

40 Table D-1a in *Monitoring the World Economy 1820-1992* by Angus Maddison, Paris: OECD 1995.

41 Page 245 in *A History of the World Economy* by James Foreman-Peck. Hemel Hempstead: Harvester Wheatsheaf, 1995.

42 Table J.2 in *Economic Statistics 1900-1983* by Thelma Liesner. London: *The Economist*,1985.

43 Correspondence with Jim Bourlet.

44 Table I-2 in *Monitoring the World Economy 1820-1992* by Angus Maddison, Paris: OECD 1995.

45 Ibid, Tables I-2 and I-4.

46 Table J.2 in *Economic Statistics 1900-1983* by Thelma Liesner. London: *The Economist*,1985.

47 Table C-16a in *Monitoring the World Economy 1820-1992* by Angus Maddison, Paris: OECD 1995.

48 Ibid, Table D-1a.

49 Page 154 in *National Accounts 1960-1992*. Paris: OECD, 1994.

50 Answer to a Parliamentary Question.

51 Table 3.19 in *Monitoring the World Economy 1820-1992* by Angus Maddison, Paris: OECD 1995.

52 Table 8.15, *Historical Statistics*. Paris: OECD, 1988.

53 Table B-110 in *Economic Report of the President*. Washington DC: US Government Printing Office, 1999.

54 Page 525, *International Financial Statistics Yearbook*. Washington DC: IMF, 1998.

55 Ibid, pages 522 and 523.

56 Page 113 in *International Monetary Statistics Yearbook*. Washington DC: IMF, 2004.

57 Ibid, pages 524 and 525.

58 Page 79 in *International Financial Statistics Yearbook 2010 and 2016*. IMF; Washington DC, 2010 and 2016.

59 Table C-16c in *Monitoring the World Economy 1820-1992* by Angus Maddison. Paris: OECD 1995.

60 Ibid, Table 3-4.

61 Ibid. Tables D-1a and D-1c.

62 Ibid, Table B-10c.

63 Page 1088 in Hutchinson's Encyclopedia. Oxford: Helicon, 1998.

64 Table C-16 in *Monitoring the World Economy 1820-1992* by Angus Maddison. Paris: OECD 1995.

65 Page 1088 in *Hutchinson's Encyclopedia*. Oxford: Helicon, 1998.

66 Table C-16c in *Monitoring the World Economy 1820-1992* by Angus Maddison. Paris: OECD 1995.

67 Ibid, Table C-16c.

68 Page 28 in *The End of History and the Last Man* by Francis Fukuyama. London: Penguin, 1992.

69 Table C-16c in *Monitoring the World Economy 1820-1992* by Angus Maddison. Paris: OECD 1995.

70 Ibid, Table D-1c.

71 Page 1088 in *Hutchinson's Encyclopedia*. Oxford: Helicon, 1998.

72 Page 133 in Monitoring the World Economy 1820-1992 by Angus Maddison. Paris: OECD 1995.

73 Ibid, Table 10c.

74 Ibid.

75 UN Website Statistics on World Population.

76 Table 1-2 in *Monitoring the World Economy 1820-1992* by Angus Madison. Paris: OECD 1995.

77 Wikipedia entry on *List of Countries by GDP (PPP) per Capita*.

78 GDP Volume Measure tables in *International Financial Statistics 2004 and 2016*. Washington DC: IMF.

79 Table 3-1 in *Monitoring the World Economy 1820-1992* by Angus Maddison. Paris: OECD, 1995.

80 GDP Volume Measure tables in *International Financial Statistics*. Washington DC: IMF.

81 Table 1-3 in *Monitoring the World Economy 1820-1992* by Angus Maddison. Paris: OECD, 1995.

82 GDP Volume Measure tables in *International Financial Statistics*. Washington DC: IMF and UN population statistics.

83 GDP Year on Year Growth Tables in *International Financial Statistics*. Washington DC: IMF, 2006 and 2016.

84 Table 1-3 in *Monitoring the World Economy 1820-1992* by Angus Maddison. Paris: OECD, 1995.

85 Ibid, Table 3-1.

86 Ibid, Table G-1.

87 Ibid, Table G-3.

88 GDP Volume Measure tables in *International Financial Statistics*. Washington DC: IMF and UN population statistics.
89 Pages 220, 534 and 1033 in *Hutchinson's Encyclopedia*. Oxford: Helicon, 1998.
90 Tables D-1b, D-1d, I-1 and I-2 in *Monitoring the World Economy 1820-1992* by Angus Madison. Paris: OECD 1995.

4. Monetarism and Neo-Liberalism

1 Pages 174 to 177 in *Main Economic Indicators*. Paris: OECD, 1999.
2 Table 20, pages 128 and 129 in *National Accounts 1960-1992*. Paris: OECD, 1994.
3 Wikipedia entry on *List of Countries by Steel Production*.
4 Wikipedia entry on List of Countries by Motor Vehicle Production.
5 Table 281 in *Statistical Abstract of the United States*. Washington DC: Department of Commerce, 2011.
6 Wikipedia entry on *A Monetary History of the United States*.
7 Table 5.2, page 228 in *Economic Trends 1996/97 Annual Supplement*. London: Office for National Statistics, 1997.
8 Pages 88 and 89 in *International Financial Statistics*. Washington DC: IMF, 1998.
9 Table B-69 in *Economic Report of the President*. Washington DC. US Government Printing Office, 2011.
10 Ibid, Table B.
11 Various tables in *National Accounts 1953-1969* and *National Accounts 1960-1992*. Paris: OECD 1971 and 1994.
12 Table 0601, *Eurostatistics03/90*. Luxembourg: The European Community, 1999.
13 ILO Labour Force Survey reports.
14 GDP Tables in successive editions of *International Financial Statistics Yearbook*. Washington DC: IMF.
15 Page 176 in *International Financial Yearbook*. Washington DC: IMF, 1998.
16 Pages 20 and 21 in *National Accounts 1960-1992*. Paris: OECD, 1994.
17 Page 122 in *International Financial Yearbook*. Washington DC: IMF, 1998.
18 *The Economics of Europe* by Edward Nevin. London: Macmillan, 1994.
19 Ibid, pages 273 and 274.
20 *The Relationship between Exchange Rates and International Trade: A Review of Economic Literature*. Geneva: World Trade Organisation, 2011. Paper WT/WGTDF/W/57.
21 Page 275 in *The Economics of Europe* by Edward Nevin. London: Macmillan, 1994.
22 Page 122 in *International Financial Statistics*. Washington DC: IMF, 1998.
23 Tables 0943 and 0955 in *Eurostatistics 5/88*. Luxembourg: The European community, 1998.
24 Table C-16a in *Monitoring the World Economy 1820-1992* by Angus Maddison. Paris: OECD, 1995 and Table 0101 in *Eurostatistics 4/99*. Luxembourg: The European Community, 1999.
25 Table D-1a in *Monitoring the World Economy 1820-1992* by Angus Maddison. Paris: OECD, 1995.

26 Page 123 in *National Accounts 1960-1992*. Paris: OECD, 1994.

27 Page 172 in *International Financial Statistics Yearbook*. Washington DC: IMF, 1998.

28 Table US.1 in *Economic Statistics 1900-1983* by Thelma Liesner. London: *The Economist*, 1985.

29 Table B-103 in *Economic Report of the President* Washington DC: US Government Printing Office, 1999.

30 Ibid, Table B-73.

31 Ibid, Broad Index in Table B-110.

32 Table D-1a in *Monitoring the World Economy 1820-1992* by Angus Maddison. Paris: OECD, 1995.

33 Ibid, Table B-12. *Economic Report of the President* Washington DC: US Government Printing Office, 1999.

34 Ibid, Table B-46.

35 Ibid, Tables B-1 and B-32.

36 Tables C-16a and D-1a in *Monitoring the World Economy 1820-1992* by Angus Maddison. Paris: OECD, 1995.

37 Table B-47 in *Economic Report of the President* Washington DC: US Government Printing Office, 1999.

38 Ibid, Table B-47.

39 Table 747 in *Statistical Abstract of the United States*. Washington DC: US Department of commerce, 1998.

40 Ibid, Table 747.

41 Tables B-1 and B-87 in *Economic Report of the President* Washington DC: US Government Printing Office, 1999.

42 Ibid, Table B-103.

43 Ibid, Table B-104.

44 Table 1295, page 791 in *Statistical Abstract of the United States*. Washington DC: US Department of Commerce, 1997.

45 Table B-2 in *Economic Report of the President* Washington DC: US Government Printing Office, 1999.

46 Ibid, Table B-63.

47 Ibid, Table B-78.

48 Ibid, Table B-110.

49 Ibid, Table 103.

50 Based on Table G-2 in *Monitoring the @World Economy 1829-1992* by Angus Maddison. Paris: OECD, 1995.

51 Table 11.13 in *Trends and Statistics – International Trade*. Geneva: World Trade Organisation, 1995.

52 Tables A-3e, F-4 and G-1 in *Monitoring the @World Economy 1829-1992* by Angus Maddison. Paris: OECD, 1995.

53 Ibid, Table I-2.

54 Pages 162 and 163 in *International Financial Statistics Yearbook*. Washington DC: IMF, 1998.

55 Ibid, pages 542 and 543.

56 Table 28 in *Trade and Development Report*. Geneva: United Nations, 1997.

57 Table 2-9 in *Monitoring the @World Economy 1829-1992* by Angus Maddison. Paris: OECD, 1995.

58 Table 25, page 200, in *Human Development Report 1997*. New York and Oxford: Oxford University Press for the UN Development Programme, 1997.

59 Table 33 in *Trade and Development Report*. Geneva: United Nations, 1997.

60 Various entries in *Hutchinson's Encyclopedia*. Oxford: Helicon, 1998.

5. World Imbalances

1 Page 63 in *International Financial Statistics Yearbook*. Washington DC: IMF, 2011.

2 Wikipedia entry on Affordability of Housing in the UK.

3 Irish Global Property Guide Internet entry.

4 Wikipedia entry on The Dow Jones Industrial Average.

5 Table 693 in *Statistical Abstract of the United States*. Washington DC: Department of Commerce, 2011

6 Page 75 in *International Financial Statistics Yearbook*. Washington DC: IMF, 2011.

7 Figures to be found in *International Financial Statistics Yearbook*. Washington DC: IMF, 2011.

8 Wikipedia entry on Bankruptcy of Lehman Brothers.

9 Xinhuanet.com Global Edition entry on German Exports.

10 www.reuters.com entry on USA losing its AAA Rating.

11 Country tables in *International Financial Statistics Yearbook 2004 and 2015*. Washington DC: IMF 2004 and 2016.

12 The year on year rate of inflation when Margaret Thatcher came to power in 1979 was 10.1% and 10.9% when she left office. Professor Tim Congdon has argued that this happened because the money supply rose during the late 1980s.

13 Wikipedia entry on Black Wednesday.

14 Ibid.

15 www.socialdemocracy 21st century blogspot,co.uk; Page 112 in *International Financial Statistics Yearbook 2000*. Washington DC: IMF, 2000.

16 Halifax House Price Index.

17 Page 981 in *International Financial Statistics Yearbook 2000*. Washington DC: IMF, 2000.

18 Ibid, page 125.

19 www.socialdemocracy 21st century blogspot.co.uk.

20 Page 165 in Ibid 2000 edition and page 75 in the 2010 edition.

21 www.bankofengland.co.uk.

22 Ibid.

23 Page 125 in *International Statistics Yearbook 2000* and page 63 in Ibid 2010.

24 www.fxtop.com.

25 www.worldbank.org.

26 Wikipedia entry on Lehman Brothers.

27 FTSE website.

28 Wikipedia entry on Sub-Prime.

29 Wikipedia entry on Government Policies and the Sub-Prime Mortgage Crisis.

30 Monetary Base and GDP Volume Measure growth tables in successive editions of *International Financial Statistics Yearbook*. Washington DC: IMF.

31 Wikipedia entry on Lehman Brothers Bankruptcy.

32 *Daily Telegraph* report 26th Feb 2009.

33 Monetary Base and GDP Volume Measure growth tables in successive editions of *International Financial Statistics Yearbook*. Washington DC: IMF.

34 Page 78 in *International Financial Statistics Yearbook 2016*. Washington DC: IMF, 2016.

35 Successive editions of Table I in *Quarterly National Accounts* London: ONS.

36 Data.worldbank.org/country/Greece.

37 Page 75 in *International Financial Statistics Yearbook 2016*. Washington DC: IMF, 2016.

38 Table B-1 in *Economic Report of the President*. Washington DC: Government Printing Office, 2011.

39 www.europa.eu site data.

40 Wikipedia entry on the Growth and Stability Pact.

41 Details provided by Goldman Sachs.

42 Figures form www.economicshelp.org.

43 Wikipedia entries on the Economies of Greece, Ireland and Portugal.

44 Page 78 in *International Financial Statistics*. Washington DC: IMF, 2016

45 Eurostat statistics on unemployment..

46 ECB website.

47 Wikipedia entry on Economic History of Argentina.

48 Quote from a newspaper article by Roger Bootle.

49 Dark Money by Jane Mayer. London: Scribe Publications, 2016.

50 Wikipedia entry on United States Public Debt.

51 Figures from www.economicshelp.org.

52 Ibid.

53 www.usgovernmentspending.com.

54 Tables A2 and I in *Quarterly National Accounts 2016 Q3*. London: ONS, 2016.

6. Unmanageable Competition

1 In 1977 the IMF index number for the real effective exchange rate on average for 1977 was 71.2 and in 1981 it was 112.2. Page 717 in *International Financial Statistics Yearbook 1989*. Washington DC: IMF, 1989.

2 Page 981 in *International Financial Statistics Yearbook 2000. Washington DC: IMF, 2000*.

3 Ibid, page 114.

4 Table 7.1, page 66, in the 2011 Pink Book. London: ONS, 2011.

5 Page 840 in *International Financial Statistics Yearbook 2016 Washington DC: IMF, 2016*

6 Ibid, taking account of 2016 exchange rate changes.

7 Pages 344 and 345 in *International Financial Statistics Yearbook 2000*. Washington DC: IMF, 2000.

8   Ibid, pages 168 and 169.
9   Ibid, pages 344 and 345.
10 Exchange rate data in successive country tables in *International Financial Statistics Yearbook 2000*. Washington DC: IMF, 2000.
11 themanufacturer website.
12 Ibid.
13 Pages 982 and 983 in *International Financial Statistics Yearbook 2000*. Washington DC: IMF, 2000.
14 Table A in *Balance of Payments 2016 Q3*. London: ONS, 2016.
15 Pages 983 in *International Financial Statistics Yearbook 2000*. Washington DC: IMF, 2000.
16 World Bank website.
17 Successive editions of *International Financial Statistics Yearbook*. Washington DC: IMF, various years.
18 Ibid.
19 www.tradingeconomics.com
20 Wikipedia entry on Purchasing Power data by country.
21 Tables UK13, 14 and 16 in *One Hundred Years of Economic Statistics* by Thelma Liesner. New York: Facts on File.
22 Ibid, Tables UK.1 and UK14.
23 Wikipedia entry on the Government Pension Fund of Norway.
24 Successive editions of Tables G and H in *Balance of Payments* reports. London: ONS.
25 Wikipedia entry on Richard Cobden.
26 Figures extracted from successive editions of *International Financial Statistics Yearbook*. Washington DC: IMF.
27 Ibid.
28 Ibid.
29 CIA website.
30 Monetary Base tables in I*nternational Financial Statistics Yearbook 2010 and 2016*, Washington DC: IMF
31 Country tables in ibid.
32 Tables I and A2 in *Quarterly National Accounts 2016 Q3. London: ONS, 2016.*
33 www.statisticstime.com, based on IMF data.
34 Wikipedia entry on GDP per head.
35 Wikipedia entry on GDP per head measured on a PPP basis.
36 *Impact of changes in the National Accounts and economic commentary for Q2 2014*. London: ONS, September 2014.
37 Tables A2 and F in Quarterly National Accounts Q2. London: ONS, 2016.
38 Page 4 in *International Financial Statistics Yearbook*. Washington DC: IMF, 2016.
39 Wikipedia entry on investment as a proportion of GDP.
40 Page 844 in *International Financial Statistics 2016*. Washington DC: IMF, 2016
41 Ibid.
42 *Annual Mid-Year Population Estimates 2014 and 2015* shows an estimate UK population increase between the midpoints of these two years of 513k.
43 Table 10.2 in the *UK National Accounts Blue Book*. London: ONS, 2013.

44 Annual Mid-Year Population Estimates, London: ONS, 2016.

45 Page 844 in *International Financial Statistics 2016*.Washington DC: IMF, 2016.

46 Ibid, page 78.

47 Ibid, page 844.

48 Ibid, page 84.

49 Table LPROD02. London: ONS, 2016.

50 Table 2 in *Regional Gross Value Added (Income Approach) Statistical Bulletin*. London: ONS, 2016.

51 Wikipedia entry on Income in the UK.

52 Wikipedia Listing of Countries by Income Inequality.

53 Table H1 in *Quarterly National Accounts Q4 2015*. London: ONS 2016.

54 Table 2.1. – Trade in Goods – in the *Pink Book*. London: ONS, 2016.

55 Quoted in www.economicshelp.org/blog/7617, based on ONS figures.

56 World Bank Database. Manufacturing value added as a percentage of GDP.

57 *International Financial Statistics 1989, 2000 and 2016*: IMF, Washington DC.

58 Page 982 in *International Financial Statistics 2000*, page 746 in the same publication for 2010 and page 771 for the latest IMF figures in the same publication for 2013. Washington DC: IMF.

59 Table B in *Balance of Payment, 2016 Q3 Statistical Bulletin*. London: ONS September 2016.

60 Ibid, Table E.

61 Ibid, Table B.

62 Table A in *Balance of Payments 2016 Q3* and Table A2 in Quarterly National Accounts Q3. London: ONS, 2016.

63 Table A in *Balance of Payment, 2016 Q3 Statistical Bulletin*. London: ONS September 2016.

64 Table H in *Balance of Payments, Q2 2014* Statistical Bulletin: London: ONS, September 2014.

65 Para 4.114 and Table 4.28 in the December 2013 OBR report to the Treasury *Economic and Fiscal Output*.

66 Table B in *Balance of Payment, 2016 Q3 Statistical Bulletin*. London: ONS September 2016.

67 Ibid.

68 Table 7.1 in the UK Pink Book 2011. London: ONS, 2011.

69 Table G in *Balance of Payments, Q3 2014 Statistical Bulletin*: London: ONS, December 2014.

70 Pages 984 and 985 in *International Financial Statistics 2000*. Washington DC, IMF 2001.

71 Website www.ukpublicspending.co.uk.

72 Figure 1, page 4 in *EU Government Deficit and Debt Return, March 2014*. London: ONS, 2014.

73 Ibid Latest Figures page 1.

74 Pages 66 in *International Financial Statistics 2016*. Washington DC: IMF 2016.

75 Tables A2 and I in *Quarterly National Accounts 2016 Q3*. London, ONS, 2016.

76 Page 66 in *International Financial Statistics 2016*. Washington DC: IMF 2016.

77 Ibid, page 81.

78 www.lloydsbankinggroup.com.

79 Halifax House Price Index.

80 Ibid.

81 www.tradingeconomics.com.

82 Halifax House Price Index.

83 Page 165 in *International Financial Statistics 2000* and page 77 in *Ibid* for 2013. Washington DC: IMF, 2001 and 2014.

84 Wikipedia entry on the Washington Consensus.

85   This paragraph draws heavily on an article in *the Political Quarterly, Vol 82, No 2, April-June 2011* by Maurice Mullard, entitled *Explanations of the Financial Meltdown and the Present Recession*.

86 *Debunking Economics*, Steve Keen, London. Zed Books, 2001.

7. Competitiveness

1   Tables UK.13 and UK.14 in *One Hundred Years of Economic Statistic* by Thelma Liesner. New York: Facts on File, Inc, 1989.

2   Ibid, Table UK.16

3   Tab le D-1a in *Monitoring the World Economy 1820 -1992* by Angus Addison. Paris: OECD 1995.

4   Table UK.8 in *One Hundred Years of Economic Statistic* by Thelma Liesner. New York: Facts on File, Inc, 1989.

5   Ibid Table US.8.

6   Ibid, Table UK.2.

7   Ibid, Table UK.8.

8   Ibid Table US.8.

9   Ibid Table UK.17.

10 Pages 62 and 63 in *International Financial Statistics Yearbook 1979*: Washington DC: IMF, 1979.

11 Table C-16a in *Monitoring the World Economy 1820 -1992* by Angus Addison. Paris: OECD 1995.

12 Page 980 in *International Financial Statistics Yearbook 2000. Washington DC: IMF, 2000.*

13 www.economicshelp.com.

14 Ibid, page 981.

15 Page 745 in the same publication for 2004.

16 Page 84 in *International Financial Statistics Yearbook 2016.*Washington DC: IMF, 2016.

17 Table A in the ONS *Balance of Payments 2016 Q3 report. London: ONS, 2016.*

18 Ibid.

19 Table A-2 in *Quarterly National Accounts 2016 Q2. London: ONS, 2016.*

20 Ibid, Table I.

21 ONS Wage Level reports.

22 Page 7 in *Economic Review, March 2014.*London: ONS, 2014.

23 www.data.OECD.org/trade/import content of exports.

24 Table A in *Balance of Payments 2016 Q3*. London: ONS, 2016.

25 Ibid.

26 World Bank database.

27 For example, a recent paper by Francesco Aiello, Graziella Bonanno and Alessia Via of the European Trade Study Group finds that 'the long run level of exports appears to be unrelated to the real exchange rate for the UK'. Quoted in an article by Lord Skidelsky in The Guardian on 21st October 2016.

28 Table A in *Balance of Payments 2016 Q3* London: ONS, 2016.

29 World Bank website.

30 These are set out in *Call to Action* by John Mills and Bryan Gould. London: Penguin Random House UK, 2015.

31 Table C in *The World Economy: A Millennial Perspective* by Angus Maddison. Paris: OECD 2001 and pages 58 and 59 in *International Financial Statistics Yearbook 1979*. Washington DC: IMF, 1979.

32 Ibid, page 981.

33 Ibid, page 125.

34 Page 66 in *International Financial Statistics Yearbook 2014*. Washington DC: IMF, 2014.

35 Ibid, pages 89 to 91.

36 www.xe.com website.

37 Wikipedia entry on the Plaza Accord.

38 Wikipedia entry on Herbert Stein.

39 Country tables in *International Financial Statistics Yearbook 2016*. Washington DC: IMF, 2016.

40 Ibid, Exports FOB Table.

41 Page 981 in *International Financial Statics Yearbook 2000*. Washington DC: IMF, 2000.

42 www.xe.com website.

43 *CALL TO ACTION: Britain's economic problems and how they can be solved* by John Mills and Bryan Gould: London: Ebury Publishing, 2015 contains the necessary calculations.

44 Producer Prices/Wholesale Prices 1970 to 1999, pages 120 and 121 in *International Financial Statistics Yearbook 2000; Prices: Home and Imported Goods for Switzerland, 1999 to 2010, page 696 and prices for manufacturing output for the UK, page 742* in *International Financial Statistics Yearbook 201*. Washington DC: IMF, 2012.

45 Table UK1 in *Economic Statistics 1900-1983* by Thelma Liesner. London: The Economist, 1985.

46 Ibid, Table UK.15

47 Ibid.

48 Wikipedia entry on Bretton Woods.

49 Page 981 in *International Financial Statics Yearbook 2000*. Washington DC: IMF, 2000.

8. Sustainability

1   *Happiness: Lessons from a New Science* by Richard Layard. London: Allen Lane, the Penguin Press, 2005.
2   Ibid, Table, page 64.
3   Ibid, Table page 64.
4   UN website.
5   Wikipedia World Population entry.
6   Page 14 in *The Skeptical Environmentalist* by Bjørn Lomborg. Cambridge: Cambridge University Press, 2001.
7   Wikipedia World Population entry.
8   Wikipedia Longevity entry.
9   Table 1-4, page 29 in *The World Economy: A Millennial Perspective* by Angus Maddison. Paris: OECD, 2001.
10 Page 141 in *Population: An Introduction to Concepts and Issues* by John R Weeks. Belmont, CA: Wadsworth, 2002.
11 Page 50 in *The Skeptical Environmentalist* by Bjørn Lomborg. Cambridge: Cambridge University Press, 2001.
12 Ibid, page 51.
13 Page 163 in *Population: An Introduction to Concepts and Issues* by John R Weeks. Belmont, CA: Wadsworth, 2002.
14 Wikipedia Fertility Rate entry.
15 Page 146 in *Population: An Introduction to Concepts and Issues* by John R Weeks. Belmont, CA: Wadsworth, 2002.
16 Ibid pages 104 et seq.
17 Page 328 in *Population: An Introduction to Concepts and Issues* by John R Weeks. Belmont, CA: Wadsworth, 2002.
18 Table on page 51 of *World Population Prospects: The 2000 Revision*. New York: The United Nations, 2001.
19 Nationmaster.com website.
20 Page 41 of *World Population Prospects: The 2000 Revision*. New York: The United Nations, 2001.
21 United Nations website on Population Trends.
22 Ibid.
23 Ibid.
24 Ibid.
25 Page 294 in *Population: An Introduction to Concepts and Issues* by John R. Weeks. Belmont, CA: Wadsworth, 2002.
26 Ibid, page 357.
27 Wikipedia, reproduced with kind permission.
28 Table C4, pages 325, 326 and 327 in *The World Economy: A Millennial Perspective* by Angus Maddison. Paris: OECD, 2001.
29 Wikipedia Growth in GDP figures show Zambia growing by 7.6% and Sierra Leone by 5.0% in 2010.
30 See Club of Rome website.
31 This section draws heavily on *The Skeptical Environmentalist* by Bjørn Lomborg. Cambridge: Cambridge University Press, 2001.

32 Wikipedia entry on cement.

33 Table 2, page 139 *The Skeptical Environmentalist* by Bjørn Lomborg. Cambridge: Cambridge University Press, 2001.

34 Ibid. The 16 raw materials are gemstones, nickel, crushed stone, sand & gravel, sheet mica, phosphate rock, silver, sulphur, cobalt, tin, chromium, asbestos, lime, molybdenum, boron, talc & pyrophite.

35 Ibid, page 137 .

36 Ibid, page 150 *et seq.*

37 Ibid, page 156.

38 Ibid page 119 *et seq.*

39 Ibid., page 126.

40 Ibid, page 133.

41 Ibid, page 136 updated to 2011.

42 Ibid, page 135.

43 Ibid, pages 176 and 177.

44 Ibid, page 189.

45 Page 259 in *The Skeptical Environmentalist* by Bjørn Lomborg, Cambridge: Cambridge University Press, 2001.

46 Wikipedia entry on carbon dioxide in the world's atmosphere.

47 Page 263 in *The Skeptical Environmentalist* by Bjørn Lomborg, Cambridge: Cambridge University Press, 2001.

48 Ibid, page 266.

49 Ibid, page 276.

50 Ibid, page 278.

51 Ibid, page 264.

52 Ibid, page 302.

53 *A Question of Balance* by William Nordhaus. New Haven and London: Yale University Press, 2008.

54 Page 317 in *The Skeptical Environmentalist* by Bjørn Lomborg, Cambridge: Cambridge University Press, 2001.

55 Ibid, page 323.

56 Ibid, page 282.

57 Ibid, page 286.

58 Ibid, page 288.

59 Leading article in *the Economist* 19th November 2011.

60 Page 247 in *Population: An Introduction to Concepts and Issues* by John R. Weeks. Belmont, CA: Wadsworth, 2002.

61 Ibid, page 19.

62 Leading article in *The Economist* 19th November 2011.

63 Page255 in *Population: An Introduction to Concepts and Issues* by John R. Weeks. Belmont, CA: Wadsworth, 2002.

64 Ibid, page 275.

65 Ibid, pages 265 and 287.

66 Ibid, page 280.

67 Leading article in *The Economist* 19th November 2011.

Index